D0385707

INCLINATIONS

BY THE SAME AUTHOR

Novels

PIANO QUINTET (1925)

THE RUIN (1926)

MANDRAKE OVER THE WATER-CARRIER (1928)

SIMPSÔN (1931)

THE SUN IN CAPRICORN (1934)

(*All published by Heinemann*)

Biography

A FLAME IN SUNLIGHT (THOMAS DE QUINCEY)
(*Cassell. 1936*)

Radio Drama

THE RESCUE (*Secker & Warburg. 1945*)

Art Criticism

GRAHAM SUTHERLAND (*Penguin Books. 1943*)

Anthology

AND SO TO BED (*Phoenix House. 1947*)

INCLINATIONS

BY

EDWARD SACKVILLE-WEST

WILMINGTON COLLEGE Library WILMINGTON N C

KENNIKAT PRESS, INC./PORT WASHINGTON, N. Y.

INCLINATIONS

Originally published in 1949
Reissued by Kennikat Press in 1967

Library of Congress Catalog Card No: 67-27642

Manufactured in the United States of America

PN571
·S15
1967

To
BUCK AND DIANA
DE LA WARR

IN DEEPEST AFFECTION

44598

The man who is completely an artist is incompletely a man, though in his art he may envisage man completely. The meaning of the artist in history, that is in life as he lives it, in the conditions under which he works, is like the meaning of history itself. History, as Niebuhr says, is meaningful, but the meaning is not yet. The history of the artist is prophetic, but the meaning of the prophecy cannot now be known.—R. P. BLACKMUR.

The only end of writing, is to enable the readers better to enjoy life, or better to endure it.—SAMUEL JOHNSON.

CONTENTS

INTRODUCTION

A GLANCE at the titles of the essays contained in this volume will, I hope, suggest a catholic taste. As a professional critic I have always tried to like as many kinds of writer as I could ; but it would be idle to attempt to conceal my predilection for art which is difficult, highly organised, ' late ',— just as in music my temperament inclines me towards chromatic rather than diatonic harmony. Most of the writers discussed here practise a very different kind of art from this : if I have chosen to write about their work, that is because I have discovered quite other reasons for admiring it. But, whatever the subject, my constant aim has been to draw attention to excellence, rather than to emphasise faults. Any conscientious critic sometimes finds himself obliged to condemn a book, more or less violently ; such a duty is usually disagreeable, and the result seldom worth reprinting.

The general title under which the essays are assembled is intended in the first place to indicate the scope of my appreciation ; in the second, as a sign of the critical attitude adopted. Though aware of the advantages of the direct approach, I have, nevertheless, here preferred to view my subjects from an oblique, or ' inclined ' angle. The method has its risks, like any other ; but at least it offers the opportunity of establishing, by suggestion and allusion, connections that might otherwise go unperceived. Thus, when writing of one art, I have endeavoured to keep constantly before me any features of the others which by analogy would throw light on the matter in hand. Art assumes many forms, but it is a unity in the sense that, whatever the medium chosen, be it music or words or pigment, it expresses the reaction to the world of an individual sensibility.

Such comparisons and connections—one might call them *vertical*—seem to me all the more justified because they enrich our appreciation of both terms. There may be danger here of inappropriate response, or even of irrelevance, but scarcely of unfairness. To criticise two writers (or two painters, or two composers) with the object of disparaging one of them, is a singularly vicious and futile procedure, for in nine cases out of ten it involves comparing what is essentially incomparable. I cannot but think that the first rule of constructive criticism should be to ask oneself the question : What is this artist trying to do ? Anyone who agrees with this view must feel nothing but abhorrence for the kind of critic who robs Peter to pay Paul, for by so doing he gives countenance to those deleterious parlour games which consist in drawing up a list of the Ten Greatest Poets, or of ' marking ' Dickens, Jane Austen, Kipling and Flaubert for specified qualities, and imagining that the result constitutes a valid judgment. Naturally it is impossible to avoid comparisons of detail, even as between artists of disparate aims ; but one should try as far as possible to assess each case on its own merits and to take account of the standards assumed by the artist in question.

★　　★　　★

The majority of these essays deal with fiction. Inescapably, the novel reflects the conflicts inherent in a society ; and when the latter becomes unstable the critical apparatus becomes unstable too. At the risk, then, of seeming portentous, I propose to set out here the critical assumptions on which these chapters are based.

(1) The style, however plain, must be *conscious*, so that the prose establishes as it were a *cantus firmus* at the back of the reader's mind.

(2) The chief persons—those whose characters and fate form the apex of the plot or idea—must possess an appreciable education and/or sensibility. I take this point to be of cardinal importance. Indifference to it, as evinced by certain American novelists and their followers, is responsible for the hollowness and the childish values which afflict much otherwise gifted contemporary fiction. Genuine tragedy at a low level of mentality is a contradiction in terms, and attempts to create it (e.g. Camus's *L'Etranger*) produce an impression of impertinence and moral chaos. Neither Shakespeare nor Racine nor even Dickens indulged this fallacy. Light comedy is possible at any level of intelligence and feeling, but the graver issues, though they may and do engulf people of all kinds, cannot receive artistic expression save through the medium of characters who

are both highly articulate and thoroughly aware of their pre-dicament. As V. S. Pritchett has said in his trenchant way, " Literature thrown into the gutter, acquires the habits of the gutter ". But this is not really a class question : moral insensi-bility, and an undeveloped, frivolous attitude to experience, are in effect the same, whether they proceed from the degenerate offspring of ancient, noble families, or from the equally degenerate offspring of middle-class or proletarian stock.

(3) Arises out of (2). I assume that, given judgment and imagination, the kind or quantity of a novelist's experience is a matter of indifference. Henry James puts this point well, in his preface to *Lady Barbarina* :

> The great truth in the whole connection, however, is, I think, that one never really chooses one's general range of vision—the experience from which ideas and themes and suggestions spring : this proves ever what it has *had* to be, this is one with the very turn one's life has taken ; so that whenever it ' gives ', whatever it makes us feel or think of, we regard very much as imposed and inevitable. The subject thus pressed upon the artist is the necessity of his case and the fruit of his consciousness ; which truth makes and has ever made of any quarrel with his subject, any stupid attempt to go behind *that*, the true stultification of criticism. . . . The thing of profit is to *have* your experience—to recognise and understand it, and for this almost any will do ; there being surely no absolute ideal about it beyond getting from it all it has to give.

(4) As a direct consequence of (1) and (2) the dialogue must proceed at a level above that of everyday life. Flat realism is not only tedious and diffuse, but conceals the idea as a charade the operative word. It is in their speech that the central characters rise above their actions.

(5) It is less the characters than the plot devised to entangle them which reveals the writer's attitude to life—his ' message ' —social, political, or philosophical. The birth of the funda-mental idea is probably always accompanied by one or more embryonic characters, or some kind of ill-defined group ; but as the plot emerges from darkness into light, it creates the characters—adding, subtracting, altering the recession, and making up the balance of personality as life itself does with living people. Take care of the plot of your novel and the characters will take care of themselves.

(6) Any novel which is to become part of a literary heritage

must aim at and achieve the effect of poetry—taking the word in its broadest acceptation. The topical, the contingent and therefore ephemeral stuff which all novels contain, must be interfused by an unflagging sense of the mysterious unity of all life. This poetic sense is at once the justification of humanity and the condition to which all art (including music) aspires. Everything else is as yesterday's newspaper—fit only for the waste-paper basket.

*   *   *

In their original form these essays appeared in the *New Statesman and Nation*, the *Spectator*, *Horizon*, *The Times Literary Supplement*, and *The Criterion*. Nearly all have been, not only drastically revised, but greatly extended ; and I have been careful to exclude anything that seemed of merely ephemeral interest. On the other hand, readers will sometimes notice observations and references which point clearly to a particular occasion. I have thought it more honest to leave such passages as they were ; trusting to the dates printed at the end of the essays to supply the occasions.

In concluding I wish to express deep gratitude to my friend Raymond Mortimer, whose encouragement and unerring critical eye have been invaluable to me in preparing this book.

LONG CRICHEL,
February 1949.

1

Dickens and the World of Childhood

I

FOR the first three decades of the nineteenth century the fabric of English social life, exposed to the hostile glare, first of Jacobinism, then of Napoleon, began to show its seams and the places where a century and more of unvarying habit had worn it thin. The aristocracy of England had good reason to fear Napoleon, but their terror of the French Revolution, as a potential source of ' infection ', was less well founded ; for, whereas the French nobles, deprived of power, but not of possessions, by Richelieu, had long since become irresponsible and effete, their English equivalents continued to govern the country in fact as well as in principle. Englishmen of this class had, at this time, as much virtue and courage as they have ever possessed ; but it is fear and misunderstanding, not courage, that clench the fist, grip the knife or the whip, and poison the fount of social confidence and good faith. English government throughout the eighteenth century unquestionably had its oppressive side ; but Fielding, in *Jonathan Wild*, and Hogarth, in *Gin Lane*, could reveal abuses without indicting the whole society which begot them. This cannot be said of *Oliver Twist*. The emotional instability of the world reflected in that lurid work of genius is revealed less by the picture of crime and poverty it contains than by a certain brutality of outlook which throws into violent chiaroscuro the opposition of the Gentle and the Unkind. When certain aspects of human nature can no longer be taken for granted they are regarded with a veneration which appears sentimental in a period concerned about other disturbances of the personality. What is sincere in one age becomes hypocritical in the next ; and it was inevitable that, at the height of the reaction to Dickens, at the opposite end of the century, cool-minded persons, firmly established in the humanitarianism of a liberal age, should have found his appeal to Pity exaggerated, embarrassing and ridiculous. And as long as that tradition obtained, we continued to feel that. The truth, of course, is that at such moments Dickens was not addressing cool-minded Victorians to whom brutality was anathema, but a governing class in whom growing terror of the new industrial proletariat had bred an indignant and ferocious resolution ; men undismayed by the sordid tragedy of Peterloo, enraged by forces they themselves had unleashed, and not yet much reassured by Sir Robert Peel's recent invention, the Metropolitan Police Force. If pity was to be aroused, it was essential to appeal in the strongest terms to people who noticed that their position was being called in question. And at that time England was a country where, in London alone, one person in twenty was a criminal of some description.

Such a state of affairs puts a premium on Tenderness. Emotions, like retail goods, rise in price during times of national stress : the early nineteenth century could not—or thought it could not—afford easy forgiveness of trepasses ; many people feel the same to-day. " For the heart must harden and a man's soul close in." Those who make it their business to open the hearts of men in the age that is upon us find it necessary to resort to methods very close to that of Dickens in his early novels. It is a vulgar error to suppose that the naked report, the prim bluebook, can do this. Only rhetoric persuades ; and Oliver Twist, Bill Sikes, Nancy, Mr. Squeers, Nell Trent, Daniel Quilp, are figures of rhetoric as well as human beings of vivid reality. Beautiful, pathetic, or merely horrible, their features are legendary and disquieting : we forget what they say and remember only what others (including their creator) said about them. When they are funny we find it easy to overlook their size ; when they are continuously tragic (Nell, Sikes) it is more than we can bear, and we express our embarrassment in terms that shift the blame from ourselves to them. We yell with laughter at Mr. and Mrs. Squeers, and even perhaps at Fagin ; but I think we may take it that they seemed less uproarious and more lifelike in 1836. For monsters, as they slip back into a distance that lends them safety, tend to disguise themselves with humour. Gilles de Rais was every bit as horrible as Haarmann, the butcher of Hanover ; but to-day he is Bluebeard in a children's book. I think it is a fair bet that Goering, Laval and Ley—perhaps even Hitler himself, if only because of his appearance—will be Guignol (rather than Grand Guignol) characters in the year 3000, if not before. Streicher is already a caricature in the pure Dickensian tradition.

Yet there is evidently a degree of wickedness which resists the humour of time : it is unlikely that Himmler or Heydrich will ever arouse laughter, for the reason that has prevented Robespierre and Fouché from becoming figures of fun. It is a question of degree, not of kind ; and now that we have moved into another period of entire ruthlessness, we should be able to see Dickens's early creations as they were intended to be seen—should be able to perceive that Fagin is really no funnier than Al Capone, Squeers and Sikes than S.S. men ; Nell not less real or pathetic than a starving Polish child, Nancy than some Czech girl haled off to a German soldiers' brothel.

★   ★   ★

The fantastic quality of Dickens's imagination distracts our attention from the extraordinary consistency of the world described in *Oliver Twist* and *The Old Curiosity Shop*—the world of criminals, Bohemians and strolling actors, where the struggle for existence, on the fringes not of affluence but of seedy respectability, is carried on in an atmosphere heavy with the fumes of hot gin and water, greasy lumps of nameless food, and flamboyant clothes seldom or never washed. In this seething world there is, nevertheless, room for everyone to have his or her counterpart : the characters reflect each other as people do in life. To disapprove of direct contrast in fiction (" mauvais procédé des romantiques ", says Gide in his *Journal des Faux Monnayeurs*) is valetudinarian and finds no confirmation in experience. Our end is often someone else's beginning, his or her beginning our end ; and the climaxes of life consist, as often as not, in the recognition of absolute disparity by those whom circumstances have forced to make common cause. Opposite characters are drawn together by the human yearning for perfection—a yearning that makes these first novels of Dickens so much more romantic, in the original sense of the word, than books like *Bleak House* and *Our Mutual Friend*, where the fantasy is planed down by a less fiercely subjective view of experience. Dickens's admiration for *Don Quixote* led him to give a picaresque surface to stories in which the element of chance turns out to play almost no part ; the typical Dickens plot is a pendulum which starts at its farthest point of oscillation, and comes to rest, the book ended, in the centre of its arc. And it is in the realisation of what his contrasts imply that the vastly *consolatory* nature of his art resides : more than any other novelist, except Balzac and Tolstoy, he reconciles us to the totality of human nature. So it is with exquisite satisfaction that we perceive that Nancy is pathetic because she began life as Nell, and that Nell claims our esteem precisely because—when it was after all the easiest solution to her distressful condition— she refrained from ending as Nancy. The statistics of child prostitution in nineteenth-century London are appalling, but are seldom taken into account by those who find Little Nell's personality distasteful. She was virtuous, gentle, unselfish, and forbearing ; one has met these qualities in combination ; no doubt Dickens's sister-in-law, Mary Hogarth, displayed them conspicuously ; but they ceased to carry conviction in an age in which extremes of character were no longer necessary to survival. We have altered all that : the survivors of the post-war world will be Oliver and Nell, on the one hand, Quilp and Monks and the Artful Dodger on the other, with Tom Scott (standing on his head as usual) in between. There will be no room for Dick Swiveller or even, I am afraid, for dear old Mr. Brownlow. In any case detractors of Nell would do well to realise that their case can rest only upon what is said about her—never upon what she herself says. When she speaks, she is sensible or affectionate or solicitous ; sentimentality only enters with Dickens's own voice or that of some other character—Marton or the sexton. In herself Nell Trent is exactly what Dickens, in the *dramatis personæ*, describes her as being : " a small and delicate child, of much sweetness of disposition ".

*   *   *

The male characters in these early novels follow the same pattern. Bill Sikes had, we may be sure, a childhood very similar to Oliver's. His behaviour to the boy is proof (if we need one) of that. Embittered experience satanically hates the innocence it has lost or destroyed in others ; so Sikes, and Fagin too, hate and maltreat Oliver, as Peter Grimes maltreats his apprentice in Crabbe's story. But the innocent are none the less perspicacious for being inarticulate, and Oliver's hysterical fear of the chimney-sweep to whom the authorities threatened to apprentice him will have been due to fear, not only of what the man might do to him, but also to some obscure but dreadful vision of what he himself might become.

The triumph of character over circumstance is seldom picturesque, and if Oliver and Nell yield nothing to Sikes and Nancy in reality, they certainly yield something to them in sheer vividness. This is in part due to the extraordinary sureness of Dickens's touch in describing the squalid and the sinister. Here a comparison with, say, the novels of Eugène Sue is instructive, for the material is roughly the same. But the Frenchman's picture is grossly overdrawn and curiously vague in outline, in spite of the muted brass and tremolando strings which blare and scrape behind each vociferous sentence. Sue had gusto, but nothing else, and we must turn to *Les Misérables*, and to parts of *Les Illusions Perdues* to find anything comparable to Dickens's symphonic poignancy of effect, in the fiction of that time. For one of the most constant features of criminal milieux is their utter inability to relax ; and a tension that never lets up is very difficult indeed to render in art. But in *Oliver Twist* Dickens succeeded in doing just this, because the nature of the plot enabled him to paint his shadows as dark as possible. In this London underworld, everyone is always on his guard : trust—and therefore ease—is impossible. If Fagin or the Artful Dodger laughs, it is always in the pleasure or anticipation of someone else's hurt ; the gin glass is never raised but a pair of suspicious eyes flickers to and fro above its rim. Sikes himself never laughs, never smiles ; the friendly sentence, the word of approval or gratitude, never reach his lips—are struck dead in the monotonous darkness of his thwarted mind. He achieves a kind of greatness through the tension which he creates. Contemporary readers complained of the unrelieved horror of this character ; but Dickens, in the preface to the book, replied that some people were indeed wholly bad and that the fact had better be faced. The reasons and the remedy are implied in the rest of the book, along with other hidden connections which I have tried to indicate. *Oliver Twist* touches upon everything —murder, torture, sexual mysteries and depravities, loneliness and despair—everything which is unbearable in human society ; but it puts its foot down *between* the danger points, not *on* them. True mystery is achieved by throwing bright light on subsidiary details—as Balzac realised when he conceived *Une Ténébreuse Affaire* and *Le Curé de Village*.

*   *   *

These early novels of Dickens attempt no picture of elegance. When he came to do this, later on in his career, the result was no more convincing than equivalent scenes in the novels of Thomas Hardy. In *Dombey and Son*, in *Bleak House* (on the whole, perhaps, his finest book), in *Our Mutual Friend*, Dickens approaches high life, but never in the expectation of finding anything enjoyable in it. He could never have understood, for instance, Disraeli's pleasure in the mere spectacle of a life in which money is no object. He had, that is to say, no directly æsthetic preoccupations, no delight in the decorative aspects of civilisation. His rich men and women are either cold and bored, like Mr. Dombey, or gross and stupid, like the Veneerings ; or they are gnawed by guilty secrets, like Lady Dedlock and the second Mrs. Dombey. As Mr. Humphry House has pointed out, in a book which is capital for the understanding of Dickens's place in nineteenth-century England, he never seems to have been visited by an inkling that money is desirable for what it can buy ; he mentions it on almost every page, but always and only with reference to the results of not having it. Dickens's standard of desirable life is represented by people like Mr. Brownlow and the Garlands, or by the stuffy cosiness in which his novels invariably land their heroes and heroines. His imagination is brilliant and profound, but its scope is relatively narrow, and nowhere does this fact emerge so plainly as in his conception of what can be done with life. It takes all sorts to make a world, and Kitty and Levin are unthinkable without their foils, Anna Karenina and Vronsky. Dickens got no nearer to Anna than Edith Dombey ; which perhaps explains his inability to devise a more comprehensive goal for his men and women than a genteel sufficiency garnished by perfect respectability.

Dickens knew that variety and colour were essential to the joy of life ; it was, indeed, the only part of his creed which could be called æsthetic, and it is to be seen at its most striking in *The Old Curiosity Shop*. This unjustly neglected novel has all the poetry of symbolism, of allegory ; the title itself is less a description of the place from which Nell and her grandfather start out at the beginning of the book and to which they never return, than of the book itself. The performing dogs in the inn at night ; Mrs. Jarley's caravan ; the waxworks of which the features are altered to suit the taste of the public ; the tartan-clad dancers on stilts encountered on the lonely country road ; Nell singing to the bargees as they glide down the river ; the Ruskinesque evocation of the furnace fire and its guardians ; the ruined Gothic house in which Nell and her grandfather at last find rest, with its neighbouring church overgrown and encrusted like a sheepdog whose face cannot be seen for hair : this secret journey through a land of fantastic marvels distils a poetry more extreme and daring than Dickens's imagination ever again achieved. Nor were his spirits, when the occasion demanded it, ever higher. Quilp and Sampson Brass are intolerable for long at a time, and just when we feel that we can bear their company no longer, the curtain rises on Dick Swiveller and the ' Marchioness ' playing cribbage :

"With which object in view, Marchioness," said Mr. Swiveller gravely, "I shall ask your ladyship's permission to put the board in my pocket, and to retire from the presence when I have finished this tankard ; merely observing, Marchioness, that since life like a river is flowing, I care not how fast it rolls on, ma'am, on, while such purl on the bank still is growing, and such eyes light the waves as they run. Marchioness, your health !"

Charles Dickens, your health !

(1944)

II

Dickens's creatures are both magical and human : we can see, touch, smell them ; they jostle us off the pavement and drive us from the room with their loud and endless loquacity. This is a commonplace of criticism ; less generally noticed, perhaps, is the manner in which the outsize figures—the monsters, of which all the novels supply a certain number—are used to set off the life-size figures of the foreground. Always background characters (*flat*, as Mr. E. M. Forster would call them), they fulfil the important function of guaranteeing the veracity of the more normal surroundings in which they strut, crawl, or posture. Pecksniff, Quilp, the Beadle in *Oliver Twist*, and—in the object of our present enquiry, *Dombey and Son*— Major Bagstock : these are essentially monsters, intended to amuse or frighten, yet always with an eye on some truth, droll or horrid. The mature novelist was too thoroughly a man of his age—the age of mid-Victorian industrial crudescence—to indulge in dreams unanchored to the everyday world. The fantasies of Lautréamont and of post-1918 poetry would have seemed to him silly—a waste of valuable time, as the spiritual inferno of Dostoevsky would have seemed to him an outrageous extravagance. His own brand of poetry consists in juxtaposing and embroidering only those notions which are common alike to educated and uneducated minds. The specialised and the esoteric held no appeal for the novelist, though the man might (and did) entertain them. Hence the vast extent and endurance of Dickens's popularity—a suffrage even greater than that of the greatest of all novelists, Balzac, who includes so much more.

But if Balzac's world is larger than Dickens's, it is ultimately less consolatory ; as a Frenchman, Balzac had no special belief in the happy ending and the tying-up of loose ends as true reflections of experience. For the same reason, perhaps, he is more chary of humorous exaggeration : Major Bagstock would have seemed to him a mere caricature. This was a limitation, and one which shut him off from the peculiar excellence of things like the apparition of Bunsby :

Immediately there appeared, coming slowly up above the bulk-head of the cabin, another bulk-head—human, and very large—with one stationary eye in the mahogany face, and one revolving one, on the principle of some lighthouses. This head was decorated with shaggy hair, like oakum, which had no governing inclination towards the north, east, west or south, but inclined to all four quarters of the compass, and to every point upon it. The head was followed by a perfect desert of chin, and by a shirt-collar and neckerchief, and by a dreadnought pilot-coat, and by a pair of dreadnought pilot-trousers, whereof the waistband was so very broad and high, that it became a succedaneum for a waistcoat ; being ornamented near the wearer's breastbone with some massive wooden buttons, like backgammon men. As the lower portions of these pantaloons became revealed, Bunsby stood confessed ; his hands in their pockets, which were of vast size ; and his gaze directed, not to Captain Cuttle or the ladies, but the mast-head.

Even Florence Dombey, brought up in the echoing desolation and stucco conventionality of the ' corner house ' (always unlucky, say the ubiquitous servants), and but newly introduced to the crowded cosiness of petit-bourgeois interiors, does not find this apparition much more disconcerting than Captain Cuttle himself, who was presumably used to it. This is Dickens's manner of showing that Florence, though in some ways a stupid girl, possessed the quick adaptability of the innocent mind, which could accept a figure like Bunsby as no more than a wonderful extension of its small but digested experience. I have described Florence as in some ways stupid, because it takes so much to make her realise her father's indifference to her. Dreadful to relate, children will put up uncomplainingly with downright ill-treatment, and even continue to be fond of their oppressors ; but they are usually quick to resent slights. Paradoxically, Florence refuses for years to draw the obvious conclusion from her father's outrageous neglect of her feelings ; yet when in a moment of exasperation he strikes her, she leaves the house (an enormous act for one in her position) and takes refuge with an old sea captain whom she hardly knows, thereafter to subside gracefully into the arms of Walter Gay. Like Miss Elizabeth Bowen's Portia, Florence experiences a death of the heart ; unlike the more modern innocent, she flies instinctively to those who will mend it for her. But she does the intelligent thing only when driven into a corner ; by the time Mr. Dombey married again, Florence was quite old enough to realise that to stage hair-brushing parties with her stepmother, night after night, would be the best way of making her father jealous, and thus of alienating him still further. Yet this is exactly what she elects to do—encouraged, of course, by the reckless and interested Edith ; and then is horrified by the consequences. Which is stupid of her.

⋆   ⋆   ⋆

Possibly Dickens intended us to draw this conclusion. Certainly we are justified in assuming so, because he was as conspicuously fair to the children of his imagination as he was unfair to those of his flesh. In this novel he is, on the whole, just even to the characters he most dislikes : to Mr. Dombey, who, when bankrupt, behaves with the utmost rectitude, and even generosity, towards those involved in his ruin ; to Mr. Carker, who is represented as having a pretty taste in interior decoration and—more importantly—as being· an able and conscientious manager ; to Edith, whose pride and foolish intransigence are redeemed by exact self-knowledge, and by an intuition of what life is really about. All this is most clever, for it throws upon us the onus of holding the balance between good and bad, a task which should always be left to the reader ; yet feebler novelists can seldom resist taking it upon themselves, thus reducing the elasticity of the moral distinctions upon which fiction reposes. " The secret of the great novelist is not in the domination of situations, but rather in the multiplicity of his intimate connivances," says André Gide, in the course of a disobliging criticism of Henry James. This fine and typically clever distinction seems to me to throw light on the real delicacy of Dickens's attitude to his creations. He did not always dominate the situations in which his people find themselves, because his improvisatory habits prevented him from seeing far enough ahead to be, in complete possession of any given moment. Sure of his virtuoso's ability to carry them through somehow, he allowed events to take care of themselves. But he took no chances with his characters, because he was anxious that, not he himself, but we, should judge them fairly.

Of course his dramatic sense, and his love of fun, sometimes caught him off his guard. In *Dombey and Son*, for instance, he allows himself to show Mrs. Pipchin (in spite of her weakness for Little Paul) a good deal less sympathy than she seems to me to deserve. In a later novel she reappears as Mrs. Jellyby, and interferes in other ways than by keeping a pack of unruly, underworked and overfed servants in order ; for which arduous service poor Mrs. Pipchin receives more kicks than ha'pence.

Even less pardonably, Dickens allows himself to be taken in by Little Paul, a slyboots if ever there was one, who battens shamelessly upon everyone, young or old, male or female, who comes within reach of his anæmic pathos. As a figure of poetry this etiolated child is, to be sure, a distinct artistic success : we are conscious, when he is on the stage, of some kind of musical beauty ; the little monster—like the big ones—exerts a spell, so that we forget, for the time being, the colossal insouciance with which he victimises his surroundings. One expects Florence to fall for his nonsense. Unused to being spoken to at any length except by Susan Nipper, Florence could not but be taken in by one who seems to have been born with the gift of serpentine eloquence. Mr. Toots would, of course, be gullible enough for anything. Mr. Dombey was prejudiced from the outset and in any case never noticed things which might not suit his book. But that all Mr. Blimber's young pupils—contemporaries of Tom Brown—should enter into a conspiracy of angelic kindness : this is altogether too much. Dickens's wish was father to his thought, so he forgot for a moment that there is nothing schoolboys resent so much as being imposed upon by one of their number. No matter how cleverly it is done—and Little Paul was certainly clever—they always spot it sooner or later, and then there is the devil to pay.

Luckily for himself, Dickens avoided the whole issue by allowing Paul to carry through his blackmail and die. Had he lived he would, I fear, have disappointed his father's hopes. With no head for figures, less than no interest in the family business, and a dilettante taste for art, he would have wandered abroad and eventually built one of those charming villas that overlook Portofino. Here he would have lived, in disgusted seclusion, with dyed hair and a male companion, a young

Italian peasant conspicuous for a mouthful of teeth, who would
have been referred to by English neighbours as 'that Mr.
Dombey's secretary', and by the indigenes as something less
respectable. Dying at the age of fifty-seven, Paul's will would
have disclosed that he had passed over his sister in favour of
the 'secretary', who, inheriting the entire Dombey fortune,
would have married a Henry James American (thus doubling his
income) and settled down in Paris (Avenue du Bois) to enjoy
the fruits of sacrifice, his teeth unimpaired and his synthetic
distinction increased by the passing of years.

The central characters of the novel—for Mr. Dombey and
Edith Granger must be allowed that position—are drawn with
a firmer, less indulgent pencil. As a representative of Money
Mr. Dombey is a forceful portrait, to which little could be added
today. Spiritually sterile, and without that sense of responsibility
inculcated by the possession of land, the rich merchant is obliged
to create a background to his life out of Pride. But pride is
undermined by a dry-rot in the form of power mania, which
always destroys the subject in the end. Love may be stronger
than death, but it is seldom stronger than the desire for power,
and we may well feel that there is something false and artificial
in Mr. Dombey's final change of heart. Far truer to fact is the
utter friendlessness of this rigid man, and the relief which he
finds in the sycophantic attentions of Major Bagstock. For
tyrants are incapable of friendship and have to put up
instead with boon companions whom they despise in their
hearts.

Equally true to fact is Mr. Dombey's irresistible attraction
to a woman in whom despair had bred the same poisons. Edith
Dombey has been written off as a figure of melodrama ; but
what exactly does this mean ? It is urged that she speaks in an
absurd, stilted fashion, and that, with her flashing eyes, her stage
gestures, and her undeviating behaviour, she is unlike a human
being. I believe this to be a misconception. The melodrama
of self-absorption mixes every emotion with pride, and expresses
the result violently. When we bang out of a room, or curse
an inanimate object that resists our efforts to displace it, we
create melodrama just as surely as Edith and Mr. Carker when
they exclaim : " Tush ! we are alone ! " or " Strumpet ! it's
false ! " All these actions and words belong to the realm of

truth ; it is but the turn of phrase which disconcerts, because this is continually being invalidated by changes in fashion. The Dombeys and Carkers speak the language of Eugène Sue and of Drury Lane, which offends the taste of some of us ; but the same language was as acceptable to Lamb and Hazlitt as that of Hemingway, which is the language of Hollywood, appears to be to many critics to-day. And behind the diction, in both cases, is a valid criticism of contemporary society. Edith Dombey—like Rosa Dartle, Lady Dedlock, Miss Havisham, and other of Dickens's terrible females—represents the vengeful and remorseless protest of Victorian womanhood against the preposterous image forced upon it by men. This revenge took many forms, and those who avoided one were usually overtaken by another equally deadly. Mr. Carker, consigning Alice Marwood to the fate ' worse than death ', meets his match from the opposite direction—in Edith. Mr. Dombey takes his first wife for granted, and she dies—but is swiftly avenged in the person of ' good ' Mrs. Brown, who strips Mr. Dombey's daughter to the skin before subsiding in maudlin self-pity upon her heap of rags.

The lesser characters are, as one might expect, nearly all delightful—not simply vivid, but comforting as a fire on a chilly day. I except Mrs. Chick, who is a bore, and Miss Tox (in spite of the Bird Waltz), who outstays her welcome. Dickens rarely knows when enough is enough—it is one of his few grave faults as a novelist—and the tiresome insistence which cannot mention Mr. Carker without harping on his teeth, spoils many an otherwise admirable passage.

It is customary to regard the earlier part of this book—up to the death of Little Paul—as by far the best ; some readers even fail to survive the appearance of Edith. Those who so fail miss one of the finest pieces of psychological and descriptive writing Dickens ever achieved ; I mean Mr. Carker's flight across France, and his death under the wheels of a railway engine. It was a clever imaginative stroke to have introduced this motive early in the book. Its sinister music, mitigated by the neighbourhood of the adorable Toodles, forms as it were a bridge between Florence and her stepmother, who meet first in the stark and unwilling mind of Mr. Dombey. The passage prepares us, in a symphonic sense, for the later chapter, where another, equally troubled mind grinds on its immitigable course :

He could not think to any purpose. He could not separate one subject of reflection from another, sufficiently to dwell upon it, by itself, for a minute at a time. The crash of his project for the gaining of a voluptuous compensation for past restraint ; the overthrow of his treachery to one who had been true and generous to him, but whose least proud word and look he had treasured up, at interest, for years—for false and subtle men will always secretly despise and dislike the object upon which they fawn, and always resent the payment and receipt of homage that they know to be worthless ; these were the themes uppermost in his mind. A lurking rage against the woman who had so entrapped him and avenged herself was always there ; crude and misshapen schemes of retaliation upon her, floated in his brain ; but nothing was distinct. A hurry and contradiction pervaded all his thoughts. Even while he was so busy with this fevered, ineffectual thinking, his one constant idea was, that he would postpone reflection until some indefinite time.

But the chapter must be read as a whole, and compared, for interest, with those greater chapters which describe the despair of Emma Bovary and of Anna Karenina. For there are points at which the greatest novelists meet each other's eyes ; and we hold our breath in astonishment, waiting for the terrible moment to pass.

(1945)

2

Middlemarch

A GREAT—above all a voluminous—writer's contemporaries enjoy one advantage over posterity which I have never seen remarked : they read his works in their entirety without strain, because these are gradually unfolded, at intervals, instead of coming out all at once, in twenty or more volumes of a collected edition. To read *all* Thackeray (or Meredith or Hardy) to-day requires the teeth of a circular saw and the stomach of an Alsatian dog ; yet I for one have been able to read everything that D. H. Lawrence and Aldous Huxley ever wrote—not to speak of Proust and Jules Romains—without the slightest sense of effort. The conscientious person who sighs heavily as he prepares to attack *The Ring and the Book*, may well think enviously of Lord Morley unpacking the four small volumes (they emerged two at a time, over a period of four months) of the first edition which he reviewed in 1869.

It is the same with George Eliot. With what excitement, with what a sense of spiritual enrichment about to be conferred on them, must that wonderful woman's devotees have opened the first parts of *Middlemarch*, in the year 1871 ! They had had nearly six years in which to digest the rather unsatisfactory *Felix Holt*, and nine in which to recover from the ambiguities of *Romola*. Yet nothing but a sour sense of duty will induce most of us nowadays to attempt any of these three novels— chiefly, I think, because we have seen them so often staring at us, Medusa-like, from the uniform opacity of a ' Complete Works '. Let us for once stare back, focus three volumes, and take them down.

★   ★   ★

The first thing that must strike anyone about *Middlemarch* is the immense seriousness of its tone. This has been said before,

and I repeat it here in order to dispose of the reproach it implies.
For if we are going to write off Dorothea Brooke as a solemn
prig we shall miss the point of Mr. Casaubon, together with
the fine balance and comprehensiveness of George Eliot's view
of life.   The moral concomitant of Christianity is stronger in
this writer than in almost all the other great nineteenth-century
novelists, including Dickens, but excluding Tolstoy, with whom
George Eliot has many interesting points of resemblance other
than the superficial one to be observed in the plots of *Adam Bede*
and *Resurrection*.   Dorothea and Mr. Casaubon (compare
Karenin) are creations of which Tolstoy might well have been
proud, not only for the rich overtones caused by their impact
on one another, but because such characters are the most
difficult of all to make vivid and sympathetic.   This can be
done only by employing the strictest fairness in delineation—a
fairness unattainable save by the most capaciously imaginative
intellects.   It is achieved, in this case, by a finely adjusted system
of checks and balances, and by a canvas sufficiently large to
allow the reader's attention to be attracted elsewhere for exactly
appropriate lengths of time.   Thus the much-abused Victorian
method of sub-plots is seen to have, when properly employed,
a distinct artistic use.   In any case George Eliot's main problem
must have been to keep us continually alive to the awful pathos
of Edward Casaubon, while preserving a perfect verisimilitude ;
for he is one of those persons whose harsh music is ill-adapted
to recording :   increase the volume only a fraction and he
would turn into a character out of Peacock, funny label and
all.   George Eliot never makes so gross a mistake.   True, she
allows a member of her chorus, Mrs. Cadwallader, to be witty
at his expense, calling him " a great bladder for dried peas to
rattle in ", but she herself has kinder words for him, as she has
for everybody ; the circumstances of her own life having taught
her charity.   To live in ' open sin ' during the Victorian age was
one of the best ways of discovering life.

      While Mr. Casaubon is definitely ' down ', Dorothea is
permitted to come up and display the purity of her heart, her
straightforward integrity.   It is of her essence that she remains
at the end of her trial what she was at the beginning, and her
answer to Mr. Casaubon's proposal both sums her up and is a
fine tribute to George Eliot's perceptiveness.   Here are no

raptures, no introspection—just eight lines of simple, dignified, exact statement of feeling.

> MY DEAR MR. CASAUBON,—I am very grateful to you for loving me, and thinking me worthy to be your wife. I can look forward to no better happiness than that which would be one with yours. If I said more, it would only be the same thing written out at greater length, for I cannot now dwell on any other thought than that I may be through life, yours devotedly, DOROTHEA BROOKE.

That is all ; true to her century, Dorothea put character before personality.

Yet when the desert-maker, Casaubon, is being given his due, the heroine is taken down a peg by a single brief remark. And it is one of this novel's characteristic subtleties that the remark is given, not to some clever person, but to Dorothea's feather-brained sister, Celia. " You always see what nobody else sees," she complains. " It is impossible to satisfy you ; yet you never see what is quite plain "—viz., that to an ordinary intelligence (which Dorothea's is not) Edward Casaubon is obviously self-absorbed, desiccated, pedantic, centreless and impotent—and that, in fine, it is stupid and obstinate to insist on marrying someone whom you cannot even help, since he is plainly an example of the Man-Who-Cannot-Bear-to-be-Wrong.

★　　★　　★

At this point a question suggests itself : What is George Eliot trying to do, in this novel of provincial life ? Her theme, as I see it, concerns the problem of Fidelity—how it is that this concept, though the only sure basis for any human relationship, involves as much of a strain on the intelligence as on the heart, so that only by integrating them both can we realise that it will pay in the end to go on enduring, when endurance, together with everything else, has ceased to seem worth while. To this end George Eliot selects two couples—Dorothea and Mr. Casaubon, Rosamond Vincy and Lydgate—suitable for displaying between them all the data, and surrounds them with a brilliantly amusing and comprehensive chorus and a *deus ex machina*, Will Ladislaw, whose role it is to unpack Pandora's box amid the spurious tranquillity of a Midland town in the

1830's. Will is a physically attractive artist in the Hawthorne tradition ; he sets the chief persons rocking on their bases, but they remain in the last resort firm, because Fidelity—even when most irksome—is a magnet strong enough to keep them all from toppling over. How much richer and more interesting, then, is the Dorothea-Casaubon-Ladislaw-Rosamond quadrangle than the equivalent treated by some smart twentieth-century novelist ! Independence of the frame of Christian morals is apt to result in a poor and monotonous response, especially when the level of intelligence is not high enough to generate a disinterested view. A stupid, immoral Christian is a more interesting object than a stupid, amoral agnostic, and Rosamond, even at her worst, carries heavier guns than her great-grand-daughter. The Madame Bovary of English fiction, she is childishly heartless and selfish, but never uninteresting, because of the moral ballast that we clearly feel to lie somewhere in her nature, if only as a force that serves to make her failure, and her husband's, the more bitter. It is the tragedy of such natures to drag others down to their own level, and this aspect of the novel is finally summed up in one of those deftly worded generalisations in which the book abounds : " We are on a perilous margin when we begin to look passively at our future selves, and see our own figures led with dull consent into insipid misdoing and shabby achievement." It could scarcely be better said.

★   ★   ★

The chorus, which is a varied and important part of the scheme, has its own disruptive factors, and here the element of mystery, thought indispensable by readers of that time, is discreetly introduced. It is fairly clear that George Eliot was sensibly less interested in the Bulstrode-Ladislaw-Raffles imbroglio than in the other parts of her story, though not to the extent of treating it shoddily. Indeed the murder of Raffles must be described as exquisitely plausible ; it is as unobtrusive as the climax of Miss Compton-Burnett's *More Women than Men*—a murder by omission.

These people—the hard-boiled business men of *Middlemarch*—can hardly be said to deserve happiness, so that their fates, if ever so slightly artificial to the modern imagination, on the whole fall into place in the general scheme. Dorothea, on the other hand, did deserve to be happy. But life is notoriously unfair, as none knew better than George Eliot, and I am not at all sure about her final resolution of her heroine's discord. Considering all that has preceded it, that happiness-ever-after with Will, achieved at the very last moment, strikes me as alleged. Long drawn-out complications, like simple absence, in the end make the strongest heart grow less fond. Hope does *not* continue to spring eternal, except in the silliest breasts, and it is not mere frivolity to accept calmly the resignation to second or third best, which it is a part of life's obduracy to enforce. To the Dorotheas of this world virtue always remains its own reward.

★   ★   ★

Of course this novel has defects, of which the *dénouement*, I believe, is one. The modern reader will observe a tendency (noted by Henry James) to proceed from the abstract to the concrete, a method before which, when it is at all strenuously pursued, credence inclines to withdraw. There are a few lapses of humour : to wear jewels in public cannot have been to sink as low as Dorothea imagined, even in early Victorian days. Finally—and this is more grave—we notice a certain absence of visual intensity throughout, due partly to lack of care for the *mot juste*. Whereas Flaubert achieved this most important quality because he proceeded on a more careful artistic principle, Balzac and Dickens arrived at it by sheer slapdash dynamics. George Eliot herself was not incapable of it in earlier days—in the *Mill on the Floss*, for example. But minds like hers tend, as they grow older, to become more analytical, less instinct with spontaneous creative vision ; and it must not be forgotten that George Eliot was already thirty-seven when her first book appeared. Thus the images in *Middlemarch* are clever and exact, but not particularly vivid—as when she describes the problem of woman as " hardly less complicated than the revolutions of an irregular solid "—a most unfeminine simile which probably owes its origin to the influence of G. H. Lewes's scientific mind. The symbols, too, are very well chosen, never obvious or too frequent : that vase, for instance (we may be sure it was an ugly one), at which Rosamond always gazed in moments of embarrassment.   But again they have not the immediate intensity and impact of Flaubert's ; there is nothing of the kind in *Middlemarch* to compare with that miraculous passage which describes Madame Bovary, convalescent after her long illness, descrying the bonfires on the distant hills.   And herein, perhaps, lies the reason why Rosamond, though a pathetic figure, cannot truly be described as a tragic one.

Middlemarch is a long book, but it is also admirably succinct : there is no padding and the length is exactly proportioned to the breadth of the subject.   A novelist must know when to skip, if only in order to prevent his reader from doing so. George Eliot never ' goes on ' :   her firmness of grasp and the intellectual ability of her analysis—unrivalled by any contemporary English novelist except Meredith—combine to give us that sense of complete adequacy in treatment, whether of a particular event or of some node of emotion, which is one of the chief sources of the enduring satisfaction induced by this majestic novel.

(1940)

3

George Meredith

OF all great novelists George Meredith has remained longest under the weather. Unread by the many, sneered at by the few who ought to know better, his books accumulate dust. Mention of his name in instructed company, at any time since the First German War, has produced an instant reaction of impatience or disgust. The alleged reason for this is usually the style—a style in fact much less rebarbative than many admired by those who sneer. The very English preference for nonchalance in art, as in social intercourse, may well have its share in the general neglect of Meredith's novels ; but the deeper reason is that, in the age of Proust and Joyce, his view of life had become exceedingly unfashionable.

Now, with the change in the intellectual climate brought about by stresses as peculiar as they are inescapable, to present generations Meredith's instrument should have the fresh power of a blade protected from rust by the very depth at which it has been buried. For this is the time, if ever, to throw off the debilitating pessimism which has brought us to the present pass, and to assume again that belief in the self-renovating power of the soul which was the foundation of Meredith's muscular agnosticism. The rise of Industrialism, ' Progress ', Darwinism (1859 saw the issue both of the *Origin of Species* and of *Feverel*) and the decline of Christian belief, had brought the men and women of Meredith's day to a stage at which a readjustment of the interacting rhythm of thought and action was taking place everywhere. It is the same to-day. The type of sensibility of which Proust is the extreme example, and which has influenced deeply numbers of people who never heard of that writer, is no longer *de mise*. For the majority of intelligent, vital men and women the piecemeal, dissociative method of conjugating the mind in action—the blade of thought ever and anon tarnished by the sour breath of an inconstant will—has ceased to be valid,

3   33

either in life or in art. Man and the present have got to be integrated, and if the result be an immediate diminution of true sensibility, it will be one of the tasks of future generations to build this back into the progressive fabric of civilisation. " The complaining millions," wrote Matthew Arnold to his friend Arthur Hugh Clough, some years before Meredith published his first novel, " want something to *animate* and *ennoble* them— not merely to add zest to their melancholy or grace to their dreams." That is as true of a people grappling with the present difficulties as it was of a generation steeped in the poetry of a previous romantic period.

" I have never started on a novel to pursue the idea it developed. The dominant idea in my mind took up the characters and the story midway", wrote Meredith in 1887— long after he had shown clearly that he belonged to that rare type of artist in whom the creative and judging faculties run in harness. One of the advantages enjoyed by those who have made their own way in life is that the struggle encourages an inductive method in the forming of principles. Thus it is with Meredith's characters, who obey his dramatic vision by living in action, all the time. Richard Feverel, Evan Harrington, Harry Richmond, Beauchamp and Romfrey, Diana, Clara Middleton, Fleetwood : all use their high intelligence in order that acts should continually proceed from the conclusions drawn. There are no Hamlets here ; these men and women act globally—with the whole of their being—and waste no time in vain regrets. " To know when a thing hath perished, or is vital, is one of the tests of wisdom ", Meredith observed to Frederick Maxse, his best friend and the ' original ' of Beauchamp ; and because these beautiful and healthy people (Meredith is never in the least afraid of making a hero or heroine look the part) know this, they have the advantage, immensely important to the reader, that they *grow* throughout the histories they precipitate. Feverel emerges from his sentimental education a man of considerably stiffer fibre than Flaubert's Frédéric Moreau ; but the effect of disillusionment is no less poignant because the final impression is something more than merely sad. For Beauchamp and Richmond the ordeal is different ; both are successful amateurs : the kind of men Meredith evidently most admired,—just as he preferred village cricket to Lords, and indeed any splendid improvisation to the more finished and cautious performance of a professional. Diana Merion's reckless vitality and confidence encompass the ruin of her love ; but the end of the novel does not find her sitting amid the ashes. Abominably treated by a self-indulgent father and a vain, deceptive lover, Clara Middleton never loses the sense of her own integrity and what the loss of it would entail ; for us, the thrilling interest of her situation lies in the spectacle she presents as, secured in oilskins and sou'wester, her hands on the tiller, she steers her course through the tempest of reinforced egotism which assails her. Loss of innocence was a theme as fascinating to Meredith as it was to Henry James and indeed must be to all novelists, just because it is among the richest of spiritual dramas ; he handles it again and again ; but its most dramatic expression, in his last completed novel, *The Amazing Marriage*, shows the victim, Carinthia Jane, by no means unequal to the humiliations she is called upon to endure at the hands of her Byronic husband. Like all Meredith's characters, both he and she are profoundly changed by their struggle with each other ; but the interest for us of their final scene (one of the best things Meredith ever wrote) lies in Carinthia's perception that for her part it was too late to forgive : life had gone on.

So it is for all, and that is why a reading of these novels makes so stimulating an impression of the victory of character over sensibility. " I cannot play at life ", exclaimed Meredith, on the occasion of his second marriage ; and when one considers that it was this marriage which was to release his finest novels—*Harry Richmond, Beauchamp's Career, The Egoist*—in quick succession, it is hardly surprising that his fundamental criticism of ' bad ' characters, such as Willoughby Patterne and Lord Fleetwood, is exactly that they do ' play at life '—as the heroes and heroines of the latter-day novel have scarcely yet ceased to do. For Feverel—for the young Meredith, as for the young people of 1925—life's answer to the enthusiastic soul was dusty ; Harry Richmond, Romfrey, Beauchamp riposte by asking it another kind of question—and the answer, this time, is a glorious affirmative.

Mr. J. B. Priestley, in his brilliant monograph on Meredith, finds the heroes too much of a good thing. " They are ", he says amusingly, " health in a hospital, where it cuts a poor

figure." To think Redworth or Beauchamp ' dull ' seems to me
to set a premium on the picturesque. For their self-confidence
alone they are fortifying to read of to-day. Also they develop,
and this is vastly to the credit of their creator. Indeed there is
hardly one of Meredith's major characters who does not strike
us, at the end of the book, as having changed importantly in
the course of it. The French critic, Ramon Fernandez, was, I
believe, the first to examine [1] in detail the dynamic aspect of
Meredith's heroes and heroines—their principle of growth ; by
this we are made to feel that the point they have reached, at
any given moment, is also that which they have reached in the
author's perception of them.

This organic method of inventing his people inspires Meredith
with images so extreme in their poetic violence that they seem
to thrust the action forward, as by jet propulsion. Thus, at the
beginning of *Diana of the Crossways*, when Redworth learns
from Lady Dunstane that Diana is already engaged to be
married :

> He bore it well. He was a big-chested fellow, and that
> excruciating twist within of the revolution of the wheels of the
> brain snapping their course to grind the contrary to that of the
> heart, was revealed in one short lift and gasp, a compression of the
> tremendous change he underwent.

And much later in the same book, when Redworth is thinking
over his relation to Diana in the light of the crisis in both their
lives :

> She was his, in a sense, because she might have been his—but
> for an incredible extreme of folly. The dark ring of the eclipse
> cast by some amazing foolishness round the shining crescent
> perpetually in secret claimed the whole sphere of her, by what
> might have been, while admitting her lost to him in fact.

It is in the power of poetry, and of poetry only, to carry us
forward like this, on the giant breaker of a single image
which by its utter adequacy transcends analysis. And with each
such image the person concerned casts a longer shadow.

At the top of the triumphs of will achieved by these people

---

[1] *Messages* (1926).

it is possible to exact even more from them, and one of the most striking features of the Meredith novel is the physical and spiritual endurance which these wonderful creatures require of themselves and of each other. Only a Meredith heroine could say, as Carinthia Jane says : " I hate sleep : I hate anything that robs me of my will." The sheer preposterousness of hating sleep, added to our complete acceptance of the remark in its context, guarantees the stature of the writer's imagination. And the same strong mind, served by a powerful physique, is seen at work in the remark, made by Meredith's last hero, but implicit in the behaviour of his first, that " the blow forgives ". This quasi-mediæval sentiment, which was strong throughout the nineteenth century and produced the best and worst of its attitudes, fits naturally into Meredith's preference (shared by Henry James) for the high milieu and the formal preoccupations which go with it. It helps also to explain his women—another source of irritation to modern readers, for whom only the latest form of wit is endurable. To a less prejudiced mind, I cannot help thinking, Diana of the Crossways conforms remarkably to Lord Houghton's account of the famous Harriet, Lady Ashburton, in whom he found " the fullest and freest exercise of an intellectual gaiety, that presented the most agreeable and amusing pictures in few and varied words ; making high comedy out of daily life, and relieving sound sense and serious observation with imaginative contrasts and delicate surprises ". This might be Devonshire House during the Regency ; but the view that feminine wit died in English society with the accession of Queen Victoria will not bear examination.

Another of Mr. Priestley's remarks, adapting the famous judgment of Henry James, bears particularly on this point. " He does the supremely difficult thing well and the easy thing badly." Whatever things may be ' easy ' for the novelist, to create a witty or humorous character is unquestionably difficult. Moral worth, innocence, caddishness, vulgarity, ambition—the writer may have a sufficient perception of these, although they form no active part of his own character. But he cannot convey the impression of a witty or humorous mind unless he possesses one himself. " Who drives fat oxen should himself be fat." Meredith's own brand of wit was not what the French under-stand by the word : it was hearty, verbose, hyperbolic—an

indirect expression, one feels, of his own good looks and
physical vitality. It was not naïve, but its sophistication was
not that of to-day ; which is, I suggest, why we so signally
fail to appreciate it. Twentieth-century wit, like that of the
Grand Siècle, is always acerb ; in the nineteenth century it was
much less often so. Anthony Trollope, who had none of
Meredith's agility, nevertheless could draw upon a similar fund
of high spirits. It would have gone ill with Lily Dale if he had
not been able to do this. I have heard this heroine described
as a bore ; but surely she has much of the 'intellectual gaiety'
Lord Houghton found in Lady Ashburton. It is largely a
question of fashion, and in dealing with Meredith especially
this question is bound to loom on every side. To take a small
but entertaining instance :

> The tempest of penitence closed with a blind look at his watch,
> which he left dangling. He had to talk to drug his thoughts.

"Which he left dangling "—how vivid this is ! Now that we
wear nothing but wrist-watches, that image is no longer current
coin. To have a sense of period is not necessarily to fail of
interest in one's own, though it may amount to that in some
cases. The little incident I have just quoted is a minor example
of Meredith's wit ; the image—poetic in its exactitude and
compression—of a rhetorician of genius.

If we look back now to Diana Warwick, I think we shall
see that, if we reject her, we cut ourselves off from a source,
not only of pleasure, but of *life*. Diana's talk is much better
than is usually allowed ; she and Clara Middleton are the
mothers of Isabel Archer and Madame de Mauves. There is
no question, it seems, of Meredith's having influenced Henry
James ; but a similar process of intuition, which analyses
character without disintegrating it, and a similar perception of
what constitutes fineness of conscience, unite the two men at
what is after all a most important point. The comparison must
not be pushed further, for Meredith's perceptions, though
always necessarily of a poetical order, were entirely unæsthetic.
His attempt to portray an artist (R. L. Stevenson, incidentally)
in Woodseer of *The Amazing Marriage* is as conventional as
anything to be found in *Punch* ; and everywhere Meredith

shows that the æsthetic approach to life, with its emphasis on contemplation and its habit of collecting sensations like bibelots, was a closed book to a man for whom experience was but an instrument for keeping an edge on the character.

All this, of course, took time to develop ; his poetry supplies a running commentary ; and to prefer—as many do—*Feverel*, or the Italian novels, or *Rhoda Fleming*, or even *Evan Harrington*, to the novels of Meredith's maturity, seems to me criminally lazy. No one would deny that the sustained lyricism and youthful beauty of *Feverel* are captivating ; but its ineptitudes, which include the tragic end, are many and excruciating. The scene of Richard's seduction by Bella Mount is surely one of the worst pieces of bathos ever invented by a great novelist (Balzac will supply parallels). No wonder it made the author's friend, Augustus Jessopp, " ill for twenty-four hours " !

On the other hand, to look for a steady artistic development in Meredith's novels would be critically maladroit. He had very little in him of the professional novelist and justifiably regarded himself as first and foremost a poet. It is clear that he could not think of a fiction in prospect as other than a *tour de force*—hence the unevenness of his novels, the lack of direction, the dire calamities. There is something amateurish about his genius, as there is about Berlioz's. Both rely upon inspiration, and when that fails we are conscious of a resonant void—or worse, a desperate fumbling after effect. If Meredith had had a more professional sense of his own scope he would not, I suggest, have attempted the Hardyesque vein in *Rhoda Fleming*, nor been satisfied with the dreadful vulgarity of *The Tragic Comedians* and the mere virtuosity of *Lord Ormont and his Aminta*.

Yet even the born improviser, provided the source of his flame does not dry up, will work his way towards the unknown centre of his genius. There may be success on the way, but it will be chancy, peripheral. In *Vittoria*—if not in *Sandra Belloni* —the miss is as good as a mile. *Harry Richmond* and *Beauchamp's Career* have Shakespearian proportions, vigour, pathos and excitement ; but it is with *The Egoist* that we reach the real centre of Meredith's life and work. In this consummately clever study in the anatomy of sentimentalism we get at last a full revelation of the well-hidden strands that wove the stuff of this very rare mind. Behind the general view of relationships stand Peacock, Spenser and Ariosto ; behind the staccato dialogue, with its perpetual ellipses, its legalistic quips, its outbursts of comic grandiloquence, stand the dramas of Shakespeare and Ben Jonson, and the novels of Jean-Paul Richter ; behind the essentially dramatic construction, the exquisite irony, the brilliant exposition of character, stand—here is the clue— La Rochefoucauld, La Bruyère, and the tragi-comedies of Molière and Regnard. The result is one of the most deeply French books ever written in English ; and to imagine what Trollope, say, would have done with such a theme is to comprehend the distinction between genius and talent.

Each of Meredith's novels is a *tour de force* ; but after *The Egoist* he was apt to turn aside into nasty thickets. *The Tragic Comedians* and *Lord Ormont and his Aminta* are parodies of their author's worst faults : heavy-footed, facetious, involved, pompous and romantical, they are written in a wildly debased Gothic which renders them unreadable to-day. It was his early passion for the Arabian Nights returning *mal à propos*. Then, miraculously, Meredith threw off these grotesqueries and gave the world, in *The Amazing Marriage*, such a novel as Browning might have written, had he chosen to cast *The Ring and the Book* in prose. All Meredith's finest qualities are here embodied in a crisp, nervous style, with less of the Gothic nimiety which mars the surface of his earlier books. And even when he indulges in a cadenza, the result has a new kind of brilliance. The description of the end of the prize fight, in Chapter XVI, comes very near to James Joyce :

> The close of the battle was on the visage of Rufus Abrane fifteen minutes before that Elgin marble under red paint in the ring sat on the knee of a succouring seconder, mopped, rubbed, dram-primed, puppy-peeping, inconsolably comforted, preparatory to the resumption of the great-coat he had so hopefully cast from his shoulders. Not downcast, by any means. Like an old Roman, the man of the sheer hulk with purple eye-mounds found his legs to do the manful thing, show that there was no bad blood, stand equal to all forms. Ben Todds, if ever man in Old England, looked the picture you might label ' bellyful ', it was remarked. Kit Ines had an appearance of springy readiness to lead off again. So they faced on the opening step of their march into English History.

Elsewhere in this astonishing book the style regains the excellence of the 'high noon' of Meredith's career as a novelist :

> Beyond the firwood light was visibly the dawn's. Half-way down the ravines it resembled the light cast off a torrent water. It lay on the grass like a sheet of unreflecting steel, and was a face without a smile above. Their childhood ran along the tracks to the forest by the light, which was neither dim nor cold, but grave ; presenting tree and shrub and dwarf growth and grass austerely, not deepening or confusing them. They wound their way by borders of crag, seeing in a dell below the mouth of the idle mine begirt with weedy and shrub-hung rock, a dripping semi-circle. Farther up they came on the flat juniper and crossed a wet ground-thicket of whortleberry : their feet were in the moist moss among sprigs of heath ; and a great fir tree stretched its length, a peeled multitude of his dead fellows leaned and stood upright in the midst of scattered fire-stained members, and through their skeleton limbs the sheer precipice of slate-rock of the bulk across the chasm, nursery of hawk and eagle, wore a thin blue tinge, the sign of warmer light abroad.

The Byronic type of man has perhaps never been more justly dealt with than in Meredith's portrait of Fleetwood. Here, and throughout the book, which describes the taming of a (male) shrew, the theme of *The Egoist*, so near to this author's heart, is explored again, finally, in its more tragic implications.

Among English writers Meredith is as isolated as De Quincey. Unlike most of his contemporaries, he preferred the unicellular scheme, eschewing the sub-plot so dear to the nineteenth-century novelist. The French and German elements in his education had given him a peculiar kind of social and artistic conscience which made him unpopular with his countrymen in his own day, but which ought to alienate them no longer. Henry James complained that he could never leave his subject alone ; " but," he added, " he did the best things best ".

I cannot think of a novelist writing in English to-day who does those things as well—unless it be Mr. R. C. Hutchinson.

(1943)

4

The Personality of Henry James

IT is in the elegance of his mask, and the adroitness with which he uses it, that a civilised personality reveals the genuineness of what is more fundamental to him : his character. The self-conscious and highly intelligent man (he is often a writer) who sets out, early in life, to construct himself a personality will probably find the labour affect his appearance. In any case his face will give him away to those with sharp eyes, for his features are like a handwriting : however carefully he may compose them, something—the angle of an eyelid, the twitch of a muscle, the set of a lip—will reveal what he is trying to hide.

This happened, conspicuously, to Henry James. By the time his personality was thoroughly ' set ', the unamenable eye of Edmund Gosse took down all the visual evidence, both for and against.

I have said that in early life Henry James was not ' impressive ' ; as time went on his appearance became, on the contrary, excessively noticeable and arresting. He removed the beard which had long disguised his face, and so revealed the strong lines of his mouth and chin, which responded to the majesty of the skull. In the breadth and smoothness of the head—Henry James became almost wholly bald early in life—there was at length something sacerdotal. As time went on, he grew less and less Anglo-Saxon in appearance and more Latin. I remember once seeing a Canon preaching in the Cathedral of Toulouse who was the picture of Henry James in his unction, his gravity and his vehemence. Sometimes there could be noted—what Henry would have hated to think existing—a theatrical look which struck the eye, as though he might be some retired *jeune premier* of the Français, *jeune* no longer ; and often the prelatical expression faded into a fleeting likeness to one or other celebrated Frenchman of letters (never to any Englishman or American), somewhat of Lacordaire in the intolerable scrutiny of the eyes, somewhat of Saint-Beuve, too, in all except the mouth, which, though mobile and elastic, gave the impression in rest of being small. . . .

At the same period Jacques-Emile Blanche noticed " l'aspect de moine bon vivant qu'il prenait parfois " ; and John Bailey remarked that in looking at James's face one had to remember that he considered Shakespeare's ' dull '. This is a far cry from the Lafarge portrait of 1861, with its naked and poetic charm—though even in that profile it is possible to discern an adumbration of the *abbé mondain* of forty years later, who would have to his credit the saving (on paper) of many a titled soul. The question of Henry James himself is quite as complicated as that of his work ; thanks to the cool-headed assiduity of Mr. Simon Nowell-Smith, we are given the means of attempting to resolve it. *The Legend of the Master* is an anthology of descriptions, anecdotes, comments and judgments, set down about Henry James by those who knew him personally between the late 1870's and 1916 (the year of his death). The result is wildly entertaining. Compiled around a ' natural ' character, such a book as this could have little point : it is the mask that gives rise to the ambiguity, the misconception, and eventually to the legend. In deciding what to include, Mr. Nowell-Smith was handicapped by nothing except lack of personal acquaintance with his subject : his intelligence, his scholarly suspicion of frivolous or dramatised evidence, his juridical sense of the germane, make him the ideal investigator.

It is evidence of the goodness of Henry James's nature that by far the most interesting of the annotations come from men and women who personally loved him. Gosse was obviously not among these ; but let us hear A. C. Benson on James's talk :

The extreme and almost tantalising charm of his talk lay not only in his quick transitions, his exquisite touches of humour and irony, the width and force of his sympathy, the range of his intelligence, but in the fact that the whole process of his thought, the qualifications, the resumptions, the interlineations, were laid bare. The beautiful sentences, so finished, so deliberate, shaped themselves audibly upon the air. It was like being present at the actual construction of a little palace of thought, of improvised yet perfect design. The manner was not difficult to imitate : the slow

accumulation of detail, the widening sweep, the interjection of
grotesque and emphatic images, the studied exaggerations ; but
what could not be copied was the firmness of the whole conception.
He never strayed loosely, as most voluble talkers do, from subject
to subject. The motif was precisely enunciated, revised, elongated,
improved upon, enriched, but it was always, so to speak, strictly
contrapuntal. He dealt with the case and nothing but the case ;
he completed it, dissected it, rounded it off. It was done with much
deliberation and even with both repetition and hesitation. But it
was not only irresistibly beautiful, it was by far the richest species
of intellectual performance that I have ever been privileged to
hear. . . . His talk . . . was not exactly conversation ; it was
more an impassioned soliloquy. . . . There was certainly something pontifical about it—not that it was ever solemn or mysterious ;
but you had the feeling that it was the natural expansiveness of a
great mind and a deep emotion, even when his talk played, as it
often did, half-lambently and half-incisively, over the characters
and temperaments of friends and acquaintances. It was minute,
but never trivial ; and there was tremendous force in the background. Like the steam-hammer, it could smite and bang an
incandescent mass, but it could also crack a walnut or pat an egg.
It was perfectly adjusted, delicately controlled.

Is not that more convincing than Thomas Hardy's curt
remark that James had " a ponderously warm manner of saying
nothing in infinite sentences " ? Probably Hardy was too
thoroughly masculine a nature to be a very sympathetic witness
in the case : all the evidence goes to show that a feminine streak
is necessary to appreciate the flavour either of James himself or
of his work. Little as women seem to have liked his later
novels, when they first appeared, there is no question that they
liked the man who wrote them. " They liked him especially
for his sympathetic and delicate discernment of their own nice
qualities ", remarked E. S. Nadal (on the whole an unfriendly
critic of James) in 1920. " He seemed to look at women rather
as women look at them. Women look at women as persons ;
men look at them as women. The quality of sex in women,
which is their first and chief attraction to most men, was not
their chief attraction to James." This might be thought a
back-handed compliment ; but, applied to a novelist, it is
simply the recognition of a merit.

There is little doubt, I think, that the feminine streak in
James himself was partly responsible for some of those features

of his literary personality which critics of his work have found disturbing and equivocal : inquisitive detachment, vagueness about practical details, squeamishness, and an over-developed taste for the dubious virtues of renunciation. Without taking too much for granted, it may, I feel, be suggested that the theme of the prying outsider, which recurs so constantly in James's plots (e.g. in *The Sacred Fount, The Aspern Papers, Confidence, The Private Life*), is a fantasy of Destruction and would therefore tend to occur insistently to a man who was as careful as James to exclude anything resembling aggression from his personal relationships. The Renunciation theme is the obverse of the same, masochistic medal. Renunciation may, of course, be a reasonable, as well as a strong-minded, act. But the evident alacrity with which James resorted to this method of solving the dilemmas of his heroes (from Christopher Newman to Guy Domville and the narrator of *The Sacred Fount*) suggests that his addiction to the idea of noble renunciation in fact concealed something less creditable—namely, lassitude, or a disinclination to face the indifference of others.

The excessive pains taken by his 'nice' characters to avoid hurting each other's feelings—the kind of verbal fuss which becomes a mania in *The Awkward Age*—is probably traceable to the same source. To attribute to other people indiscriminately your own delicacy of feeling is an amiable trait, even when seen to be ridiculous ; but if transferred by a novelist to the characters of his own creation it is bound to take the edge off many a situation. Not that James was unaware of the danger in his own case : in *Notes of a Son and Brother* he observes, as early as 1860 (when he was seventeen), his " wasteful habit or trick of a greater feeling for people's potential propriety or felicity or full expression than they seemed able to have themselves ". He met the danger, as we see, not by trying to correct the habit—that would have involved sacrificing an integral part of his genius—but by deliberately narrowing the field of his concentration. If, as I disengage, the supreme test of an artist's intelligence is his ability correctly to judge his own scope, then Henry James rarely betrayed the faculty for which, as a novelist, he is perhaps most justly famous.

Rarely, but not never. There is, after all, *The Princess*

Casamassima. This embarrassing novel displays the author as a good and clever, but curiously naïve spinster who has rashly agreed to give a lantern lecture to a boys' club in a slum district. Her goodwill is not in question, but it is impossible not to titter. So entirely at sea did James find himself, when faced by the theme he had undertaken to illustrate, that his very first chapter recalls—unthinkably—the *Mystères de Paris* of Eugène Sue. Unthinkably, because in any context with which he was familiar James would not—at this date—have thought it desirable to employ the spotlight of crude melodrama. Like all James's large canvases, this one has well-realised passages, and the single character who bears signs of having been observed—Millicent Henning—is a distinct success, in spite of the conventional Cockney in which she is made to speak. The impression of objectivity is striking—until we realise that for once James was not in a position to be anything but objective. It might, however, be argued that he chose the right moment at which to write this book : we may safely assume that if he had attempted it earlier in his career, it would have been even worse than it is ; later on, he would not have wanted to write it at all. We can, if we like, call the novel ' a brave effort ', so long as we remember that to write outside one's scope usually indicates a desire for approval from quarters that have hitherto withheld it.

★   ★   ★

James's excursion into the theatre was an error of judgment of a different kind. There is plenty of evidence in the novels that theatrical effect, even of quite a crude order, was not outside James's scope. It seems improbable that he realised how melodramatic his plots often were. To face this fact might have disconcerted him seriously : he preferred to complain, with some emphasis, that " I *may* be made for the Drama (God only knows !) but am not made for the theatre ! " The result was that when he sat down to write for the stage his eye was only half on the ball. It seems almost too obvious to point out the futility of attempting a medium of which one feature—and that the most important—repels your taste ; yet this is just what James did. The effort was not even brave.

Had he lived in the era of broadcasting he might have perceived in radio drama a solution to his problem. We cannot suppose that in this event he would have ceased to write fiction ; but on occasion he might have found microphone technique, with its fluid sequences, its power of suggestion, its capacity for juggling with time and space, a fascinating medium for the kind of theme which appealed to him. How much better, for instance, *The Outcry* or *Covering End* would be ' on the air ' than they are as stories, or than they would ever have been on the stage !

It is pleasant to dream of the triumphs James might have won in the Third Programme. In reality, however, we are faced by the dismal failure of *Guy Domville* ; and here, I feel, we move back, out of the public sphere of the artist, into the private world of James himself. An atmosphere of mystery surrounds this play and its production. It has never been published and there is some reason to suppose that the text has vanished altogether. The reports of the first-night calamity contradict one another : some speak of a tempest of booing, others say the commotion was in reality very small. Whispers of a cabal rose, fell, then rose again. Those who saw the play have shown themselves curiously unwilling to be drawn on the subject : not one has given a detailed account of the plot. Mr. Shaw, with his customary generosity, spoke up for the play and had a scathing word for the booers ; otherwise his notice is unusually reticent.

What are we to make of all this embarrassment, which could hardly have been greater if James had appeared before the audience without his trousers ? After all, unsuccessful playwrights (and successful ones too) had been greeted with boos before 1895. Even the alleged cruelty of George Alexander, in deliberately hiding from James the temper of the house which he was about to face, is not, judged by the standards of public life, very heinous.

I think we must conclude that the cause of all the shame and embarrassment, and of the subsequent desire of all concerned to draw a veil over the incident, was the personality of James himself. With the possible exception of De Quincey, no eminent man of letters was ever less of a ' public ' character (in the sense that Mr. John Strachey is a public character) than

Henry James. With his New England urbanity, his squeamishness, and the overscored minuet of his habitual speech, he displayed the peculiar—the touching and exasperating—innocence
of the quintessentially private person. Wherever he went he
expected everyone to be as courteous to him as he was to them,
and you would have had to be grossly insensitive—not to say
ill-natured—to disappoint this expectation. It is fatal for such
people to invite a *direct* relationship between themselves and the
general public. So long as they confine themselves to printed
publication, all may be well. The results, if ungratifying, can
be ignored or explained away. But the man who exposes
himself, immediately, to the jeers and hisses of a crowd of
strangers, is assuming the responsibilities of a public personality.
It must have been painfully evident on the first night of *Guy
Domville* that Henry James had put himself in a false position.
He had expected the minimum politeness and deference in a
sphere where such confidence is misplaced. Thus—obscurely,
indefinably perhaps—it seemed unfair, as well as rude, to have
booed Henry James in person, for the reason that would make
it not unfair, or even rude, to boo a professional politician.

If James's extreme urbanity, and his peculiar form of
innocence, were a transformation of aggressive impulses to
which his conscious nature refused all overt expression, his
notorious, and often comic, ignorance of practical life was due
to the purely idealistic cast of his mind, to which material
particularities appeared irrelevant and even absurd. It is entirely
possible that James himself did not know what the humble
domestic object was by which Mr. Newsome *père* had made
his pile. We are free, if we will, to conclude that it was a
chamber pot ; but this conclusion is strictly irrelevant to James's
purpose. At the emotional level on which *The Ambassadors*
proceeds, exactitude of this type is as intrusive as a curiosity to
know what Mélisande had for breakfast. If one feels the need
of these facts, it is a sign that one had better let James and
Maeterlinck alone. As Stuart P. Sherman has argued, [1] with
some force, James was interested, first and last, in Beauty ; and
this exclusive devotion led naturally to the elaborations of his
personal demeanour. Paradoxically, the eye can be innocent

---

[1] In *The Question of Henry James*, a symposium edited by F. W. Dupee.
(Allan Wingate, 1948.)

and yet know that it is innocent. To so highly conscious and withal so clever a man—and one who so clearly was able to look on at the spectacle of himself—it is rash to attribute *any* degree of unawareness or naïvety. Such people love to act ' in character ' : it flatters their self-esteem and amuses their friends at little or no cost to themselves. When James, taking tea with E. F. Benson at a golf club, referred to the game as " some beflagged jam-pots, I understand, my dear Fred, let into the soil at long but varying distances. A swoop, a swing, a flourish of steel, a dormy " : when he spoke thus, we may take it that he knew perfectly well how hugely Benson—and posterity, too—would enjoy the joke.

★   ★   ★

Some kinds of reticent people cannot unbutton even in correspondence. James was not one of these : his letters are not a mere by-product of his life, they are an integral part of his *œuvre*, and it is in them—quite as much as in his reported conversation—that we find him enjoying, tongue in cheek, the delicious fun of being Henry James. When Lamb House was being got ready to receive him, in 1898, his friend Miss Muir Mackenzie sent him from Winchelsea a report on the progress of the work. His reply strikes the ingenuous note which, in middle-aged men of letters, seldom fails :

> . . . I am content enough with the bathroom—but hopeless about the garden, which I don't know what to do with, and shall never, *never* know. I am *densely* ignorant—only just barely know dahlias from mignonette—and shall never be able to work it in any way. So I shan't try—but remain gardenless—only go in for a lawn ; which requires mere brute force—no intellect ! For the rest I shall do decently, perhaps—so far as one can do for two-and-ninepence. I shall have nothing really ' good '—only the humblest old fifth-hand, 50th hand, mahogany and brass. I have collected a handful of feeble relics—but I fear the small desert will too cruelly interspace them. Well, *speriamo*. I'm very sorry to say that getting down before Saturday has proved only the fondest of many delusions. The whole place has to be matting-ed before the rickety mahogany can go in, and the end of that—or, for aught I know, the beginning—is not yet. I have but just received the ' estimate ' for the (humblest) window-curtains (two tiers, *on*

the windows, instead of blinds : white for downstairs, etc., greeny-blue for *up*, if you like details), and the ' figure ' leaves me prostrate. Oh, what a tangled web we weave !—

Best of all, perhaps, because so richly funny, is his description, in a letter to A. F. de Navarro, of the alarm of fire at Lamb House in the following year :

> Drama—tableau ! My dear Tony, you are literally my saviour. The above row of stars represents midnight emotions and palpitations of no mean order. As I finished the line just before the stars I became aware that a smell of smoke, a sense of burning that had worried me for the previous hour, had suddenly very much increased and that the room was full of it. *De fil en aiguille*, and in much anxiety, I presently discovered that the said smoke was coming up through the floor between the painted dark-green planks (*dark* green !) of the margin—outside of matting and rugs, and under a table near the fireplace. To assure myself that there was no source of flame in the room below, and then to go up and call my servant, do you see ? (he long since snoring in bed—for it's now 2.15 a.m.) was the work of a moment. With such tools as we could command we hacked and pried and sawed and tore up a couple of planks—from which volumes of smoke issued ! ! Do you see the midnight little flurry ? Bref, we got *at* it—a charred, smouldering—*long*-smouldering, I suppose—beam under, or almost under, the hearthstone and in process of time kindled— that is heated to smoking-point by its temperature (that of the hearth), which was very high. We put him out, we made him stop, with soaked sponges—and then the relief : even while gazing at the hacked and smashed and disfigured floors. Now my man is gone to bed, and I, rather enlivened for immediate sleep, sit and watch by the scene of the small scare and finish my letter to you. . . .

★   ★   ★

This kind of thing prompts us to ask how Henry James would have reacted to any kind of serious violence. As he reacted to the hostile reception of *Guy Domville*, no doubt—with icy horror, silence, retreat. But the question is academic, not so much because serious violence was in fact never offered him, as because he belonged to the small but distinct race of people who are shunned by events. These people " to whom nothing ever happens "—you can call them fortunate or unfortunate, according to taste—have been admirably touched off by Henri de Montherlant, in one of his published *Notebooks* :

> Certains hommes éloignent d'eux le tragique. Dans le petit et dans le grand. Cela va de l'écrasé dans la rue, qu'ils ne sont jamais là pour voir, aux bombes et aux mitraillades qui les entourent de toutes parts sans les toucher. Ils ne sont pas plus timorés que d'autres, et ne se mettent pas plus à l'abri. Au contraire, leur imagination peut avoir le goût et quelque désir de l'épreuve tragique. Rien à faire : le drame ne frappe pas où ils sont. Ils traversent la guerre et les révolutions sans avoir vu une seule fois un cadavre, sans savoir comment cela est fait. Incurablement préservés, et bourgeois malgré eux.

★   ★   ★

" Bourgeois in spite of themselves "—the phrase applies to Henry James as it applies to Proust, with whom he had a good deal in common. The enormous statement, " L'homme commence au Baron ", attributed to an " eminent French naturalist " (unnamed and seemingly untraceable) in Sutherland Edwards's *History of Lyrical Drama*, would have delighted both James and Proust, though neither would have been naïve enough to subscribe to it. In its simplest form, the passion of the middle-class person for a ' title ' is probably a sign of emotional underdevelopment—the child's awe of the grown-up. The persistently naïve snob always displays other signs of arrest as well. Yet what is comprehensively described as snobbishness has not always been so unintelligent as it is nowadays universally assumed to be. Like James, Proust was interested, first and last, in Beauty ; and it was the beauty of history, its colour and variety and romance, which attracted both these writers to the relational complexities of Debrett and the Almanach de Gotha. Those who harp on the futility of social gatherings, dinner parties and gossip about family connections, overlook the fact that such relaxations are games played according to rules : they exercise the faculties of mental agility and finesse as golf or football exercises those of the body. James was never in any danger of forgetting this. The man who, during his first London period, dined out nearly every night, must often have been supremely bored—but clearly he remembered that the ability to conceal boredom is part of any social life above the level of a schoolroom.

Nevertheless, the fact that Henry James considered a position in London Society of the *fin-de-siècle* " a légitimate subject of ambition ", did not prevent him from soon assuming an ambivalent attitude towards it. It was a love affair, and as such had its ups and downs ; but the balance was never completely upset. James found wickedness shocking, and the evil in his chosen themes was often a result of the social system of the times. But from this it does not follow that he believed a cultured civilisation such as he cherished could survive a collapse of the hierarchic structure. In fact it is the contrary belief, implicit in everything he wrote, said and did, which, more than anything else, annoys American critics of Henry James—especially those, like Mr. Edmund Wilson and Mr. Van Wyck Brooks, who hang on to the tradition of Mark Twain, despite all the demonstrable rubbish talked by that man of genius. They do not, however, avoid the issue, as Mr. Stephen Spender does in *The Destructive Element*, by pretending that in his last period James's admiration for the European nobility had turned to contempt, and that his three largest canvases—*The Ambassadors*, *The Wings of the Dove* and *The Golden Bowl*—were intended as a kind of time-bomb. Those who want an indirect indictment of nineteenth-century society would be better advised to look for it in *Lucien Leuwen*, *L'Education Sentimentale*, and the novels of George Gissing.

*   *   *

A prolonged study of James's work (as of Proust's) brings us up against the ultimate absence of an inclusive philosophy. Of religion, in either the institutional or the mystical sense, it is obvious that he had little idea. At the age of fifty-five we find him acknowledging receipt of his brother William's lecture on *Immortality*, with " great appreciation of the art and interest of it ". He continues : " I am afraid I don't very consciously come in to either of the classes it is designed to pacify—either that of the yearners, I mean, or that of the objectors. It isn't the difficulties that keep one from the yearning—it is somehow the lack of the principle of the same." The habit of intellectual analysis had by this time destroyed any basis for an act of faith such as may originally have been there. In a letter of condolence, written earlier in 1883, James seems to come as near as he could to the formulation of a creed :

> . . . I am determined not to speak to you except with the voice of stoicism. I don't know *why* we live—the gift of life comes to us from I don't know what source or for what purpose ; but I believe we can go on living for the reason that (always of course up to a certain point) life is the most valuable thing we know anything about, and it is therefore presumptively a great mistake to surrender it while there is any yet left in the cup. In other words consciousness is an illimitable power, and though at times it may seem to be all consciousness of misery, yet in the way it propagates itself from wave to wave, so that we never cease to feel, and though at moments we appear to, try to, pray to, there is something that holds one in one's place, makes it a standpoint in the universe which it is probably good not to forsake.

This kind of belief is vague enough to be thoroughly comfortable, is in no sense active and can safely be left to look after itself. The term ' stoicism ' is symptomatic ; in modern times it means little more than that the person who applies it to himself has come to terms with the irreducible sadness of life.

Possibly Henry James must be numbered among those artists (and there have been many) who remain satisfied with the *spectacle* presented by the universe. Certainly it was the drama of moral beauty which appealed to James in his most characteristic inventions—from Catherine Sloper to Maggie Verver —rather than any supernatural sanction which might be supposed to guarantee its value. In his ' ghost ' stories, in *The Turn of the Screw* and *The Sense of the Past*, James took over the supernatural apparatus of Poe and Hawthorne as elsewhere he took over the female confidant of French classical tragedy and the lightly caricatured secondary character of Balzac. He uses the supernatural element as a mere device whereby to express a psychological state—a climactic intensity of spirit. There are no overtones.

This is the *ne plus ultra* of the æsthetic outlook, and there is no evidence that James ever felt the need to go beyond it. His curiosity was infinitely deep, but it was confined to the

relations of men and women to each other. In the sphere of
his own life we are not permitted more than an oblique glimpse
of feelings that might have endangered the tenor of his way.
Few artists can have had a stronger sense of vocation ; but over
and above this, James possessed the invalid's temperament,
which knows, within a hair's breadth, how much of anything
it can stand. The question of his health had preoccupied him
from the first, yet his references to it have the vagueness
characteristic of neurotic anxiety. He died, we are given to
understand, of intestinal atrophy brought on by the obstinate
pursuit of a dietetic fad known as ' Fletcherising '. The whole
situation, so far as we know it, suggests hypochondria, closely
bound up with groundless worry about his financial position,
which, if not exuberant, was in fact perfectly secure.

Hypochondria is perhaps never wholly emotional, although
from the way James dances round the physical ailment or
incapacity which prevented him from taking an active part in
the American Civil War, we gather that he was not anxious to
go into details. It has been suggested, on the basis of certain
pages in *Notes of a Son and Brother*, that James suffered from a
life-long sense of guilt at not having participated actively, as his
brothers did, in the Civil War. This kind of view is dangerous
because, once suggested, it looms disagreeably and seems able
to explain so much. Moreover, in this case it is based solely on
the *tone* of James's statements about his physical and mental
condition at the time. Nevertheless, if we are careful not to
press the point, we must, I think, admit that there is something
equivocal about the crucial passage :

> Scarce at all to be stated, to begin with, the queer fusion or
> confusion established in my consciousness during the soft spring of
> '61 by the firing on Fort Sumter, Mr. Lincoln's instant first call
> for volunteers and a physical mishap, already referred to as having
> overtaken me at the same dark hour, and the effects of which
> were to draw themselves out incalculably and intolerably. Beyond
> all present notation the interlaced, undivided way in which what had
> happened to me, by a turn of fortune's hand, in twenty odious
> minutes, kept company of the most unnatural—I can call it nothing
> less—with my view of what was happening, with the question of
> what might still happen, to everyone about me, to the country
> at large : it so made of these marked disparities a single vast

visitation. One had the sense, I mean, of a huge comprehensive ache, and there were hours at which one could scarce have told whether it came most from one's own poor organism, still so young and so meant for better things, but which had suffered particular wrong, or from the enclosing social body, a body rent with a thousand wounds and that thus treated one to the honour of a sort of tragic fellowship. The twenty minutes had sufficed, at all events, to establish a relation—a relation to everything occurring round me not only for the next four years but for long afterward— that was at once extraordinarily intimate and quite awkwardly irrelevant. I must have felt in some befooled way in presence of a crisis—the smoke of Charleston Bay still so acrid in the air—at which the likely young should be up and doing or, as familiarly put, lend a hand much wanted ; the willing youths, all round, were mostly starting to their feet, and to have trumped up a lameness at such a juncture could be made to pass in no light for graceful. Jammed into the acute angle between two high fences, where the rhythmic play of my arms, in tune with that of several other pairs, but at a dire disadvantage of position, induced a rural, a rusty, a quasi-extemporised old engine to work and a saving stream to flow, I had done myself, in face of a shabby conflagration, a horrid even if an obscure hurt ; and what was interesting from the first was my not doubting in the least its duration—though what seemed equally clear was that I needn't as a matter of course adopt and appropriate it, so to speak, or place it for increase of interest on exhibition.

Hernia ? A strained heart ? It seems a pity that not even on this occasion could James bring himself to state the case in plain terms. And he only makes matters worse by his coy approaches to the subject of the war itself :

My appreciation of what I presume at the risk of any apparent fatuity to call my ' relation to ' the War is at present a thing exquisite to me, a thing of the last refinement of romance, whereas it had to be at the time a sore and troubled, a mixed and oppressive thing—though I promptly see, on reflection, how it must frequently have flushed with emotions, with small scraps of direct perception even, with particular sharpnesses in the generalised pang of participation, that were all but touched in themselves as with the full experience. Clear as some object presented in high relief against the evening sky of the west, at all events, is the presence for me beside the stretcher on which my young brother was to lie for so many days before he could be moved, and on which he had lain during his boat journey from the South to New York and thence again to Newport, of lost Cabot Russell's stricken father, who, failing, up and down the searched field, in respect of his own irrecoverable boy—then dying, or dead, as afterwards appeared, well within the enemy's works—had with an admirable charity brought Wilky back to a waiting home instead, and merged the parental ache in the next nearest devotion he could find.

The gluttonous enthusiasm of the non-combatant for the ardours and endurances of the fighting man is always embarrassing to contemplate ; and in a passage like the following we cannot help noticing how near James approaches to the luxurious vanity of Proust relating the tender solicitude for his health and comfort displayed by Saint-Loup and his brother officers of the garrison at Balbec :

This (the animating principle of his memories) was, for me, at the time neither more nor less than that the American soldier in his multitude was the most attaching and affecting and withal the most amusing figure of romance conceivable ; the great sense of my vision being thus that, as the afternoon light of the place and time lingered upon him, both to the seeming enhancement of his quality and of its own, romance of a more confused kind than I shall now attempt words for attended his every movement. It was the charmingest, touchingest, dreadfullest thing in the world that my impression of him should have to be somehow of his abandonment to a rueful humour, to a stoic reserve which could yet melt, a relation with him once established, into a rich communicative confidence ; and, in particular, all over the place, of his own scanted and more or less baffled, though constantly and, as I could not have it, pathetically, ' knowing ' devices. The great point remained for me at all events that I could afterwards appear to myself to have done nothing but establish with him a relation, that I established it, to my imagination, in several cases—and all in the three or four hours—even to the pitch of the last tenderness of friendship. I recover that, strolling about with honest and so superior fellow-citizens, or sitting with them by the improvised couches of their languid rest, I drew from each his troubled tale, listened to his plaint on his special hard case— taking form, this, in what seemed to me the very poetry of the esoteric vernacular—and sealed the beautiful tie, the responsive sympathy, by an earnest offer, in no instance waved away, of such pecuniary solace as I might at brief notice draw on my poor pocket for. Yet again, as I indulge this memory, do I feel that I might if pushed a little rejoice in having to such an extent coincided

with, not to say perhaps positively anticipated, dear old **Walt**—
even if I hadn't come armed like him with oranges and pepper-
mints. I ministered much more summarily, though possibly in
proportion to the time and thanks to my better luck more
pecuniarily ; but I like to treat myself to making out that I can
scarce have brought to the occasion (in proportion to the time
again and to other elements of the case) less of the consecrating
sentiment than he.

The patronising reference to Walt Whitman is particularly
unfortunate, since it suggests that James was far from possessing
the older man's breadth of sympathy—and to assume this would,
I think, be a superficial judgment.

★   ★   ★

To distinguish the false from the true in a nature so subtle,
and withal as elaborately constructed, as that of Henry James, is
no doubt an impossible task for the historian. Only personal
intimacy could suffice—and perhaps not even that, for emotion
(affection, dislike, vexation, self-love) intervenes to hide clues
and distort understanding. In some sense it is easier to arrive
at a fair judgment of a cold, unsympathetic, self-sufficing
character, than of someone who gives himself, as generously as
did Henry James, to his friends. The touching comedy of his
assumption of British nationality was, we may take it, typical
of the partisanship which he brought to his friendships. The
strong feminine streak in his nature forbade criticism as disloyalty, once he had given his affection. It is loyalty, and the
quest for perfectly balanced relationships, which inspired the plots
of his most moving stories, at all stages of his career as a novelist.
However great an artist we may think him, James hardly belongs
to the type of creator who disappears behind his work. We
can admire, say, Titian and Brahms without being much interested in them as men. With James this is not so : although
at his best he is among the few classically perfect novelists, his
work prompts intense curiosity about the man himself, because
his style, even at its most elaborate, is as personal—as conversational even—as that of a letter.

The past ten years have produced a considerable crop of
Jamesiana, and there is probably still more to come. But even

when the last extant letter has been published, and the last comment made by the last personal friend, critics will continue to speculate and argue and disagree ; for the personality of Henry James—like his work—is inexhaustibly rich.

(1948)

II

The Portrait of a Lady

The code of ladyhood received its first attacks (from within) just before the 1914–18 war. After that war it was generally buffeted, both from within and from without ; now there are few representatives of the species still extant, and they are mostly old, living apart and—as a standard—generally unregarded. Where a lady is detected, her vulnerability is contemptuously exploited. Virtue may be its own reward, but the adage comes ill from those who flout it. What is—what was—that virtue ? To be a lady meant to possess a high degree of social responsibility and a sensitiveness to *taste* in behaviour. It was primarily an æsthetic, only secondarily a moral, position : the lady did certain good things because to do them was implied by her condition, and she avoided certain others because they were (to her) obviously ugly. If she was kind it was because she was, in the nature of her case, disinterested. She was not expected to be an angel, but was continuously required to be something of an artist. In order to fulfil these responsibilities it was necessary for the lady to be relieved from certain others. She was not expected to cook, do housework, or look after her own children from morning till night. These tasks entail virtues of their own, which are not the virtues proper to ladies. H. G. Wells sneered at Henry James for thinking that there was any difference between a lady and a woman. An æsthetic sense at all times meagre may help to account for this failure of comprehension; in any case, other Socialists have shown themselves less insensitive to a distinction which, as I have said, reposes less on a moral than on an æsthetic basis. Yet it is Socialism, with its egalitarian tenets, that will have been responsible for the liquidation of the lady. One does not have to be Henry James to be alarmed at this prospect. The values of culture, which are in the widest sense those of religion and art, have in the past owed to the institution of ladyhood, and to the activities expected of ladies, a steady nourishment with which these values cannot dispense. It is an institution based on leisure—not necessarily more leisure than is possible in a classless society, but a leisure differently distributed and admitting of inequality in the incidence of sacrifice.

In 1881 ladies were the rule, and in drawing the portrait of one Henry James set himself to make explicit what novelists like Disraeli and Meredith took for granted, and to isolate and set in relief the specific qualities of the situation. The result is by the highest standard a most beautiful and distinguished piece of work. If, as a novel, it is not quite in the first class, the reason lies, not in any failure to realise the chief end, but rather in the relative weakness of two of the other characters portrayed. Nevertheless the standard of conduct represented by Isabel Archer will not soon be matched by any code of social behaviour we are likely to see emerge from the opening era. Indeed, to read *The Portrait of a Lady* to-day is to take the measure of the relational poverty to which modern men and women have condemned themselves.

Perhaps I can best establish this by reminding you of the plot, which is, generally speaking, that of almost all of James's larger fictions. A beautiful young girl, brought up in a happy, but strict, New England home, comes to England at the invitation of her aunt, the selfish but intelligent wife of a rich old Anglo-American banker. At the latter's country house Isabel receives attentions, first from her cousin, Ralph Touchett, a prematurely wise and generous-minded invalid who hopes for nothing but friendship from her; secondly, from the local landowner, Lord Warburton, who is as good as the gold of which he disposes in so large a quantity; thirdly, from an old admirer, Caspar Goodwood, a strong silent business man who has followed her from America and does not intend to be shaken off. But Isabel refuses all three. Why? Because none of them touches her imagination. The Young Girl is still in the ascendant; the Lady awaits the test of experience. This is not long in coming. While yet in England Isabel meets a friend of her aunt's, a clever, charming, accomplished, somewhat mysterious woman of the world, Madame Merle—and succumbs to the romance of charm. Later, when she accompanies her aunt to Florence, she is taken by Madame Merle to visit a friend of hers, one Gilbert Osmond, a dilettante living in distinguished poverty with a young daughter, in a beautiful house full of precious objects picked up ' on the cheap '. Against the advice of everyone, in spite of the horrified warnings of Ralph Touchett, the more discreet approaches of Lord Warburton, and the overt attacks of Caspar Goodwood, Isabel insists upon marrying Osmond, who, primed by Madame Merle with the information that Isabel is her uncle's heiress, has alone guessed how to appeal to her imagination. Defiant, persuaded she is doing a fine thing, Isabel marries in haste and repents at gradual, dreadful leisure. She is not long in discovering that her husband is heartless, pig-selfish, a snob, and pettily cruel ; but it takes her longer to realise that with his low mind, which always attributes the base motive, he actually hates her for being what she is—a lady. The climax is reached only when she discovers that Pansy Osmond is her husband's illegitimate child by Madame Merle, who married Isabel to her old lover for the sake of a common convenience. At this point Isabel's isolation is complete, for she has deliberately cut herself off from all those who could, and would, help her. After Ralph Touchett's death, Goodwood makes a last appeal to Isabel to leave her odious husband and return to America with him ; but she refuses, preferring to lie on the bed she has made for herself.

Such is the story, which is unfolded with Victorian leisureliness but with a serpentine guile in the ' placing ' of events and the juxtaposition of characters. As far as the creation of living character goes, James's later elaborations of method never enabled him to do better than here. As the years went on he took mother-of-pearl opera-glasses to look at things he could already see quite clearly. The result was a completeness of detail, fascinatingly absolute, and a soft yet bright light beautifully diffused over the whole canvas—at the cost of lively impact and of clear-cut dialogue. It is possible that at least once (in *The Wings of the Dove*) James treated a situation with wider and deeper implications and an even greater intrinsic pathos ; he never told a more poignant story with more perception and directness.

The poignancy lies in the sweetness of Isabel's character and the brutal disillusionment to which her Bovarysme exposes it. She may have " enjoyed puzzling a lord ", but she declined to marry even the nicest of them. To have chosen so much—so very much—worse would seem to argue a failure of intelligence. But this is precisely the crux of Isabel's character, for we are told quite early in the book that her view of life reposed on a considerable self-esteem. Now innocence such as hers is made doubly vulnerable by this quality, which creates a vicious time-lag after innocence has been destroyed. So that, even when Osmond sneered most outrageously at her, " she still wished to justify herself ; he had the power, in an extraordinary degree, of making her feel this need. *There was something in her imagination he could always appeal to against her judgment.*" (Italics mine.) That something was the romantic dream which such characters as Isabel never wholly relinquish.

Such dreams, however, have nothing to do with being a lady, and life would in any case have posed Isabel some problem or other involving that conception of how to behave. It was not for nothing that James was steeped in French literature, and this novel in especial rings with the sharp, clear voices of La Bruyère and La Rochefoucauld, as well as the graver tones of Corneille. For the Lady is a Cornelian conception and *The Portrait* a typically Cornelian tragedy. Yet these sacrifices have attendant satisfactions, and Isabel rightly felt that they left her " in a better position for appreciating people " than they were for appreciating her. Even in the ultimate abyss of disillusion, during her last meeting with the woman who has grossly betrayed her friendship, she enjoys the luxury of silence, where mere words would spell a vulgar revenge. Such private subtleties are the reward of a Cornelian conception of duty which bids us embrace danger and unhappiness in the æsthetic fulfilment of personality.

" L'esthétique est une justice supérieure," said Flaubert.

Superior or not, Henry James is a novelist who never flinches from judging his characters. Neither in this book nor elsewhere does he pretend to impartiality ; we are told, in no uncertain terms, what to think of his people. This, where the novelist is quite certain of his ground, may be a gain ; where he is not, it merely creates prejudice. No one is likely to object to the way in which the Touchetts, Madame Merle, Henrietta Stackpole, the Warburton family, or Isabel herself are presented. Caspar Goodwood and Gilbert Osmond are less completely successful. The former, intended to seem stiff, is in effect wooden ; while in Osmond, carefully and fairly as he is drawn, we are conscious of being led up the garden path of an ever so dim theatricality ; which is, of course, disappointing. In fact the best portrait of Osmond is the shadow he casts on Isabel herself. Evil is contagious, and what we are permitted to see of Osmond's ill effects on his wife, is among the many evidences we possess of James's sensitiveness to what Hazlitt called " the air of truth ".

To quote La Rochefoucauld : " When loyalty in love does violence to our feelings, it is no better than disloyalty." This is very un-Cornelian and no lady would agree with it ; yet Isabel (and here is one of the incidental beauties of this rich novel) allowed poor Ralph, on his death-bed, to perceive, though not to hear, that she loved him more than anyone else, at long last. They discuss death and Ralph says : " Dear Isabel, life is better, for in life there is love. Death is good—but there's no love."

So Isabel chose life, and the love that is disclosed by the renunciation of love. There is no ' full close ' to this novel, and the scene of Goodwood's final appeal is not among the best in the book. The last page flings open the door on to a room as empty as the heart that has just vacated it. We are left to imagine the years of silent resignation and gnawing doubt—for she will sometimes have doubted—that must have followed Isabel's return to Italy and her husband. Here, in this unresolved and diminishing chord, we feel some of that ineffable quality of mystery that envelops two of Balzac's finest stories—*Le Lys dans la Vallée* and *Le Curé de Village*. Mme de Mortsauf ended by preferring death to the ' love ' of her impossible husband (a better man, however, than Gilbert Osmond) ; but Mme

Graslin, fortified by the Catholic religion and the ruthless support of the priest who knew her secret, found a better way of sticking it out. We may indulge the hope that, on her return to Italy, Isabel may have solaced her loneliness with care for the peasants around her. In any case, all these heroines have one important quality in common : they are, first and foremost, ladies, and know how not to notice the rolling eye of the Devil, even when he speaks sweetest reason.

(1943)

III

The Sacred Fount

" I have just finished . . . a fine flight . . . into the higher fantastic, which has rather depleted me, or at any rate, affected me as discharging my obligations in that quarter." Thus Henry James in a letter to W. D. Howells, written after completing *The Sacred Fount*, in August 1900.

The remark serves to remind us that throughout his career (from *The Last of the Valerii* and earlier, up to *The Sense of the Past*) James considered himself as under ' obligations ' to fantasy. In cases other than this he is thought to have shown a peculiarly happy hand ; but I have yet to come across more than two critics of James's work who have a good word to say for *The Sacred Fount*. Indeed, it is considered unreadable even by amateurs of the master's last phase, many of whom affect not to understand what the book is about. The two exceptions are James's friend Howells, and a later critic, R. P. Blackmur. The first makes a point which, though it seems obvious enough when made, I have not seen used elsewhere, to justify the artist who explores the mysteries of human personality without attempting to explain them.

That troubled source, I will own, " is of a profundity ", and in its depths darkles the solution which the author makes it no part of his business to pull to the top ; if the reader wants it, let him dive. But why should not a novel be written so like to life, in which most of the events remain the meaningless, that we shall never quite know what the author meant ? Why, in fact, should not people come and go, and love and hate, and hurt and help one another as they do in reality, without rendering the reader a reason for their behaviour, or offering an explanation at the end with which he can light himself back over the way he has come, and see what they meant ? Who knows what anyone means here below, or what he means himself, that is, precisely stands for ? Most people mean nothing, except from moment to moment, if they indeed mean anything so long as that, and life which is full of propensities is almost without motives. In the scribbles which we suppose to be imitations of life, we hold the unhappy author to a logical consistency which we find so rarely in the original ; but ought not we rather to praise him where his work confesses itself, as life confesses itself, without a plan ? Why should we demand more of the imitator than we get from the creator ?

It is not necessary to agree with Howells's unhappy description of fiction as an " imitation of life ", in order to feel the cogency of his plea for the validity of James's attitude towards the characters of *The Sacred Fount*.

If we turn now to Mr. Blackmur we shall find a more accurate definition of this extraordinary book, and one which provides a clue to its enigma. In his view it is " not a novel at all but a vast, shadowy, disintegrating parable, disturbing, distressing, distrait, indeed distraught, [which] remains in the degree of its fascination quite ineluctable. It is the nightmare nexus, in James's literary life, between the struggle to portray the integrity of the artist and the struggle to portray, to discover, the integrity of the self."

If, bearing in mind that acute description, we now attempt to say what *The Sacred Fount* is ' about ', I think we shall not find it so very difficult. Put briefly, the theme is that of two people, one of whom, in any relation of intimacy, battens upon the other's vitality. In an image which should spring as naturally to our own minds as it did to James's, the relationship is likened to that of a blood transfusion. Surely there is nothing very obscure or esoteric in this situation : life-givers and spiritual vampires are a frequent subject of comment in all circles at all times.

In *The Sacred Fount* the process is displayed as in one case adulterous, since two of the four people involved are married out of this relationship, which is the reason why they are driven to seek it. The turn which James habitually gave to any screw that came to hand here involves a two-fold character for the sought supply : in the case of Gilbert Long it is mental liveliness which gushes from the sacred fount, in that of Mrs. Brissenden a rebate of physical vitality. I take this distinction to be sufficiently clear from the moment at which James himself (the novel is told in the first person) chooses to reveal his characters. Mr. Edmund Wilson, from his position of dead-pan hostility to the whole book, concludes that what causes the apparent change in the balance of the couples is, simply, love. This view seems to confuse the means with the end : whether or not a sexual relation is involved (and James leaves this in doubt) some degree or kind of ' love ' is clearly essential, for without it the tie would be too weak to operate the mysterious trans-fusion. For mysterious it is, however recognisable ; and the hiding-place of the sacred fount is at least as much the object of James's detective investigation as the various results of its flow. This dubiety, of which Mrs. Brissenden, in the final scene of the book, makes full use, in order to cover her own tracks and cast ridicule on the detective's work, is the chief cause of the generally ambiguous atmosphere of which Mr. Wilson complains. But it is an error to assume that, because it was in the characters' interest to obscure the issue as much as possible, therefore James himself did not really know what it was. It was indeed his habit, in the later novels, to confess his intention explicitly on an early page ; and in *The Sacred Fount* he is careful to expose, in plain terms, the position of his chief characters with regard to one another :

Gilbert Long might die, but not the intensity he had inspired. The analogy with the situation of the Brissendens here, I further considered, broke down ; I, at any rate, rather positively welcomed the view that the sacrificed party to *that* union might really find the arrest of his decline, if not the renewal of his youth, in the loss of his wife. Would this lady indeed, as an effect of *his* death, begin to wrinkle and shrivel ? It would sound brutal to say that this was what I should have preferred to hold, were it not that I, in fact, felt forced to recognise the slightness of such a chance. She would have loved his youth, and have made it her own, in death as in life, and he would have quitted the world, in truth, only the more effectually to leave it to her. Mrs. Server's quandary—which was now all I cared for—was exactly in her own certitude of every absence of issue.

Since this is a detective story, the essential criminality of the beneficiaries is established at an even earlier point in the story. "The agents of the sacrifice are uncomfortable, I gather," says the narrator, "if they suspect or fear that you see." And James makes sure that Gilbert Long and Mrs. Brissenden come to seem more and more baleful to us, as do Charlotte Stant and the Prince in *The Golden Bowl*. After two days' proximity with Henry James, Mrs. Brissenden realises that he is not to be put off the scent, and it is then that she makes her final—and successful—bid to escape conviction. This she does by persuading him that the supposititious process has existed entirely in his sense of it, a contention which does not in the least impair the beauty of the drama ; for it is at this point that we become, at last, fully conscious of what Mr. Blackmur calls " the nightmare nexus ".

* * *

Such, then, in this particular case, is H. G. Wells's " egg-shell, dead kitten, and piece of string ". From the pooh-pooh standpoint, of course, the plot of *The Sacred Fount* will certainly appear tenuous and unreal—but not more so, surely, than *Pelléas et Mélisande* or one of James's own most admired stories—*The Beast in the Jungle*, say, or *The Altar of the Dead*. At the same time, I know that, in sustaining the view that *The Sacred Fount* is one of James's most remarkable and characteristic performances, I am up against his own decision to exclude it from the collected edition of his works. Exactly how much of actual dislike that decision implied cannot now be decided, since James seems to have kept silence on the subject ; merely mentioning the exclusion, without comment, in his preface to the *Daisy Miller* volume. If Mr. Blackmur (as I think) is right, *The Sacred Fount* is James's most *personal* performance, for in it he lifted a corner of the opaque curtain that covered his most private feelings. It is at least possible that he did not realise this until the book was in the hands of the public. The bewilderment and sense of outrage shown by the critics may have warned him that he had ventured on dangerous ground— dangerous, that is, to the safety of much that he intended should remain his own secret. If the sacred fount flowed for James too, it is understandable that he should have desired to let silence fall round his hints about it. As matters stand at present, we cannot know for certain. Further evidence may come to light ; but for the time being we are entitled to feel astonished at the capriciousness that rejected this novel but remained satisfied with a story like *Maud-Evelyn*, of which the *donnée* is considerably more far-fetched and in general terms less ' rich ' than that of *The Sacred Fount*.

★   ★   ★

To turn now from the theme to its treatment is immediately, I feel, to leave debatable ground behind us : as an artistic *tour de force* the book is extraordinarily perfect. By the time he came to write it Henry James had digested, with great fortitude, the bitter lesson of his disastrous venture into the theatre. This meant realising that, although his imagination was in the deepest sense a dramatic one, the tempo of his invention was not well adapted to the stage. His solution—a bold one—was a series of novels which possess all the advantages of theatrical con- struction as well as the discursive qualities of nineteenth-century fiction. I can name only one other author who attempted this fusion successfully : George Meredith ; but even *The Egoist*, much as it owes to the example of Molière, does not attempt the daring symmetry, the absolutely consistent atmosphere, and the resolute values, of *The Sacred Fount*. For in this book James hedged himself in with more restrictions on freedom of move- ment, action and scene, than in any other of his large canvases. The classical unities are strictly observed : if we exclude the brief prologue, which takes place during the train journey from London to Newmarch, the action plays itself out in under twenty- four hours (allowing for sleep) ; within the confines of a country house and its surrounding park ; and without the slightest deviation from the single theme. This severe programme imposes as much strain upon the reader's attention as it seems to have imposed upon James's technical ingenuity. Those who find the price too high cannot be proved unreasonable ; but, as Sainte-Beuve remarked, in denigration of Balzac's *Le Lys dans la Vallée*, " on n'improvise pas toute une atmosphère morale " ; and it can, I think, be agreed that the moral atmosphere in which James was involved by his subject demanded the narrow intensity of classical drama.

Henry James's sense of drama was inextricably bound up with his sense of evil as a positive force, so that he was bound to unfold his story in terms of the waxing and waning of that unstable power in Long and Mrs. Brissenden. But since it was part of his genius to be incapable of neglecting *any* facet of a situation, the action of the novel also involves glimpses of the ' victims ', Guy Brissenden and Mrs. Server, who are represented as huddling together for mutual comfort in their state of dilapidation.

This quadrangular intrigue (there are, of course, the usual subsidiary confidants) is simple enough in outline, but very highly organised in a series of ' set ' scenes which mount steadily, like a grand staircase, up to the final climax of the detective's discomfiture at the hands of Mrs. Brissenden. True to his dramatic scheme, James keeps the dialogue strictly relevant to the situation—a procedure which necessarily limits the number of scenes, but at the same time gives him his opportunity for a decor of the utmost splendour. He had described English country houses before, and was to do so again ; but in creating Newmarch he did the stately home prouder than it has, I think, ever been done, outside the novels of Disraeli. The portrait is in no sense ' built up ', for the detail is too sparing for that ; but the suggestion of fleets of Palladian rooms, opening out of each other and (through French windows) upon wide scapes of lawn and terrace ; the sense of space and of an eternity of still summer trees basking in a hush of unclouded sunlight ; the taste of civilised ripeness, as of a pear just before it turns woolly ; the aptness with which each phase of the drama is lit by the appropriate hour—rising quickly to the sultry grandeur of noon, then dipping more slowly towards night, so that, scene by scene, the human figures throw longer and longer shadows upon the grass : all these calculated features, laid into the background of our consciousness, leave us with the impression—brilliant as a

canvas by Monet—of those " accumulations of expression " in
which for James the fascination of a great country house con-
sisted. Because of the mysterious nature of the intrigue the
characters move in an ambience of magic—of a world where
the mere process of living is taken for granted and occurs out
of sight. Even the host and hostess play no overt part : we never
see them, never even learn their names : they are the invisible
genii who invoke the setting in which the spring is to flow,
suspected but unhindered.

So important to James is this ' magical ' atmosphere that he
sets his most crucial scene with poetic exactitude. The passage
is among his finest flights of prose :

There was a general shade in all the lower reaches—a fine clear
dusk in garden and grove, a thin suffusion of twilight out of which
the greater things, the high tree-tops and pinnacles, the long crests
of motionless wood and chimneyed roof, rose into golden air.
The last calls of birds sounded extraordinarily loud ; they were
like the timed, serious splashes, in wide, still water, of divers not
expecting to rise again. I scarce know what odd consciousness I
had of roaming at close of day in the grounds of some castle of
enchantment. I had positively encountered nothing to compare
with this since the days of fairy-tales and of the childish imagination
of the impossible. *Then* I used to circle round enchanted castles,
for then I moved in a world in which the strange ' came true '.
It was the coming true that was the proof of the enchantment,
which, moreover, was naturally never so great as when such
coming was, to such a degree and by the most romantic stroke
of all, the fruit of one's own wizardry. I was positively—so had
the wheel revolved—proud of my work. I had thought it all
out, and to have thought it was, wonderfully, to have brought
it. Yet I recall how I even then knew on the spot that there was
something supreme I should have failed to bring unless I had
happened suddenly to become aware of the very presence of the
haunting principle, as it were, of my thought. This was the light
in which Mrs. Server, walking alone now, apparently, in the grey
wood and pausing at sight of me, showed herself in her clear dress
at the end of a vista. It was exactly as if she had been there by the
operation of my intelligence, or even by that—in a still happier
way—of my feeling. My excitement, as I have called it, on seeing
her, was assuredly emotion. Yet what *was* this feeling, really ?—of
which, at the point we had thus reached, I seemed to myself to
have gathered from all things an invitation to render some account.
Well, I knew within the minute that I was moved by it as

by an extraordinary tenderness ; so that this is the name I must
leave it to make the best of. It had already been my impression
that I was sorry for her, but it was marked for me now that I was
sorrier than I had reckoned. All her story seemed at once to look
at me out of the fact of her present lonely prowl. I met it without
demur, only wanting her to know that if I struck her as waylaying
her in the wood, as waiting for her there at eventide with an idea,
I shouldn't in the least defend myself from the charge. I can scarce
clearly tell how many fine strange things I thought of during this
brief crisis of her hesitation. I wanted in the first place to make it
end, and while I moved a few steps toward her I felt almost as
noiseless and guarded as if I were trapping a bird or stalking a
fawn. My few steps brought me to a spot where another perspective crossed our own, so that they made together a verdurous
circle with an evening sky above and great lengthening, arching
recesses in which the twilight thickened. Oh, it was quite sufficiently
the castle of enchantment, and when I noticed four old stone seats,
massive and mossy and symmetrically placed, I recognised not only
the influence, in my adventure, of the grand style, but the familiar
identity of this consecrated nook, which was so much of the type
of all the bemused and remembered. We were in a beautiful old
picture, we were in a beautiful old tale, and it wouldn't be the
fault of Newmarch if some other green *carrefour*, not far off, didn't
balance with this one and offer the alternative of niches, in the
greenness, occupied by weather-stained statues on florid pedestals.

★   ★   ★

The narrator of *The Sacred Fount* has been taken to task, in
some quarters, for the indiscretion he shows in failing to mind
what these critics conceive to be his own business. So extreme
an interest in other people's private affairs is felt as ill-bred.
This is a typically Anglo-Saxon criticism, which would seem
futile in a Latin country—or indeed any in which the habit of
psychological discussion is considered natural, and the reality
of amorous intrigue (in one form or another) taken for granted.
Furthermore, what is a novelist's business, if it is not just that
detective interest which stops short at *no* stage of analysis ?
True, the narrator of the novel is not explicitly identified with
James himself. Yet whom else could he conceivably be meant
to represent ? As a revelation of the novelist's reaction to the
raw material of his art the book is peculiarly interesting (this
point has been noted before), and perhaps it is not very sur-

prising that people should be dismayed by the possibility of themselves providing material of this kind. But, as moths devour wool, so novelists devour people, and James follows Stendhal in valuing the social occasion (here a large week-end party) for its power to heighten the awareness, to sharpen the wits and competitive instincts, of the personalities he wishes to observe.

" Try to be one of the people upon whom nothing is lost ", wrote Henry James to a young aspirant : advice that came naturally from one who so clearly belonged to those " minds for which the vision of life is an obsession ". By 'life' is to be understood above all the mind in action, struggling to conceal—and yet preserve—emotion below the unbroken urbanity of the social surface. This contest (it is the ground-bass of James's whole œuvre), is the distinguishing mark of civilisation, in the sphere of human relationships. Seen as a profound enquiry into the cost of these tensions, *The Sacred Fount* appears a supreme exercise in the spirit of poetic analysis.

(1947)

5

The Moment of Silence

THE decision of Teodor Josef Conrad Korzeniowski to write his novels in the English language was the kind of compliment which nations, unlike individuals, seldom receive. To be sure, it had in this case been preceded by what many Englishmen might consider an even greater act of esteem—the future writer's wholehearted adherence to the life and traditions of the British Merchant Navy. The two compliments were really complementary, for the qualities which Conrad found to admire in England and the English were exactly those which, as a member of the Polish upper class, he had been brought up to admire ; but in our case they were combined, and, as it were, systematised, in a manner which made a special appeal to Conrad's most un-Polish love of reserve. There is no reason to suppose that he found the English braver or more honourable than his own countrymen ; but he will have found them gentler in the expression of their virility and more inclined to make light of the grimmer sides of personal experience. It was, in fact, the Public School tradition (then, as now, unconfined to Public School men) which Conrad admired and set himself to celebrate—in Lord Jim, in Captain Lingard, in the heroes of *Youth* and of *The Arrow of Gold*, in the saturnine, pipe-chewing narrators of so many of his stories.

The nineteenth-century English gentleman is a mysterious figure ; and here Conrad was admirably placed, by the nature of his temperament and imagination, to grasp the outline and significance of a type which reaches back, beyond Corneille, to the ideals of fifteenth-century Spain. Love, Duty : in the widest acceptance of these two words are contained the conflict and resolution within a view of life which needs nothing else for its fulfilment. Such a system is only by accident associated with Christian belief ; essentially it is Stoic, and in our own day it has often reverted to its origins. It is a conception in which Silence plays an important rôle, analogous to the gigantic rests in Beethoven's musical style : silence which is not mere void but a form of transition. At such moments of spiritual crisis words are necessarily a kind of betrayal—a dilution of the personality. So that taste here means knowing by instinct how to *define the inexpressible*. In his masterly variations on this ghostly passacaglia Joseph Conrad shows himself the last of the great nineteenth-century novelists, and it was fitting that he should have survived Henry James, whom he greatly admired and to whom he owed much, by only a few years. For all their elaborate articulateness, both these writers place the highest value—the most brilliant accent—on the peak of silence. In a sense their plots are so constructed as to lead up to it. It is, as James might have said, their beautiful moment. Thus Millie Theale dies without telling Kate and Densher what she thinks of them ; Isabel Archer returns to her disgusting husband without the final word to Caspar Goodwood which would explain—and explain away—her action. 'The rest', for Lord Jim, as for Hamlet and Madame Bovary, is silence ; the hero and the heroine of *The Rescue* become articulate only after their crisis has passed ; and the charm of Mrs. Gould's character, for Nostromo as for us, arises from everything she refrains from saying.

★   ★   ★

On a spiritually lower level, but of correspondingly higher dramatic tension, is the silence of suspense of which Conrad is so fond. Let me quote an example of this, on its smallest scale, from the scene in *The Rover* where the lovers, Arlette and Réal, are spied upon by the *sans-culotte*, Scévola :

> She lay down on the very edge of the bed, the kissed hand tucked under her cheek. The faculty of thinking abandoned her altogether, but she remained open-eyed, wide awake. In that position, without hearing the slightest sound, she saw the door handle move down as far as it would go, perfectly noiseless, as though the lock had been oiled not long before. Her impulse was to leap right out into the middle of the room, but she restrained herself and only swung herself into a sitting posture. The bed

had not creaked. She lowered her feet gently to the ground, and by the time when, holding her breath, she put her ear against the door, the handle had come back into position. She had detected no sound outside. Not the faintest. Nothing.

From scenes like this, broken, if at all, by a sharp gesture, an intake of breath or a whispered warning, Conrad derives some of his most striking effects. Similar passages, though on a much larger scale, form the climaxes of *Victory* and of *The Arrow of Gold*. Think, too, of that wonderfully contrived moment in *Nostromo*, when the hero, after his long disappearance from the scene, slides back like a shadow into our ken. And all these passages could be considered as so many studies for the biggest canvas of all, in which Suspense—the waiting for something thought of but unspoken—is the very atmosphere in which all the characters move. In that remarkable novel— surely one of the most impressive fragments in the history of fiction—a bearable tension persists right up to the point where the novelist's own death created a suspense that still endures.

★   ★   ★

An acute sense of the human mystery, which has landed many novelists of to-day in despair and contempt of life, led Conrad to a high opinion of men and women. His disgust when they betrayed the standard he expected of them was incompatible with resignation to human frailty. As a novelist he was no less intransigent ; when the creatures of his imagination fail to rise to his occasions, then the nervous exasperation, which was so striking a feature of his own personality, shows itself in bursts of violent disdain. This cavalier treatment is responsible for much that is bad in his high-toned novels. Scévola, for instance, might have been plausible enough if Conrad had been able to restrain his contempt for a type of fanaticism that was foreign to his own nature ; and in stories like *Victory* and *Nostromo* the lavishly exotic decor favours a too picturesque distortion in the drawing of character. The sense of romance (the feature of his work which seems to ' date ' most strongly just now) gave Conrad his preference for melodramatic plots, unaccompanied by any love of telling a story for its own sake. He has left it on record that in his opinion the point of the universe is probably spectacular. Such a view is perfectly consistent with a strong sense of man's responsibility to develop his powers to the utmost. In slightly varying forms it was the view accepted by the great Elizabethans, and by nineteenth-century figures like Beddoes, Vigny, Meredith, Hardy and (I would add) Henry James. In our own day it is typified by two great novelists—Malraux and Kafka (compare Conrad's shipping-office scenes with the bureaucratic circles of Kafka's hell), and finds original expression in the level narrative and the compassionate understanding of Camus's *La Peste*.

The mainspring of all these writers, from Marlowe to the Existentialists, is the absolute compensation attainable through courage. In a sense this is also Conrad's single theme, concealed in countless variations but most searchingly explored in what many consider his finest novel : *Lord Jim*. This would seem, on the face of it, a most objective work ; but objectivity in fiction is never more than apparent. To the extent to which we may credit Flaubert when he exclaims : " Madame Bovary, c'est moi ! " we are entitled to believe that Conrad might have said, " Lord Jim, c'est moi ! " That Conrad was an efficient sea captain there is no reason to doubt ; hidden in the depths of his reserve were the anguish and the self-distrust which visit all men who are responsible for the lives of others, and supremely, perhaps, in that great symbol of life, the sailing ship. To have imagined the tragedy of Lord Jim's final lapse was to have carried that lapse always in his own heart, and towards the end of his life Conrad gave a further expression to it, in a story which makes little effort to conceal its nearness to his own experience. At the end of *The Shadow Line*, near the height of the long-drawn crisis, the narrator transcribes a portion of his diary, ending with these sentences :

Ships have been dismasted in squalls simply because they weren't handled quick enough, and we have no power to whirl the yards around. It's like being bound hand and foot preparatory to having one's throat cut. And what appals me most of all is that I shrink from going on deck to face it. It's due to the ship, it's due to the men who are there on deck—some of them ready to put out the last remnant of their strength at a word from me. And I am shrinking from it. From the mere vision. My first command.

Now I understand that strange sense of insecurity in my past. I
always suspected that I might be no good. And here is proof
positive ; I am shirking it, I am no good.

The weaknesses that great men successfully overcome tell
us more about them than the façade they present to the world.
To dramatise these frailties becomes their most cherished
ambition. In Conrad's case the moment of silence could have
been filled only in this manner ; which perhaps explains the
fact that, although comparatively slight in texture, *The Shadow
Line* is one of his most satisfying stories. To read this *nouvelle*
after, say, *The Nigger of the Narcissus*, is to be made sharply aware
how greatly Conrad improved his style between 1897 and 1917.
None of us would wish to deprive *The Nigger* of its deserved
status as a minor classic, but we can hardly avoid observing
how often in that novel Conrad has recourse to the swell pedal,
to pompous insistence and un-English phraseology. In other
passages he writes supremely well ; but in *The Shadow Line*
there is everywhere a greater ease and fluency, a clearer outline,
and a lack of emphasis which exactly balances character against
event in a design of great poetic power. And as an essay in
symbolism the story is a masterpiece, for the planes of reality
are kept level to the end.

*   *   *

A highly conscious artist, Conrad believed thoroughly in
the absorption of 'atmosphere' and the collection, on the spot,
of characteristic detail. He did not care to be caught out in
a matter of fact. When I knew him, in the last years of his life,
he had begun work on *Suspense*. Well as he already knew
the Mediterranean scenes among which the story was to be set,
he had no thought of relying on his memory, and his last
journey was undertaken with the object of refreshing it. This
care for detail, for soaking oneself in the atmosphere of the
intended scene, was the chief lesson which he chose to impress
upon one aspiring writer. Hunched like a wary bird in his
upright chair, his face a triangular mirror always tilted towards
the light, he would look down the point of his beard at the hero-
worshipping boy who had walked across the summer park at

Bourne to interrupt the solitude of his study. Perhaps it was
with some idea of correcting my ill-judged enthusiasm for the
novels of D'Annunzio that he shot out at me, in one of his
sudden bursts of jet-black animation : " Go to Venice. And
don't stay at an hotel ; take a room in an old palace and live
there for some time. It's the only way to get the *feeling* of the
place."   And then, if I remember right, he escaped—as so often
—into French, in which language, for conversational purposes,
he seemed still to be more at home than in English. He spoke
of the difficulty he had recently had in recapturing the mood
of *The Rescue*, in order to finish it after a lapse of over twenty
years. In everything he said I recognised the writer I so greatly
loved—the undeviating artist, unsatisfied, treating his novels
as so many surmounted obstacles on the path of an endless quest ;
impatient of admiration—as of so much else—yet never in
doubt of the essential truth of his vision.

The suspended conclusion of *Suspense* is curiously prophetic :

" Where is his star now ? " said Cosmo, after looking down in
silence for a time.
" Signore, it should be out," said Attilio, with studied intonation.
" But who will miss it out of the sky ? "

For some twenty-five years it has been missed neither by
the reading public nor by other writers. It is ·high time it
emerged from behind the cloud.

(1946)

6

Ladies whose bright Pens . . .

I<small>T</small> might be thought that Miss Elizabeth Bowen and Miss Ivy Compton-Burnett were writers too dissimilar to be brought together in a single essay. It is true that a close comparison of their methods and achievements could scarcely fail to be unfair to both of them. But I hope to show that there are points of resemblance, as well as of contrast, which make it worth while to consider them together.

That both are women is already important. Disagreeing with Dr. Johnson's low opinion of feminine ability, I find that when women take the trouble to form a literary style it tends to be a sharper and more flexible instrument than most men command. Gifted with rapidity, the female intelligence is far less given to pedantry and sententiousness. Its characteristic weapons are the adroit phrase, the cunning sentence, the startling yet homely image, the eye which pierces to the heart of a complex personal relationship, and a refreshing freedom from those political obsessions which nag and distort the visions of men. And for kindred reasons women writers seem on the whole more careful than we to keep within their scope. Nowadays it is a common occurrence to find male novelists describing milieux which they have obviously never even visited, simply because they fear the critics' parrot cry : " Mr. So-and-So leaves too much out of his picture." If the picture is properly composed and true to its subject, it is complete : what is omitted is strictly irrelevant. Only the Marxian bigot despises Jane Austen for writing of what she knew and ignoring certain aspects of her times (and she ignores less than appears on the surface). Both Miss Bowen and Miss Compton-Burnett know their limitations ; and knowing them means turning them to account. Miss Bowen marches with the times in the sense that the scenes of her stories are roughly contemporaneous with their publication ; while Miss Compton-Burnett's world is the comparatively

distant and static one of the late Victorian days. At the same
time it should be noticed that both novelists exhaust their
material ; there are no loose ends ; their books are sonatas of
which the subjects are very thoroughly explored. Fascinated,
like all considerable artists, by the richness and profundity of a
single subject, they concentrate all their powers on the gradual
unravelment—volume by volume—of the situation to which
their temperaments have given them the key. And a precise
consciousness of their scope dictates the unit of composition :
in Miss Bowen's case the individual trembling on the verge
of irreconcilable ties ; in Miss Compton-Burnett's, the
family.

★   ★   ★

The family. . . . The disintegrating effect of two wars
has tended to drive novelists away from the direct treatment
of this subject. For Miss Compton-Burnett it is not only the
source of her ideas—and therefore of her plots—but also the
focus of all other relationships. Her characters are in the first
place (as the titles of her novels imply) sons, daughters, wives,
brothers, etc., and only in the second place separate individuals
with lives of their own. Like the Greek dramatists, with whom
she has sometimes been compared, Miss Compton-Burnett
finds in the family the central meeting-place of love and hate ;
so that in the working out of her books tragedy takes the form
of a tightening of the family tie, comedy that of a loosening of
the same tie, when those who have enough courage escape into
the world. (We never follow them into that world, the
advantages of which are taken for granted.) In a scrap of
dialogue worth quoting for other characteristic features, Miss
Compton-Burnett implies her view of this situation :

" What is a little impatience, hastiness—tyranny, if it must be
said—compared with a real isolation and loneliness ? "
" I am afraid it must be said, and they are a great deal
worse."

Two more quotations should serve to explain the richness and
fascination of the subject to which this novelist devotes her

astonishing powers. The first is from the same book (*Daughters and Sons*).

> " What I can't understand about that family," said Rowland, " is how they say what they like all the time, and yet seem to be afraid. Can anyone explain it ? "
>
> " No one yet," said Miss Marcon. " Alfred may be able to presently. But families can seldom be explained, and they make better gossip without any explanation. To know all is to forgive all, and that would spoil everything."

In the end of these novels we *do* know all, and forgive all, and everything *is* spoilt, in the sense that nothing—absolutely nothing—further remains to be said. The material is exhausted and our satisfaction with the work of art is complete.

My third quotation is from a later book, *Parents and Children* : " You should not want to know the things in people's minds. If you were meant to hear them, they would be said." So much is in fact said in these novels, which are nine-tenths dialogue, that the suppressed idea or emotion assumes the importance that in other novelists requires a whole scene, or sequence of scenes, to build up. One of the advantages of Miss Compton-Burnett's exquisite conversation is that any direct statement of feeling or intention has the force of a violent gesture. The ' cast ' is always assembled in such a way that there is one character, and one only, who by making such statements carries the plot a step forward. Like flying bombs, these stories proceed by jet propulsion, and the explosion, when at last it occurs, hits those who were least prepared for it.

A society, the members of which are so highly conscious of their interdependence, creates its own destiny ; and the flying bomb becomes a boomerang. If they could, they would leave stones unturned ; but their circumstances make this impossible. To them, all life is one long process of more or less painful discovery. " When people shut themselves up they cease to separate occasions " ; and—with equal inevitability—they become like actors intoxicated by their own eloquence, wit, self-pity and self-love. Indeed, the degree of articulateness displayed by everyone—from servants and children to the tyrant of the household (an invariable figure)—seems alleged, until it is realised that this is a stylistic convention such as every

artist has the right to adopt.   That everyone in these novels
employs the same tone and the same large and scholarly
vocabulary does not, strangely enough, impair the vigour of
the characterisation, except in a few instances where the dimness
of the outline is due to other causes as well.   Indeed, Miss
Compton-Burnett's signal triumph in this field seems to me
quite sufficient to justify repudiation of the modern insistence
on naturalistic dialogue.   In *Manservant and Maidservant*, for
example—a story in which the convention is carried to its
furthest extreme—the characters whose idiom is least natural
are precisely those who emerge as most real and pathetic.   I am
thinking of George, the footman, Miss Buchanan, the keeper of
the village shop, and at least three of the children (Marcus,
Jasper and Avery).   Their characters emerge in what they say—
not in their manner of saying it—and, still more perhaps, from
the occasions they choose for displaying loss of patience in a
short, stinging sentence.

★   ★   ★

It need not be supposed that this remarkable invention owes
nothing to former novelists ; but those who seek its origin in
an obvious place (e.g. in Henry James) will return empty-
handed.   The true hiding-place, I suggest, is perhaps rather an
unexpected one.   No one would be surprised to discover a
resemblance between the Compton-Burnett milieu and that of
Cranford ; but in a finer, lesser-known novel by Mrs. Gaskell—
Wives and Daughters—another kind of resemblance is too
startling to be accidental.   I quote, for example, the scene in
which Cynthia Kirkpatrick and her half-sister, Molly Gibson,
are discussing the local grandees, Lord and Lady Cumnor, with
Osborne, the elder son of Squire Hamley.

" Are the family coming to the Towers this autumn ? "
" I believe so.   But I don't know, and I don't much care.   They
don't take kindly to me," continued Cynthia, " and so I suppose
I'm not generous enough to take kindly to them."
" I should have thought that such a very unusual blot in their
discrimination would have interested you in them as extraordinary
people," said Osborne, with a little air of conscious gallantry.
" Isn't that a compliment ? " said Cynthia, after a pause of

mock meditation. "If anyone pays me a compliment, please let it be short and clear ! I'm very stupid at finding out hidden meanings."

"Then such speeches as ' you are very pretty ', or ' you have charming manners ', are what you prefer. Now, I pique myself on wrapping up my sugar-plums delicately."

"Then would you please to write them down, and at my leisure I'll parse them."

"No ! It would be too much trouble. I'll meet you half-way, and study clearness next time."

"What are you two talking about," said Molly, resting on her light spade.

"It's only a discussion on the best way of administering compliments," said Cynthia, taking up her flower-basket again, but not going out of the reach of the conversation.

"I don't like them at all in any way," said Molly. "But perhaps, it's rather sour grapes with me," she added.

"Nonsense ! " said Osborne. "Shall I tell you what I heard of you at the ball ? "

"Or shall I provoke Mr. Preston," said Cynthia, "to begin upon you ? It's like turning a tap, such a stream of pretty speeches flows out at the moment." Her lip curled with scorn.

"For you, perhaps," said Molly ; "but not for me."

"For any woman. It's his notion of making himself agreeable. If you dare me, Molly, I'll try the experiment, and you'll see with what success."

"No ! don't, pray ! " said Molly in a hurry. "I do so dislike him ! "

"Why ? " said Osborne, roused to a little curiosity by her vehemence.

"Oh ! I don't know. He never seems to know what one is feeling."

"He wouldn't care, if he did know," said Cynthia. "And he might know he is not wanted."

"If he chooses to stay, he cares little whether he is wanted or not."

"Come, this is very interesting," said Osborne. "It is like the strophe and anti-strophe in a Greek chorus. Pray, go on."

Osborne takes the words out of our mouth : they are an oblique tribute to the patness of the dialogue Mrs. Gaskell always had it in her to write.

Further on in the same book occurs another and shorter passage, which I cannot resist quoting, for it is even closer to the style of Miss Compton-Burnett. Cynthia and Molly are

discussing with Mrs. Gibson the illness of Osborne Hamley and
his brother Roger's chances of succeeding to the property—a
Compton-Burnett situation, if ever there was one.

> " Why, my dear, it is a very natural thought. For poor Roger's
> sake, you know, one wishes it not to be so very very long an
> engagement ; and I was only answering Molly's question, after
> all. One can't help following out one's thoughts. People must
> die, you know—young, as well as old."
> "If I ever suspected Roger of following out his thoughts in a
> similar way," said Cynthia, "I'd never speak to him again."
> " As if he would ! " said Molly, warm in her turn. " You
> know he never would ; and you shouldn't suppose it of him,
> Cynthia—no, not even for a moment ! "
> " I can't see the great harm of it all, for my part," said Mrs.
> Gibson plaintively. " A young man strikes us all as looking very
> ill—and I'm sure I'm sorry for it ; but illness very often leads to
> death. Surely you agree with me there, and what's the harm of
> saying so ? Then Molly asks what will happen, if he dies ; and
> I try to answer her question. I don't like talking or thinking of
> death any more than anyone else ; but I should think myself
> wanting in strength of mind, if I could not look forward to the
> consequences of death. I really think we're commanded to do so,
> somewhere in the Bible or the Prayer Book."
> " Do you look forward to the consequences of my death,
> Mamma ? " asked Cynthia.

It must be admitted that Miss Compton-Burnett's people
have a good deal more to talk about than Mrs Gaskell's.
Murder, incest, suicide, theft, immolation, relentless mental
cruelty, self-martyrdom, forgery, burning of legal papers : the
worst of which human nature is capable is examined on the
level of a solecism, between the dropping of a teacup and the
entrance of a parlour-maid to collect the fragments. Apart
from physical violence and starvation, there is no feature of the
totalitarian regime which has not its counterpart in the atrocious
families depicted in these books. That this is not immediately
obvious is due partly to the Cranfordian background—the
quiet, dignified, medium-sized country house standing in what
Lady Catherine de Bourgh would have described as a ' small '
park, with its village, its rector, its doctor, its retired couple
living on savings or a ' genteel sufficiency '. These people live

too intensely to have time for enjoying their material world. If
anything, the roses round the door make them love mother
less—and she is seldom lovable, in any case. Money is always
important to them, but only in so far as it affects their relationships. They are mildly snobbish. Their sense of social responsibility is implicit, and if lacking is remarked on. Perfect urbanity
is the first rule of their intercourse. In these embowered, rook-
enchanted concentration camps (the landscape is evoked, hardly
ever described) the horrors are made acceptable, but not blunted,
by Politeness and Wit. That is, after all, what manners are for ;
without them, men and women are incomplete. Self-control is
rarely lost in these novels, but where it is lost the result is
proportionately upsetting to everyone, the reader included.
Anger, despair, exasperation, increase the loftiness of the speech,
so that the characters seem to exult in the eloquence of their
feelings. Thus, in *Brothers and Sisters*, Dinah Stace, exceeded by
grief and by her mother Sophia's demands upon her forbearance,
speaks her mind to the housekeeper whose clumsy inquisitiveness
has revealed the family skeleton :

> " Oh, well, Patty, if people will listen at doors, we are
> helpless. . . . We can't allow for that ; though it does seem the
> rule of the house. And we have to talk to Sophia about it. She
> can't keep it off her mind. How is she to make an effort now,
> for the first time in her life ? If people will leave no stone unturned,
> to find out what they ought not to know, they must go on turning
> stones. There are some more to turn. Sophia must be served until
> the end."

Here exhaustion induced by strong feeling is evident, but so is
the control, which is apparent in the short, measured phrases,
and the moderation of the words. But when, as seldom happens,
Miss Compton-Burnett decides that the moment is appropriate
for somebody to lose his or her head, the tempo changes. In
the following speech, taken from the end of *Daughters and Sons*,
the author shows what she can achieve by directness :

> John gave his sister a look and turned away, and she suddenly
> rose and spoke in a harsh, stumbling voice, in tense, stumbling
> sentences, which seemed to be torn from some depth within her
> below the level of speech.

" So Edith is everything, is she ? Edith, whom you married because you thought she had given you money and would give you more ! Edith, whom you married for the paltry sums you thought she would earn and go on giving you ! You did not want her for herself ! You did not want to earn for your wife ! She was to earn for you. And the plan was an empty one after all. It is France who earned the money, France who gave it to you, France who wrote the book that won it ! She hid behind Edith's name, because you were jealous of her. Jealous of your daughter ! She had to hide because she was afraid of your jealousy ! Oh, I know it ; I know it all. I know how Mater thought she found out ; I saw her tamper with the letters ; I saw her read the one addressed to Edith, which was meant for France. I know when she told you ; I know when you talked about it ; I know how you told each other that Edith would have other money in the end. And Edith knows why you married her. She found it out and did not dare tell you. She did not dare tell her husband that for the time she had only herself to give ! She was afraid of the power of your feelings. Oh, people are afraid of you, though you think they are only afraid of me. It is not only of women that people are afraid. What a welter of deceit I have found in my family ! What a moral mess I have stumbled on unawares, stumbled on because it was everywhere. First Mater must deceive us all ; then she deceived you ; then you deceived Edith. Now Edith has begun to deceive you, though I admit she was afraid. France had already deceived you, though I admit she was afraid. Think of the feeling she had for you, when she wanted to save you the humiliation of not being able to earn ; and did not dare to face your jealousy, and so took refuge behind that letter from a stranger ! She knew what you wanted ; she knew you. And I know you now ; I know you. I am not going to do anything more ; I am not going to serve you. I am going to live for myself, as you do. You have taught me how to do it, and I have learned. You tell me you have learned the lessons I have taught, and I can tell you the same. It is Edith who will have to serve you, because she cannot work, cannot earn the petty sums that mean so much to you. They are so paltry, these sums of money that mould your life."

In the finely managed arc of this torrential speech I seem to descry the pattern of Miss Compton-Burnett's literary heritage. Though the resemblances are in some ways misleading, her novels are conceived on the same moral and intellectual level as those of Henry James ; behind both writers, at a distance which, because of their excellence, seems less great than it is, stand the vehement yet composed rhetoric of the Grand Siècle, and the later, more bitter knowledge of Laclos.

★　　　★　　　★

Miss Compton-Burnett's progress in her art has been more considerable than might. appear, in view of the curious and no doubt deliberate uniformity of her novels. For, like a sculptor obsessed by the human figure, she recommences the same task in each successive book, and relies for variety on the endless combinations of spoken language. Her characters are comparatively few and reappear constantly under different names ; but each incarnation reveals some new facet of experience. Her first book, *Dolores* (published in 1911), is indeed not very characteristic and is chiefly interesting for the few glimpses of her later style which it contains. A lachrymose, amateurish book, it occasionally startles one with things like this :

" How do you do, Mrs. Cassell ? " said Mrs. Blackwood. " We were all beginning to wonder if anything had prevented your coming."
" How do you know we were, mother ? We have none of us said so," said Elsa.

This foreshadows the portentous domestic tyrants of *Brothers and Sisters*, *A House and Its Head* and *Daughters and Sons*, as well as the disillusioned, completely intelligent, but dutiful children who suffer under them.

With *Pastors and Masters* (1925) the mature style is already formed in all essential features : it only remained for the artist to exploit the potentialities of so remarkable an invention. Her own view of the matter is set out, in modest but very illuminating fashion, in a dialogue with Miss M. Jourdain published in *Orion*. But to the present writer the effect of her art recalls the aims of the Cubist movement in painting, at its inception. Like a Picasso of 1913, a Compton-Burnett novel is not concerned with decoration or with observation of the merely contingent, nor is it interested in exhibiting the author's personality or in exploiting a romantic dream. It is constructive, ascetic, low in tone, classical. In enquires into the meanings—the syntactical force—of the things we all say, as the Cubist enquired into the significance of shapes and planes divorced from the incidence of light and the accidents of natural or utilitarian construction. These novels contain very few descriptive passages, and none where description is indulged in for its own sake, or for Impressionistic ends ; and in this connection it is significant that Miss Compton-Burnett seems to scorn the aid of images. This does not, I think, strike us at the time of reading ; it is not until we take up some other book that we realise to what extent nearly all novelists rely on metaphor and simile to enliven their scene.

I have described these novels as being nine-tenths dialogue, which gives the measure of the space Miss Compton-Burnett allows herself for noting the scene, the aspect and movement of persons, and any comment she may find necessary. All this is reduced to the absolute minimum and in its abrupt succinctness hardly amounts to more than what one expects to find in the stage directions of a play. The result is something unique, though it has affinities with the tradition of the dramatic legend which was instituted by Plato and includes Fontenelle, Diderot and W. S. Landor.

But it is her zeal for measuring the *temperature* of emotion— the graph described from moment to moment by the action of the plot on the alert sensibilities of her characters—which is responsible both for the continuously witty surface of her writing and the deeper truth of her picture. Like Henry James, Miss Compton-Burnett is much concerned to preserve an amusing surface, as well as a polite one ; and this remains true of the tragic passages in her books. Indeed, in those which deal with the most frightful happenings (*Brothers and Sisters*, *Men and Wives*, *More Women than Men*, *A House and Its Head*) the comic relief is more pronounced and more evenly distributed than in the later novels, of which the plots are considerably less lurid. But it is her anxious attention to Truth which, more than anything else, gives to her books their quality of timeless relevance. Her wit has many sides, but it excludes absolutely the wise-crack, the smart epigram, the modish or private sally. " People don't feel as much as you want them to." This assumption is fundamental to all these novels : it is the arrow on the thermometer which marks 98.4°. And the movement of the book is the to-and-fro rhythm of a tug-of-war between those who do not wish to feel too much and those who are determined to make them feel more than they can bear—until the rope breaks.

I do not want to give the impression that I consider these novels faultless. In common with other important artists Miss Compton-Burnett has a number of failings which are perhaps inherent in her very personal idiom. They are easily described :

(1) She tends to fill her canvas too rapidly, and this mistake is aggravated by the perfunctory way in which she describes her characters, so that we are in constant danger of forgetting or confusing them. It must, however, be pointed out that in her later novels this fault is less apparent.

(2) She cannot manage masculine men. Her males are either overtly effete (e.g. Alfred Marcon in *Daughters and Sons*), or possessed by a feline power-mania (e.g. Duncan Edgeworth in *A House and Its Head*).

(3) Her plots are not easily remembered in detail, or distinguished one from another. This is not a serious charge, for her emphasis lies elsewhere ; but it argues a certain rigidity of imagination and probably has some connection with

(4) Her subsidiary characters are often (but by no means always) too ' flat '. Even regarded as a chorus, they are too dim in outline and tend, moreover, to be always of the same type.

(5) Her chief characters do not develop in the course of the book, they only loom larger or dwindle, according as the author lengthens or shortens her opera-glass.

(6) When Action supervenes, she skates over it as quickly as possible, in the manner of Jane Austen. At such moments a kind of deadly calm descends on the page ; which is in a way effective, but tends to spoil what in music is called the balance of parts.

These faults, although they add up to something, do not seriously affect the brilliance and gravity of these amazing books, or the intense satisfaction that arises from submitting oneself to Miss Compton-Burnett's regime. If her novels are tiring to read, that is because the non-stop rallies, the wonderful patness, the immense logical sequences, make it difficult to decide where to put the book down, when it becomes necessary to attend to something else. Once launched on the stream one must attend completely to every word, until the end is reached. But although these difficulties render her work no light undertaking for the reader, the reward is proportionate—not only in the illumination of so much in life that other, and perhaps more scopious, novelists agree to ignore, but in irresistible laughter. For these books are, one and all, monumentally funny.

★　　★　　★

Cleverness, with which the great Victorians were so liberally gifted and which, in all centuries until the present, was accepted as the nervous system of the intellect, has fallen into disrepute in England (but not, however, elsewhere in the British Isles). This distrust of nimble-mindedness has naturally accompanied the decline in elegance and quality, and the admiration for mediocrity, which are the inevitable outcome of an unjustified belief in ' natural ' equality. In public life this tendency led to preferring Mr. Baldwin to Lord Curzon—a course the results of which many people now agree to deplore ; while in matters of art it is perhaps not surprising that a public which cannot respect Bartok, Hindemith and Picasso should find it easier to applaud John Ireland, E. J. Moeran and Stanley Spencer. Where literature is concerned the distinction is not so clear ; but it remains true that to call a novelist clever is tantamount to accusing him or her of superficiality or of underhand appeal to a reactionary minority.

Both Miss Elizabeth Bowen and Miss Compton-Burnett are extremely clever, though in different ways. The latter, as I hope I have conveyed, enjoys a special ability akin to that of a logician or a statist ; and the beauty of her books arises from the harmony and symmetry of a carefully constructed world. Miss Bowen, on the other hand, is clever in the generally accepted sense of the word : her style, at once smooth and sparkling, is constantly tasselled with fresh and startlingly apt images ; in narrative she is mistress of the oblique and suggestive ; her dialogue is economical but highly characterised ; her plots (described by herself as " the knowing of destination ") are sufficiently ingenious and perfectly adapted to the idea ; and she is supremely sensitive to the poetic moment. As her " Notes on Writing a Novel " show, she is as highly conscious an artist as Miss Compton-Burnett ; but the reader who is uninterested in technique will be less aware of this fact, while reading one of Miss Bowen's novels or stories, because her method of rendering life is not (as painters say) pushed nearly so far. She stands in the same relation to Miss Compton-Burnett as Vuillard stands to Braque, or Sickert to Ben Nicholson.

· Miss Bowen's scope of reference has a wider variety than Miss Compton-Burnett's, but whatever she writes of she knows. It is the same world—that of highly educated, civilised people— but altered and extended by the general loosening up and over-lapping that have taken place in the last thirty years. A single sentence from one of Miss Bowen's most recent stories nicely implies the point of view from which her comment originates :

> " As you know, I was at Sandyhill yesterday : they are taking two more of cousin Rosanna's servants, so she has decided to close some more of the house, including that little ante-room through to the library."

A less careful novelist would probably have written simply ' the library ' ; it is that little ante-room which shows, not only how completely Miss Bowen dominates her ambience, but her precise awareness of the visual situation offered, at all points, by her choice of scene. For, just as Miss Compton-Burnett is essentially an *ear*, Miss Bowen, despite the unquestion-ably real quality of her dialogue, is above all an *eye*. Her business is with the complexities of the heart, light with per-ceptive wonder or heavy with some burden of unwelcome knowledge. But it is always the visual accompaniment of emotion which gives to that emotion its force and colour, and so fixes it in our minds. The scene, however fleeting, is always *set* ; the characters may not give voice to their thoughts, but a sudden sunbeam, a shape of cloud, a sly look, a door ajar, a smouldering cigarette—these speak for them.

Like Miss Compton-Burnett, then, Elizabeth Bowen exhausts her material, but in pursuit of a very different theme. This— to put it briefly—is the conflict between Innocence and Guilt (using those words in the Christian sense). It is the same theme which fascinated Henry James in so many stories, from *The*

American to *The Wings of the Dove* and *The Golden Bowl*. I
say 'conflict', but 'attraction' better describes this most
poignant of all situations ; and it is in the corruption of guileless
persons by those who simultaneously love and hate them,
that Miss Bowen finds her clue.   Innocence is not the prerogative
of girls, but although she has portrayed at least two innocent
males (Colonel Bent in *The House in Paris*, Major Brutt in *The
Death of the Heart*), it is natural that women should be her main
target.   Intense feeling—perhaps the most intense *personal*
feeling he ever knew—kept Henry James at a respectful distance
from Daisy Miller, from Milly Theale and Maggie Verver.
Miss Bowen takes the analysis a step further, into the dead centre
of the personality, exploring that distressful limbo which rings
with the faint cries of those whose trust has been betrayed.
She is adept at conveying to us the fateful calm in which,
at the outset of her novels, the heroine waits for something
to happen. And it is always the worst that happens—the
humiliation that injures the soul so much more direly than
physical rape.

> *Heiss mich nicht reden, heiss mich schweigen,*
> *Denn mein Geheimnis ist mir Pflicht;*
> *Ich möchte dir mein ganzes Innre zeigen,*
> *Allein das Schicksal will es nicht.*

Portia (*The Death of the Heart*), Emmeline (*To the North*), Lois
(*The Last September*), Karen (*The House in Paris*) : these fine-
grained creatures—*jeunes filles en fleur* trembling on the brink
of 'life'—are the descendants of Mignon, but for them fate
(*das Schicksal*) is less foreseen.   They all experience the heart-
break which is not (save in one instance) irreparable, either
through the insouciance of philanderers (Portia, Emmeline,
Karen), or through the selfish conventionality of their immediate
surroundings (Lois).   Evil, as a motive, has not in these novels
the impersonal, terrifying power, working *from outside*, that it
acquires in the work of François Mauriac or Graham Greene ;
but its precipitation in the alembic set a-boil by a chance encounter
is the measure of Miss Bowen's seriousness as a critic of life, and
of her importance in the history of English fiction.   For it should
be noticed that her most characteristic creations are distinctively

English : one would not expect to find Portia or Emmeline or Lois in a Latin country, nor yet in the United States of to-day.

★   ★   ★

As if to defend the subtlety of her theme, Elizabeth Bowen's plots are usually simple and well-defined ; unlike Miss Compton-Burnett's they are impossible to forget or to confuse one with another. Uninterested in complexity for its own sake, she never attempts a sub-plot, and the many subsidiary lives which surround the object of attention are never allowed to engage too much of the reader's interest. Nevertheless, the air in these books is easier to breathe than that of Miss Compton-Burnett's secret sessions. Miss Bowen enjoys a large , cast : her people and places are open on all sides. There is a general air of busy-ness, of work in the background ; light and space surround her characters, even in their tenser moments. These novels are full of movement, in the literal as well as the figurative sense, and this is perhaps why we never feel crowded out of the page—as we sometimes do in a novel by Miss Compton-Burnett.

Though true of all her novels, these assertions need to be modified in the case of what I consider Miss Bowen's finest achievements, *The Last September* and *The House in Paris*. The first of these is an idyll, and therefore more static than (for instance) *To the North*. The setting has some of Miss Compton-Burnett's enclosed quality. But the discursive style, light and quick as a dragonfly, dispels any sense of difficulty. Perhaps because this is an early book, a slight self-consciousness mars the surface ; but the picture of an Anglo-Irish country-house, spell-bound in the lovely autumnal calm that precedes its extinction, could hardly be better done. The double tragedy, with which the book ends, completes the structure without weighing it down. Miss Bowen's debt to Jane Austen shows here (more clearly than in her first novel, *The Hotel*, which happens to be lighter in tone) in an uncommon ability to treat tragedy on the same level as comedy. This could not always be a suitable impression to produce ; that she has chosen it here is an example of her cleverness in discerning the exact tone of feeling with which Lois, her uncle and aunt and her lover, will respond to events.

" People do not feel as much as you want them to."

Miss Bowen would not agree to that, and in her most artistically successful—her most mysterious and poetic—novel, *The House in Paris*, she gives us the full range of her subtle imagination. In this extraordinary and very beautiful book the innocent and the guilty are less sharply distinguished than elsewhere in Miss Bowen's work, and the atmosphere is more sinister. Although there is plenty of movement the dark little house of Mme Fisher dominates the whole book and casts its ambiguous shadow across the Channel into the sunlit, spacious, everyday world of the Michaelis family, which is the author's natural milieu. The contrast is most skilfully suggested, and its influence, like that of a leitmotiv, knits together into a plausible whole the several dramas of the two children, strangers to one another, shut up together for a whole day ; of Karen and Max Ebhardt ; of Max and Mme Fisher ; of Max and Naomi Fisher : until the carefully controlled surface of the book is felt to be underpinned by one of those cat's-cradles which, in life, cause us to exclaim : "How small the world is ! "

The plot itself has the fascinating ambiguity of the supernatural ; caught up in something larger than themselves, outdistanced by their own acts, the characters rise to their creator's occasion in words that have the precise eloquence we have noticed in Miss Compton-Burnett. It was a master-stroke of imagination to have made the children, at the moments of crisis in the story, appear less innocent than most of the adults who surround them. (If we feel sometimes that these children use expressions which are beyond their years, it is because Miss Bowen's dialogue is, on the whole, far less stylised than that of Miss Compton-Burnett, who presents children in the same light.) And when words fail them at last, and they cling together with tears of disappointment and desolation, that is the author's moment of poetry—perhaps the best among the many she has imagined, both in this and other books.

Until *The Heat of the Day*, *The House in Paris* was Miss Bowen's largest, most far-reaching novel. It was eclipsed in public esteem by the later *Death of the Heart*, which is more direct, more scathing, and more consistently amusing. In a sense it is its author's most spirited book. Miss Bowen has always been able to make us laugh aloud by her portraits of second-rate people. Mark Linkwater (*To the North*), Mrs. Vermont and Livvy (*The Last September*), are observed with the virulent exactitude of extreme distaste. The results are in the best tradition of feminine humour ; but it is not till we come to the dreadful Heccomb family, in *The Death of the Heart*, that we find Miss Bowen really stamping on the accelerator. The section of this long novel entitled ‘The Flesh’ is indeed appallingly funny. The moral shoddiness, the callous opportunism, the tastelessness, the threadbare emotional background of this very ordinary English household of the provincial middle class, are rendered with a technical brilliance that astonishes. But it is, I think, possible to feel that the author has overweighted her book here : the last section is too short for what has gone before. My final impression of this novel is that it suffers from the author's having enjoyed herself too much in it : the control is less perfect than in *The House in Paris*, the invention spread thinner, the whole conception less poetically bold. And amusing as the Heccombs are, I prefer the passages of delicious observation, of humour less purely satiric, which abound elsewhere in these novels.

“ What are men one is engaged to like ? ”
“ Very worried and kind,” said Marda, blotting a sheet of her letter. “ Business-like, passionate, and accurate. When they press you against their chests a paper crackles, and when you sit up again to do your face and arrange your hair, they cough and pull out the paper, all folded and say : ‘ While I think of it, I just wanted to consult you about this.’ Dinner services come crashing through the air like in a harlequinade. You feel you have been kissed in a shop. I cannot be adequate. I suggested writing to those public schools for vacancies for our three little boys, but that was not nice apparently. When you are engaged you live in the future, and a large part of the future is improper till it has happened.”
                                                    (*The Last September.*)

Though seen through a woman's eyes, the men in these novels are more various than those of Miss Compton-Burnett.

They tend, it is true, to be definitely either gentlemen or cads (Miss Bowen makes no bones about the reality of this distinction, which is part of her view of life) ; but there are intermediate types, such as Max Ebhart and Julian Tower, and on these she expends the best of her analytical subtlety. The following passage conveys, I think, her method of getting round a character :

> In fact, it was less the niece than the uncle that worried Julian : something in him that would not bring off the simplest relationship, that could be aware of any relationship only as something to be brought off; something hyperconscious of strain or falsity. This descent of an orphan child on his life might have been superficially comic, or even touching. But the disheartening density of Proust was superimposed for him on a clear page of Wodehouse. The poor child's approximation to what she took to be naturalness parodied his own part in an intimacy. She mortified him on his own account and on account of the woman so drearily nascent in her immaturity : he confronted again and again in her look, as she chattered and romped, the unavowable anxiety of the comedian. He was estranged from her, as though she were transparent, as he was estranged from almost all women, by a rather morbid consciousness of fraternity. After three days of her company, he felt like a pane of mean glass scrubbed horribly clean, like a pool dredged of its charming shadowy water-weeds. Those inexactitudes of desire that sent him towards Cecilia, those bright smoky movements of fancy became remote and impossible. Sobriety, peopled with nudes, became unseemly as a Turkish bath ; he could look nowhere without confusion, least of all at himself.
>
> (To the North.)

Miss Compton-Burnett would, almost certainly, have contrived this impression by a cross-fire of argument ; but it should not be assumed (as it so often is) that dialogue is necessarily superior, as a method of exposition, to discursive analysis. Dialogue is of course always more *dramatic* than narrative, but as long as this is taken into account in planning the lay-out of the book, there is no moral obligation to put into dialogue what you prefer to explain in ' your own ' words.

*   *   *

In her latest novel, *The Heat of the Day*, Miss Bowen achieves by subtlety what a male novelist, treating a similar subject, would have tried to achieve by power. For the first time since *The Last September* she has chosen a theme which takes her outside the bounds of private life. Yet she avoids, with extraordinary adroitness, the threats to her scope offered by an international plot to sabotage the Allied war effort during the autumn of 1942. In creating the figures of the traitor, Robert Kelway, and the counter-spy, Harrison, the temptation to strain her imagination beyond bearing must have been considerable. For the world in which these men move, when they are off the stage—the world behind the life, public and private, of Stella Rodney—is that which writers like Simenon and V. S. Pritchett and Graham Greene do not have to invent because they know it. Miss Bowen does not attempt to invent it : as Jane Austen would have done, she takes it for granted, but without losing sight of its effect on character and behaviour. She loads her three central figures with the heaviest possible responsibility : the fate of nations is assumed to depend, at least to some extent, on the good faith and intelligence required by the work in which they are engaged ; and their 'reality', as characters of fiction, is to be measured by our awareness of the ways in which their humanity is modified by what they are compelled to do.

This bringing of public to the bar of private life gives weight and solidity to a story which is painfully dramatic, but never merely sad. Finer and subtler in the analysis of complex feeling than *The House in Paris*, wider in range than *The Death of the Heart*, *The Heat of the Day* is cunningly built up in scenes each of which concentrates the light upon a portion of the displayed canvas. Time plays—is meant to play—little part in the drama, which is superficially laid out in the first few chapters. All that is left is for us to discover, through Stella's eyes, what is really there. The characters do not change : what changes is our attitude towards them. In the process of gradually stripping her people Miss Bowen shows a control that only occasionally falters—though when it does falter, in the case of Robert Kelway, the result is nearly disastrous. Her portrait of the counter-spy, Harrison, is her most brilliant feat. We end by feeling something like affection for this unbearable creature whose unlovability is the clue to his comfortless self. (Incidentally, this figure is an ironic comment on the possible results of a complete victory of character over personality.) It was clever of Miss Bowen to

have seen Harrison, not as sub-, or super-, but as pseudo-human
—provisional—mechanical—sinister and rigid as a being invoked
by a sorcerer's spell.

His concentration on her was made more oppressive by his
failure to have or let her give him any possible place in the human
scene. By the rules of fiction, with which life to be credible must
comply, he was as a character 'impossible'—each time they met,
for instance, he showed no shred or trace of having been continuous
since they last met. His civilian clothes, though one could be
remotely conscious of alternation in suit or shirt or tie, *seemed* to
vary much less than Robert's uniform ; the uninterestingly right
state of what he wore seemed less to argue care—brushing, pressing,
change of linen—than a physical going into abeyance, just as he
was, with everything he had on him, between appearances.

Perceived with the acuteness of extreme distaste, but not
entirely without sympathy, Harrison is much more convincing
than Robert Kelway, who suffers from Miss Bowen's inability
to invest him with any charm. Apart from the fact that he is
alleged to be good-looking, tall, and lame in one leg, it is
difficult to see why Stella (whose attractiveness we never for a
moment doubt) should have been drawn to so null a man.
There are signs of fumbling here : astonishment that Robert
should be capable of treachery somehow gets confused with a
more general wonder that men should be the odd creatures
they are.

This one failure is not enough to spoil the book, though it
does rob the climax of intensity—and even, perhaps, of plausi-
bility. But if the positive aspects of Robert go by default, the
author manages, in brilliant fashion, to account for the flaw in
his character which has produced the spiritual vacuum. Readers
of Miss Rebecca West's *The Meaning of Treason* will recognise a
similar method of putting two and two together. Both have a
characteristically feminine eye for the details of an ambience, but
Miss Bowen, although writing a novel, is the less emphatic.
'Holme Dene ', the house (it is not a home) of the Kelways, is
the counterpart of ' Waikiki ' in *The Death of the Heart*, and of
the London house of Mark Linkwater and his sister in *To the
North* : all of them suggestions that Miss Bowen is unceasingly
concerned with the opposition between poetry and that which

is foreign or hostile to it. These houses, and their inhabitants, are outside the world of poetry because they are emotionally sterile and have no spring of being save the will to survive. For those to whom the poetic is an absolute value there is moral evil in the resistance to it. Even Harrison, we are made to feel, is preferable to the Kelways, because he aspires to poetry through the possession of Stella. His angry refusal to take her, when she at last offers him the shell of herself, gives him a pathos of which the Kelways and their kind are wholly incapable. ' ' Holme Dene '—" the abode of The Thing ", as Charles Addams would call it—is a triumph of Miss Bowen's satirical vein. It is better done than ' Waikiki ', because the author enjoys it less ; the issues being graver, the fun is less hyperbolic.

Everything that *implies* the character of Robert Kelway is more successfully rendered than the man himself. These implications include an opponent who is essentially more formidable even than Harrison : Stella's son, Roderick, who has—and is—everything that Robert lacks. The human excellence of Roderick, and his very evident charm, are enhanced by a tinge of pathos inherent in his exposed condition—exposed, I mean, by the fact of being shovelled, straight from school, into the army, in war-time. This portrait is a wholly admirable one, partly because it is drawn so delicately, and without explanatory emphasis. Roderick's dry humour, and his respectful love for his mother, win the reader's affection at once. His *raison d'être*, where the plot of the novel is concerned, depends on our comprehension of his implicit standards. Before his unexpected inheritance of Mount Morris he is presented simply as a nice boy waiting to see what life may have to offer. Then, the quiet resolve with which he accepts the inheritance (Miss Bowen is careful to deprive this of the more obvious attractions, as well as saddling it with a grave drawback in the form of a supposedly mad female cousin) shows us the quality of his character. In no other kind of person—certainly not in Robert Kelway—should we accept as plausible the same blind grasp of the offered responsibility, the same unhesitating rejection in advance of all other chances, including those of special talents yet undiscovered. To Roderick, a dilapidated ' place ' in Ireland, which he has not even seen and which he has every reason to fear may be a white elephant, is the first of all claims

on his allegiance, just because to make such a choice is part of
a gentleman's heritage.

Roderick is necessary to Miss Bowen's design because he
alone aspires, by the nature of his choice, to rescue certain values
from a world in dissolution. I wish I could feel equally certain
about the propriety of letting Louie Lewis, and her friend
Connie, into the story. In herself Louie is, of course, a gloriously
amusing figure, but she is *necessary* only if the novel is intended
to give an inclusive picture of war-time London—an assumption
which, I feel, the author would be the last to sanction. As if
aware that Louie's position in the book could be thought
anomalous, Miss Bowen defiantly entrusts her with the final
chapter—an act of unwisdom aggravated by a certain sentimentality inherent in the scene itself.

Nevertheless, *The Heat of the Day* is literaturé : as a whole
it will stand up to serious criticism of detail because its effect, as
a work of art, is homogeneous and impressive. Miss Bowen
has gone to school with Henry James, but in order to learn how
best to express an original vision. The result is an analytical
prose continually enlivened by deft allusion and clever imagery.
And her idiom is poetic because it is sustained—like that of
James and Conrad—at the level of drama.

> The very soil of the city at this time seemed to generate more
> strength : in parks the outsize dahlias, velvet and wine, and the
> trees on which each vein in each yellow leaf stretched out perfect
> against the sun, blazoned out the idea of the finest hour. Parks
> suddenly closed because of the time-bombs—drifts of leaves in the
> empty deckchairs, birds afloat on the dazzlingly silent lakes—
> presented, between the railings which still girt them, mirages of
> repose. All this was beheld each morning more light-headedly :
> sleeplessness disembodied the lookers-on.
> In reality there were no holidays ; few were free however
> light-headedly to wander. The night behind and the night to come
> met across every noon in an arch of strain.' To work or think was
> to ache. In offices, factories, ministries, shops, kitchens, the hot
> yellow sands of each afternoon ran out slowly ; fatigue was the
> one reality. You dared not envisage sleep. Apathetic, the injured
> and dying in the hospitals watched light change on walls which
> might fall to-night. Those rendered homeless sat where they had
> been sent ; or, worse, with the obstinacy of animals retraced their
> steps to look for what was no longer there. Most of all the dead,

from mortuaries, from under cataracts of rubble, made their anonymous presence—not as to-day's dead but as yesterday's living—felt through London. Uncounted, they continued to move in shoals through the city day, pervading everything to be seen or heard or felt with their torn-off senses drawing on this to-morrow they had expected—for death cannot be so sudden as all that. Absent from the routine which had been life, they stamped upon that routine their absence—not knowing who the dead were you could not know which might be the staircase somebody for the first time was not mounting this morning, or at which street corner the newsvendor missed a face, or which trains and buses in the homegoing rush were this evening lighter by at least one passenger.

These unknown dead reproached those left living not by their death, which might any night be shared, but by their unknownness, which could not be mended now. Who had the right to mourn them, not having cared that they had lived ? So, among the crowds still eating, drinking, working, travelling, halting, there began to be an instinctive movement to break down indifference while there was still time. The wall between the living became less solid as the wall between the living and the dead thinned. In that September transparency people became transparent, only to be located by the just darker flicker of their hearts. Strangers saying " Good night, good luck ", to each other at street corners, as the sky first blanched then faded with evening, each hoped not to die that night, still more not to die unknown.

Such writing has the exaltation and gravity of music, its boldness and freedom. And in small sketches of people, where appearance, character and environment are to be rapidly and simultaneously conveyed, Miss Bowen has recourse to the same, musical method. For example, the portrait of the Irish peasant girl, Hannah Donovan, reaches us through the same channels of sensibility as would an orchestral leitmotiv in an opera :

Hannah so far had stood with her forehead raised in docile imitation of her father. After his last words she seemed to search the view and the morning, but to find their shining calmness as unchanged as her own. The oblation to victory being taken by her to be now ended, she stepped down quietly from the parapet and began to wander towards the house. Perhaps unwilling to leave the sunshine for the chilly shadow of Mount Morris, or just hoping her father might call her back to declare that, for whatever reason, this was a holiday, she looked back once, her face a moon in daylight between divided hair. Hannah was beautiful—a year older, yet somehow further back, than her sister Mary. This was Stella's first full view of her in daylight : she stayed below stairs over her cooking, or was to be heard calling her poultry in a low, wary voice, shy while a stranger was in the house. Now, to find herself standing in this open sweep in front of the mansion seemed to amaze her : she was a flower only out to-day. Childish for sixteen years, she wore the gravity of her race ; something was added to her beauty by her apartness from what was going on ; her mountain-blue eyes had inherited the colour of trouble but not the story. Having not a thought that was not her own, she had not any thought ; she was a young girl already upon her unmenaced way to Heaven. Her roughened hands hung folded loosely over her apron.

★   ★   ★

Miss Bowen's method is the traditional one ; in this, as in other features of her technique, she is the reverse of an experimental writer ; her originality—like Charlotte Brontë's—derives from poetic vision and a completely sane grasp of the human mystery. Both of these qualities are displayed at their most arresting in her descriptive paragraphs, whether these concern people or natural appearances.

Mme Fisher was not in herself a pretty old lady. Waxy skin strained over her temples, jaws and cheekbones ; grey hair fell in wisps round an unwomanly forehead ; her nostrils were wide and looked in the dusk skullish ; her mouth was graven round with ironic lines. Neither patience nor discontent but a passionate un-resignation was written across her features, tense with the expectation of more pain. She seemed to lie as she lay less in weakness than in un-willing credulity, as though the successive disasters that make an illness had convinced her slowly, by repetition. She lay, still only a little beyond surprise at this end to her, webbed down, frustrated, or, still more, like someone cast, still alive, as an effigy for their own tomb. Her illness seemed to be one prolonged mistake. Her self looked, wildly smiling, out of her body : what was happening in here was too terrible to acknowledge ; she had to travesty it and laugh it off. Unserene, she desperately kept her head.

(The House in Paris.)

That is clever, but not *merely* so : the writer, it is clear, is not enjoying the spectacle, but feeling with her object, and intensely.

My final quotation, from a book which is not a novel at all, has a different aim ; but it would not be so beautiful if it were not also as accurate and concrete as the picture of Mme Fisher.

> In the woods round the house there are rookeries. In September, after harvest, the rooks' existence concentrates feverishly : after sunset they cross the sky over the house in their black thousands, back from the stubblefields. Their swirling, diffused pattern has an intense core ; their return has succeeding movements, like a long dance. They pivot on one another in wide whorls, dissolve in the glaring twilight, look like a black snowstorm. Their cries fill the upper silence ; for minutes together a tree is charged with them and rustles with them, then they spill out to make their pattern again. Slowly the darkness smoking out of the trees absorbs them ; for a long time stragglers continue to cross the sky ; it is quite dark before the last cry is heard.
>
> (*Bowen's Court.*)

*   *   *

The fascination exercised by her novels is apt to make one forget that Miss Bowen is also a voluminous writer of short stories. Of these the longest are also distinctly the most successful. *The Disinherited*, for instance, belongs to the best of her work. But she is the kind of writer who needs space for her best effects, and although her shorter stories are executed with epigrammatic verve and adroitness, their qualities tend to be of the magazine order. If one regrets these *tours de force*, it is because, in a writer of Miss Bowen's attainments, one resents any lowering of standards ; also—and more importantly—because the faint whiff of vulgarity which rises from the pages of a volume like *Look at all Those Roses* can also be discerned, as a disintegrating factor, in *The Death of the Heart*.

However, in her latest collection of stories, *The Demon Lover*, as well as in *The Heat of the Day*, this disheartening fault is altogether to seek. Indeed, I wonder if Miss Bowen has ever written better, or risen to greater heights of imaginative excellence, than in things like *The Happy Autumn Fields* (she manages the supernatural without a hint of whimsy), *The Inherited Clock*, *Ivy Gripped the Steps*, *Sunday Afternoon*. In the last-named story she joins hands with Miss Compton-Burnett, whose style may be said, without derogatory intent, to have influenced the whole tone of the dialogue. Yet 'influence' is probably the wrong term to use here : mature writers do not imitate those with whom they have not already more than a little in common, and it is fairer to regard Miss Bowen and Miss Compton-Burnett as complementary to one another in the positions from which each has chosen to evolve her complex, but neatly exhaustive, art.

*   *   *

Wider in scope but less perfect than Jane Austen, superior to Susan Ferrier (whom in many ways she strongly resembles), at her best the equal of Charlotte Brontë, Elizabeth Bowen is already assured of a distinguished place in any civilisation capable of appreciating, say, *Middlemarch*. The rich background of Anglo-Irish life from which she springs must be presumed in the main responsible for her extraordinary gifts : there is little object in probing further in this direction. A dedicated novelist, she adds, in each successive book, to the private history of English life in our times.

Miss Compton-Burnett's value is easier to assess, because she has set herself a more special, and perhaps on the whole a still harder task. Though her scene is apparently so confined, the moral implications of her art reach into every corner, not only of her own world, but of those worlds the existence of which she only implies. That is the advantage of the high degree of 'abstraction' involved by her method : it achieves universality by dint of excluding what is not essential to the completeness of the design. Like an expert piquet player, she prefers the bird in her hand to the dubious number she might pick up in the *talon*. The results are self-evident, timeless, there-fore proof against the hysteria of fashion and the blight of political theory.

(1946, 1949)

7

The Patient

FEW have had the courage to write a detailed study of physical disease from the patient's point of view. Of the older writers Burton is too objective to enter the category ; nor would I count the drug-addicts who, with Crabbe, Coleridge, De Quincey, Baudelaire, Poe and others, have extended the scope of poetry with the visions of their torture and ecstasy. Of course illness, too, includes extremes of sensation, but they are of a different nature ; the sudden and violent diseases that befall healthy people have not produced a characteristic literature. The reason for this is fairly obvious : while the disease lasts the patient alternates between pain and the precarious relief of a semi-comatose condition, neither of which conduces to reflection ; and once he is cured he is only too anxious to forget the experience and return to his ordinary preoccupations.

To another class of chronic invalid belong those who suffer —and die—in silence. There are always plenty of these, as any hospital Matron will tell you. They are ordinary people unburdened by particular ambition or by the consciousness of any outstanding talent, and their merit lies in the nobility of their resignation. The most selfless of martyrs, they are uninterested in the spectacle of their own suffering, knowing well that it lacks the æsthetic appeal of dramatic destinies.

More psychologically interesting than these triumphs, and much less often examined, is the day-to-day battle against ill-health waged by the chronic invalid who is *not* resigned to his condition. " The tedious thing about illness," said Flaubert, " is that you have to take the trouble to get well, and it is then that you feel the weight of mere existence." No doubt ; but the tedium felt by basically healthy people who know they will eventually recover completely, however troublesome their complaint, is as nothing compared to the Sisyphean task imposed on those who know their condition to be insusceptible of any but slight temporary improvement, as long as they live. It is this razor-edge condition, usually referred to as simply ' feeling ill ', that is difficult to describe because of its lack of positive features.

A few important writers have touched upon it, usually as part of a larger context : one thinks of Montaigne, of Amiel, of Rilke (in *Malte Laurids Brigge*), of D. H. Lawrence (in his *Letters*)—especially perhaps of Virginia Woolf, whose essay " On Being Ill ", says some new things and is extraordinarily accurate. This is a capital point. Objectivity is here neither possible nor really to be desired ; but it is important to be very precise. Precision involves an intensity of concentration that is not always available ; for concentration is very difficult, if not impossible, so long as the body insists on making its presence felt. This insistence need not involve actual pain. A slight but continuous pressure on some inward part, comparable to the tug of friendly but restraining fingers, is a torture in the long run more errosive than acute pain ; for pain admits—indeed requires—interludes of relief, whereas the hands of disquiet never need to relax their steady hold. With obdurate gentleness the attention is distracted from within, the mind divided against itself. Yet the struggle goes on, for the opponents are evenly matched and for a long time the outcome seems uncertain. Thus the patient finds himself in a position analogous to that of K, in Kafka's *The Trial*. Although he is hopelessly constrained, violence is not suggested, let alone offered. His warders show him the politeness of perfect indifference, and even his execution is as ceremonious as all the rest : no more force is used than is necessary to plunge the knife into his heart. From beginning to end of the story, K's own attitude implies a measure of *consent*. Although unaware of having committed any particular crime, and to that extent indignant with the authorities who refuse to disclose the reason for his arrest, K is paralysed, Hamlet-like, by the consciousness of a more general sin. He has no positive aim —only the negative one of being freed from accusation and arrest. He fails in this aim, because in his soul he consents to the authorities' view of himself.

In the same way, to ' consent to ' his sickness is the gravest—

the most desperate—condition into which the chronic invalid can fall. In such a state he relinquishes a primary aim in favour of a secondary one. To regain health is no longer envisaged, for that sun has already sunk below the horizon. He cannot hope to get well because he does not 'deserve to' do so. All that is left to him is a struggle to keep his end up against the Accuser whose aim is to compel him to lose control—to give himself away—to disclaim any place whatever in the sphere of normality. Retiring, like a King at the end of a game of chess, from prepared positions to others less or not at all prepared, he may lose hope so gradually that, when it is all gone, he fails to realise it. Meanwhile, his opponent may himself have few pieces left, but he wins because the King has abdicated ("I am too tired now to shoulder the burden of Hope again"), at the behest of a Castle, a Knight and a single Pawn.

The problem is one of perpetual vigilance. What has to be charted is a graph of awareness : the patient is concerned to discover the point beyond which he knows he can no longer guarantee the minimum integration of thought and feeling ; and it was, I believe, because she felt herself approaching the region (she had been there before) where such a guarantee becomes permanently impossible, that Virginia Woolf decided upon an abdication which was all the more courageous because she knew well that obtuse people would call it the reverse.

In a sense, then, a permanent watch upon the validity of this guarantee is the principal—often the only—activity of an invalid's existence ; it is his ambition, his 'moment of truth'. Life, which once seemed a rocket-shower of enticing possibilities, is narrowed into a focus so tiny that the patient is obliged to develop some day-dream or other with which to counterbalance this exasperating stint. "W. N. P. Barbellion", whose real name was Bruce F. Cummings, who wrote the *Journal of a Disappointed Man*, who died before he was thirty of disseminated sclerosis, who despite this made a small but definite name for himself as a biologist, has described the battle with this particular angel so accurately and so comprehensively that what remains to be added to his account must take the form of comment and illustration. The *Journal* is a minor classic ; it is also one of the most depressing books ever written, partly because Barbellion lost his battle, partly because there was something in him which wanted to lose it, as well as much more that wanted to win.

> The intense internal life I lead, worrying about my health, reading (eternally reading), reflecting, observing, feeling, loving and hating—with no outlet for superfluous steam, cramped and confined on every side, without any friends or influence of any sort, without even any acquaintances excepting my colleagues in journalism (whom I contemn)—all this will turn me into the most self-conscious, conceited, mawkish, gauche creature in existence.

His dread was not unfounded, although his self-pity bred a self-contempt which prevented him—except in rare moments of physical ease—from recognising his own unquestionable superiority of mind and spirit. The next entry, dated a month later, gives another turn to the screw.

> The facts are undeniable : Life is pain. No sophistry can win me over to any other view. And yet years ago I set out so hopefully and healthfully—what are birds' eggs to me *now* ? My ambition is enormous but vague. I am too distributed in my abilities ever to achieve distinction.

That was in 1910. Barbellion was twenty, and had rather less than ten more years to live. In his long and deeply interesting Preface to the posthumous *Last Diary*, Barbellion's brother, Mr. Arthur J. Cummings, takes the critics of the *Journal* to task for describing its author as egotistical and self-pitying, and for their failure to discern the love of life which underlay the expressions of despair. I do not think he entirely succeeds in making his point. No one who did not know Barbellion personally would dream of denying the testimony of those who did, that in fact the joy of living was his salient characteristic, right up to the end. What can be objected is that, although both diaries are full of passages which bear witness to an almost inexhaustible courage, the aggregate effect of Barbellion's self-revelation is depressing. No man has ever been able to put the whole of himself into his work—even when that work is an intimate diary ; and it is even more difficult for the autobiographer to display the *balance* of his character as it appears to his friends. Nor is it desirable he should do so, for the truth is manifold, and only by collating disparate recensions can we arrive at it. As Barbellion himself remarked, in *A Last Diary* : " It is almost impossible to tell the truth. In this journal I have tried, but I have not succeeded." Perhaps he succeeded better than he knew ; at all events he was conscious of the dilemma.

Meanwhile it is evident, even to one who had not the privilege of knowing Barbellion personally, that this man had a remarkable capacity for positive happiness. This was bound up—as in Englishmen it so often is—with the sense of adventure and the thrill of discovery. Probably the happiest hours of his life, apart from those which his wife helped him to snatch from death, were those of his boyhood, before his body began to assert its tedious presence—hours spent in observing birds and insects in the West Country. From his brother's account we learn that Barbellion was " a puny, undersized child, nervously shy, with a tiny white face and large brown melancholy eyes ". This is the kind of child for whom the Accuser lies in wait. To play at chess with him, and win, requires solid inner defences, the signs of which appear on the outside. The description, far more detailed, of the grown man shows how striking was the impression of feverish vitality :

His appearance, notwithstanding his emaciation, was striking. His great height, causing him to stoop slightly, produced an air and attitude of studiousness peculiar to himself. A head of noble proportions was crowned by a thick mass of soft, brown hair tumbling carelessly about his brow. Deepset, lustrous eyes, wide apart and aglow with eager life, lighted up a pale, sharply pointed countenance with an indescribable vividness of expression. His nose, once straight and shapely, owing to an accident was irregular in its contour, but by no means unpleasing in its irregularity, for it imparted a kind of rugged friendliness to the whole face ; and he had a curious habit in moments of animation of visibly dilating the nostrils, as if unable to contain his excitement. His mouth was large, firm, yet mobile, and his chin like a rock. He had a musical voice, which he used without effort, and when he spoke, especially when he chose to let himself go on any subject that had aroused his interest, the energetic play of his features, the vital intensity which he threw into every expression, had an irresistible effect of compulsion upon his friends. His hands were strong and sensitive, with a remarkable fineness of touch very useful to him in the laboratory, and it was always a pleasure to watch them at work upon a delicate dissection. His hands and arms were much more active members than his legs. In conversation he tried in vain to control a lifelong and amusing habit of throwing them out and beating the air violently to emphasise a point in argument. But he moved and walked languidly, like a tired man, as indeed he was.

This was the man who wrote in a letter that " if life were the sheer wall of a precipice, I should stick to it by force of attraction ! " So strong an image would hardly occur save to one who had perceived a threat to his dearest possession.

Again, only *joie de vivre* can account for the persistence of Barbellion's sense of humour in the last year of his illness :

November 26th, 1918.—My old nurse lapses into bizarre mala-propisms. She is afraid the Society for the *Propagation* of Cruelty to Animals will find fault with the way we house our hens ; for boiling potatoes she prefers to use the camisole (casserole) ! She says *Mr. Bolflour, arminstance, von Tripazz*, and so on. Yesterday, in the long serenity of a dark winter's night, with a view to arouse my interest in life, she went and brought some heirloom treasures from the bottom of her massive trunk—some coins of George I. " Of course, they're all obsolute now," she said. " What ! absolutely obsolute ? " I enquired in surprise. The answer was in the informative.

The sense of adventure is vividly present in the following passage, where the observation has a minuteness and a sensitive-ness which recall the Notebooks of Gerard Manley Hopkins :

I arrived only on the outside of the fringe in my study of the habits of the Greater Horseshoe Bat, but I got a lot of enjoyment out of the risky adventure of exploring the disused mines. The wooden struts were rotten, and the walls and roofs of the galleries had fallen in here and there. So we had sometimes to crawl on hands and knees to get past. All the borings were covered with a red slime, so we wore engineers' overalls, which by the time we had finished changed from blue to red, speckled with grease dropping from our candles. Occasionally, in turning a corner, a sudden draught would blow the candles out, and in one rather lofty boring we were stopped by deep water, and, boy-like, meditated the necessity of removing clothes and swimming on with candles fastened on our foreheads. One boring opened into

the side of a hill by a small, insignificant, and almost invisible hole
at the bottom of a steep slide. We slid down with a rope, and once
inside the little hole at the bottom, found a big passage with a
narrow-gauge line and abandoned truck—great excitement !
Another entrance to the mines was by way of a shaft no bigger
than an ordinary man-hole in a drain pipe, its mouth being overgrown with brambles. We fixed a rope round the trunk of a tree,
and went down, hand over hand. We crawled along a narrow
passage—three of us, leaving no one at the top to guard the
rope—and at intervals espied our game, hanging to the roof by
the hind legs. We boxed three altogether, gently unfixing the
hind legs, and laying the little creatures in a tin carefully lined
with wool. The Horseshoe Bat is the strangest sight in the world
to come upon in a dark cave hanging upside down from the roof
like an enormous chrysalis in shape. For when roosting, this bat
puts its two thin hind legs and feet very close together, making a
single delicate pedicle, and wraps its body entirely in its wings,
head and ears included. When disturbed, it gently draws itself up
a little by bending its legs. When thoroughly awakened, it unfolds
its wings and becomes a picture of trembling animation : the head
is raised, and it looks at you nervously with its little beady dark,
glittering eyes, the large ears all the while vibrating as swiftly as a
tuning-fork. These with the grotesque and mysterious leaf-like
growth around its nose—not to mention the centrepiece that
stands out like a door-knocker—make a remarkable vision by
candle-light in a dark cave.

It is clear that such a man ought never to attempt to live in
a town—above all, not in London, for many years Barbellion's
exterior prison. But poverty nagged—as it had nagged George
Gissing, another of those victims of whom the *Journal* irresistibly
reminds us. There is about these unfortunate men a peculiar
aura of ill-ventilated middle-class misery, so much more distressing to read about, because of its pathetic attachment to
intangible values, than the cruder wretchedness of the very poor
whose lives are more liable to be suddenly brimmed by some
concrete satisfaction. The world of the genteel boarding-house,
with its livid gaslight, shooting-gallery ornaments, bamboo
furniture and hairy sofas, its smell of cabbage and stewed steak
and Jeyes' Fluid ; its grimy windows, creaking wardrobe and
looking-glass which tips forward ; its brown-leaved fern, its
gamboge cake from the grocer's ; a world where lovers hold
timid hands over a plopping gasfire and where those whom

love has ignored hug to their scrannel bosoms some political or
religious quackery : this was the world, and this the atmosphere,
in which the central movement of Barbellion's pathetic symphony reached an inconclusive end. It is a picture by Sickert,
of the Camden Town period. The early volumes of Miss
Dorothy Richardson's *Pilgrimage*, and Mr. William Plomer's
The Case is Altered, are there for those who wish to document
themselves still more fully in the evasions of this repellent
milieu ; but in Barbellion's case the surroundings do not loom
so large because his illness, and its attendant self-absorption,
burst the gimcrack framework of his life. His standard of
happiness was not really low, in spite of references to " dream
pictures of a quiet studious life in the Cromwell Road ", and a
taste for the milk-and-soda ecstasies of Eugénie de Guérin : not
low, because of his bright peculiar gift, his microscopic eye ;
because he so evidently loved the highest when he saw it—which
was seldom, though that was hardly his fault ; and because he
fought his battle with the Accuser open-eyed.

But the end was not yet. Despite the mock announcement
of his death (a joke in rather dubious taste, whether or not it
was intended to deceive) with which Barbellion concluded the
Journal, he lived for two more years, and the tone of *A Last
Diary* is subtly different from that of the preceding volume. In
Kafka's *Diary* for 1911 there is a passage of which the tone
recalls Barbellion :

It seems so dreadful to be a bachelor, to become an old man
struggling to keep one's dignity while begging for an invitation
whenever one wants to spend an evening in company, having to
carry one's meal home in one's hand, unable to expect anyone
with a lazy sense of calm confidence, able only with difficulty and
vexation to give a gift to someone, having to say good night at
the front door, never being able to run up a stairway beside one's
wife, to lie ill and have only the solace of the view from one's
window when one can sit up, to have only side doors in one's
room leading into other people's living rooms, to feel estranged
from one's family, with whom one can keep on close terms only
by marriage, first by the marriage of one's parents, then, when
the effect of that has worn off, by one's own, having to admire
other people's children and not even being allowed to go on
saying " I have none myself ", never to feel oneself grow older
since there is no family growing up around one, modelling oneself

in appearance and behaviour on one or two bachelors remembered from our youth.

When we read the diaries and autobiographies of bachelors we are, I think, always more or less aware of the exasperating solitude against which, by some means or other, they have to provide. For there will always be times when the burden of self becomes too heavy to be borne. However busy the life, however many the friends, the single room, glumly empty, bides its moment. In the *Journal of a Disappointed Man* it is this nasty little room which we can never forget. But Barbellion had the sense, and the courage, to get out of it. He married, in spite of everything, and went to live in the country. It was his final act of defiance, his challenge to the Accuser, with his derisory company of Knight, Castle and Pawn. And the tone of the *Last Diary* is proof that in losing his life he saved it.

When the *Journal* was first published, many readers were, as I have recalled, shocked by its egotism, to which, indeed, Barbellion himself draws constant attention. I wonder now what those readers expected, in the circumstances. Healthy people are judged by what they do, sick people by what they say ; and surely the value of that resides in its honesty. But Barbellion is more than honest : his introspection has that supercharged quality, often found in German and Russian, but very seldom in English, literature—at all events since understatement became a national characteristic. It was not an accident that Barbellion saw himself reflected in Lermontov and Marie Bashkirtsev. Let me collate a few examples from the *Journal* :

Feel like a piece of drawn threadwork, or an undeveloped negative, or a jelly fish on stilts, or a sloppy tadpole, or a weevil in a nut, or a spitch-cocked eel. In other words and in short—ill.

Before now I have tried going off to bed. But that does not work—I don't sleep. Moreover, I have been in the grip of a horrible mental unrest. To sit still in my chair, much less to lie in bed doing nothing seemed ghastly. I experienced all the cravings of a dissolute neurotic for a stimulus, but what stimulus I wanted I did not know. Had I known I should have gone and got it. The dipsomaniac was a man to be envied.

February 20.—Am feeling very unwell.   My ill-health, my isolation, baulked ambitions, and daily bread-winning, all conspire to bring me down.   The idea of a pistol and the end of it grows on me day by day.

February 21.—After four days of the most profound depression of spirits, bitterness, self-distrust, despair, I emerged from the cloud to-day quite suddenly (probably the arsenic and strychnine begin to take effect) and walk up to Exhibition Road with the intention of visiting the Science Museum Library so as to refer to Schaefer's *Essentials of Histology* (I have to watch myself carefully so that I may act *at once* as soon as the balance of mind is restored).

So many rubrics for an anthology of Discomfort. . . . The last of these is of especial interest, because it reveals the importance, for the chronic invalid, of acting *at once*, whenever the cloud happens to lift.   Hence the feverish haste to accomplish the most trivial business of life, the anxiety to cram as much activity as possible into the precious hours of relief, until the Accuser wakes up and those persuasive fingers close again round the vitals.

Unlike other writers on illness, who dance round the subject, or embroider it, Barbellion pierces to the inmost cell—that of nervous depression, which is the ultimate, featureless hell always liable to open and swallow up the sufferer.   This prison is perfect. No warder is needed, because there is no door ;   there is no light, because no window, and printed words might be in Etruscan, for all the pleasure or instruction they communicate ;   no sound, except the lame Alexandrine of the blood ;   nothing but sensa-tion—the body crammed with milling centipedes, from the roots of the hair to the soles of the feet.   In such case nobility of nature can assert itself only in gestures of despair.   The voice crying, " This is not I ! " recedes beyond human earshot.   But, because this horror must somehow be expressed, its results excused, the hand continues to write :

December 15.—I simply do not believe the conclusions I have drawn from my present condition, which has already lasted almost a year, my condition is too serious for that.   Indeed, I do not even know whether I can say that it is not a new condition.   My real opinion, however, is that this condition is new—I have had similar ones,

but never one like this. It is as if I were made of stone, as if I
were my own tombstone, there is no loophole for doubt or for
faith, for love or repugnance, for courage or anxiety, in particular
or in general, only a vague hope lives on, but no better than the
inscriptions on tombstones. Almost every word I write jars against
the next, I hear the consonants rub leadenly against each other and
the vowels sing an accompaniment like Negroes in a minstrel show.
My doubts stand in a circle around every word, I see them before
I see the word, but what then ! I do not see the word at all, I
invent it. Of course, that wouldn't be the greatest misfortune,
only I ought to be able to invent words capable of blowing the
odor of corpses in a direction other than straight into mine and
the reader's face. When I sit down at the desk I feel no better than
someone who falls and breaks both legs in the middle of the traffic
of the Place de l'Opéra. All the carriages, despite their noise, press
silently from all directions in all directions, but that man's pain
keeps better order than the police, it closes his eyes and empties
the Place and the streets without the carriages having to turn about.
The great commotion hurts him, for he is really an obstruction to
traffic, but the emptiness is no less sad, for it unshackles his real
pain.

That quotation is again from Kafka's *Diaries*. If we turn now
to Barbellion's *Journal*, we find the tone essentially the same.

My sympathy with myself is so unfailing that I don't deserve
anybody else's. In many respects, however, this Journal I believe
gives the impression that I behave myself in the public gaze much
worse than I actually do. You must remember that herein I let
let myself go at a stretch gallop : in life I rein in, I am almost
another person. Here I stand revealed as a contemptuous arrogant
malcontent. My life has embittered me *au fond*, I have the crabbed
temper of the disappointed man insufficiently developed yet to be
very plainly visible beneath my innate affable, unassuming, humble,
diffident, cheerful characteristics.

To complain of the egotism of such passages is beside the
point ; even so, no reader can fail to be struck by the scarcity
of references to the 1914–18 war, the course of which coincided
with more than half of this *Journal*. But it is in the nature of
illness to exclude what interests the healthy : " Nothing matters,
provided the tongue is not furred " (March, 1915). There is
the truth ; to have stated it so baldly is perhaps shocking, but
also courageous, since it is evident that Barbellion was acutely

aware of the impression his *Journal* would create, as well as
anxious that he should be given the benefit of the doubt.   In
the long run I believe he will be justified in his hopes, because
fundamentally he was not disconnected either by illness or by
temperament from love in any of its aspects.

> This morning how desirable everything seemed to me !   The
> world intoxicated me.   Moving again among so many human
> beings gave me the crowd fever, and started again all the pangs
> of the old familiar hunger for a fuller life, that centrifugal *élan* in
> which I feared for the disruption and scattering of my parts in all
> directions.   Temporarily I lost the hegemony of my own soul.
> Every man and woman I met was my enemy, threatening me
> with the secession of some inward part.   I was alarmed to discover
> how many women I could passionately love and with how many
> men I could form a lasting friendship.   Within, all was anarchy
> and commotion, a cold fright seized me lest some extraordinary
> event was about to happen :   some general histolysis of my body,
> some sudden disintegration of my personality, some madness,
> some strange death. . . . I wanted to crush out the life of all these
> men and women in a great Bear's hug, my God !   this sea of
> human faces whom I can never recognise, all of us alive together
> beneath this yellow catafalque of fog on the morning of the
> announcement of world famine and world war ! . . .

A passage like that throws all the windows wide open :
the Cromwell Road, the stuffy lodging-house, disappear in a
flash, and the free gift of humanity is revealed as the superpersonal
spirit it is.

But our beginning is also our end.   The child of thirteen
who noted :   " *Sept.* 8 :   Toothache.   *Sept.* 9 :   Toothache.
Sept. 10 :   Toothache.   *Sept.* 11 :   Toothache."—was father to
the man who closed his *Journal*, thirteen years later, with the
entries :   " *Oct.* 14–21 :   Miserable.   *Oct.* 21 :   Self-disgust."
It is the dates which horrify :   six whole days given over to one
ungovernable, destructive emotion.   And then another.   Then
silence, for three months, of which we divine the dragging
length.

The final entry in *A Last Diary*—"To-morrow I go to another
nursing home "—can be taken in a hopeful sense.   To my mind
the phrase tolls like a bell, and would do so in any context.
Between this statement (but it is also something more) and those

I have quoted from the end of the *Journal*, Barbellion is far less laconic. As Death creeps nearer his spirit seems to widen out. Having learnt resignation to pain, if not to death, he could recollect in comparative tranquillity. But there were days of complete lassitude . . . " I expect I am wrong, and I am past hammering out what is right." Barbellion's cry is that of the French poet of the sixteenth century, Jean de Sponde :

> Ton Mal, c'est ta prison, et ta prison encore
> Ce Corps dont le souci jour et nuit te dévore :
> Il faut rompre, il faut rompre enfin cette prison.
> Tu seras lors au calme, au beau jour, à la plaine !
> Au lieu de tant de vents, tant de nuit, tant de gêne,
> Qui battent, qui noircit, qui presse ta raison.
>
> O la plaisante Mort qui nous pousse à la Vie,
> Vie qui ne craint plus d'être encore ravie !
> O le vivre cruel qui craint encore la Mort !
> Ce vivre est une Mer où le bruyant orage
> Nous menace à tous coups d'un assuré naufrage :
> Faisons, faisons naufrage, et jetons nous au Port.

But ultimately the word resignation does not apply to Barbellion ; he was never more vividly himself than when his thoughts turned to the war which was approaching its end :

> Man made the war and we know his reasons. God made the world, but He keeps His own counsel. Yet if man, who aspires to goodness and truth, can sincerely justify the war, I am willing to believe—this is my faith—that God can justify the world, its pain and suffering and death.

And at the time of the Armistice he let fall a sentence—" After the aeroplane, the soul "—which shows how far his own spirit had voyaged in search of the desirable life.

(1945)

8

The Significance of
The Witch of Edmonton

THE character of Hamlet is, on even the most superficial view, an interesting one : that is to say, it presupposes a problem, whatever the circumstances. The same is true of Macbeth, Bussy d'Ambois, Bosola, Orgilus ; and the continued vitality of the dramas in which these figures occur is in large part due to this sense of the problem of personality as arising in any case and in spite, so to speak, of their creators' surrounding inventions. A play like *The Witch of Edmonton*, on the other hand, in which the characters are less obviously complex, and in which the faults of construction and the simple luridity of the plot distract attention from the underlying significance of the action—such a play as this tends to elude revival, or, when by a lucky chance it achieves one, has its point altogether missed by those critics who have one eye firmly fixed on the box-office. It is indeed profoundly saddening that such a masterly performance as the one now to be seen at the Old Vic, under a producer of genius, should have given the majority of critics an impression that the play was something merely quaint—a period piece—a minor hotch-potch by a number of very minor Jacobean poets. Such a view is very superficial, for the problem with which this play deals—briefly that of Good and Evil—is as actual to-day as it was in 1623, and the symbols chosen to represent the conflict have the heart-rending poignancy of a very real humanity. As the Witch herself protests, witchcraft is not confined to poor and hideous old women who seek protection and revenge from a demon against the world which has reviled and cast them out. Expensive, fashionable women,

> " Upon whose eyelids lust sits, blowing fires
> To burn men's souls in sensual hot desires . . .
> Are not these witches ? "

So might the modern fortune-teller, sentenced to prison for pursuing her illegal trade, arraign her clients portrayed in the *Sketch* and the *Tatler*.   Or again :

> " She on whose tongue a whirlwind sits to blow
>   A man out of himself, from his soft pillow
>   To lean his head on rocks and fighting waves,
>   Is not that scold a witch ? "

Mother Sawyer must have made a fine figure at her trial, at which we regret not being allowed to assist ; for she is swift at repartee and has a superb flow of images at her command. It is to Dekker's eternal credit (this part of the play is almost certainly his) that he should have realised—rather surprisingly, in that age—the underlying causes of witchdom.   In her first speech Mother Sawyer voices her bewilderment and the self-distrust which is to lead her to destruction.

> "Some call me witch,
> And being ignorant of myself, they go
> About to teach me how to be one ; urging
> That my bad tongue—by their bad usage made so—
> Forspeaks their cattle, doth bewitch their corn,
> Themselves, their servants, and their babes at nurse.
> This they enforce upon me, and in part
> Make me to credit it."

From this frame of mind to that in which *any* relief from obloquy seems expedient, is a short step ; and it is made within the compass of a single scene by the agency of a last straw in the form of the clowns who ridicule the poor old woman.

> " 'Tis all one
> To be a witch as to be counted one,"

she concludes ; and so fine has been her foregoing speech that we are moved to suspend judgment in her favour.   Her personality as a whole has a vivid intensity, whether she be cursing ; or taking a satiric flight, as in the semi-comic scene with the Justice ; or indulging in horrid merriment with her familiar, the

Dog. But it is in her final despair that she rises to her greatest heights,—that moment when she begins to realise that her demon has no more need to attend her, for her soul is at last split quite in two :

> " I'm lost without my Tomalin ; prithee come,
> Revenge to me is sweeter far than life ;
> Thou art my raven, on whose coal-black wings
> Revenge comes flying to me. O, my best love !
> I am on fire, even in the midst of ice,
> Raking my blood up, till my shrunk knees feel
> Thy curled head leaning on them : come, then, my darling ;
> If in the air thou hover'st, fall upon me
> In some dark cloud ; and as I oft have seen
> Dragons and serpents in the elements,
> Appear thou now so to me. Art thou i' th' sea ?
> Muster-up all the monsters from the deep,
> And be the ugliest of them : so that my bulch
> Show but his swarth cheek to me, let earth cleave
> And break from hell, I care not ! Could I run
> Like a swift powder-mine beneath the world,
> Up would I blow it all, to find out thee,
> Though I lay ruined in it."

The passionate intensity of a perverted love finds here a rhetorical expression equal to, and recalling, that of Baudelaire.

★   ★   ★

But if the witch herself, who provides one crux of the plot, is interesting, the other, Frank Thorney, is even more so. The Jacobean hero-villain never had a subtler exponent in his own age, though for the perfect example we must turn to the work of a later poet—to *Paradise Lost*. The Satan of Milton (and of Blake too, for that matter) was an angel who was damned because he had acquired individuality and could not bear the idea of relinquishing it. Rather than lose it, then, he embraced the worst in himself—all those self-destructive desires and instincts which are the essence of evil. But the will to self-destruction (and it will be remembered that Christ himself could not obtain pardon for Satan, because he did not *wish* to be pardoned) cannot operate alone ; it must disintegrate those

around it as well ; hence the desire for proselytes that devils
have always displayed.

Such is Frank Thorney, and the intensity with which he
feels the conflict between good and evil within his soul is the
cause of his crimes. Had he been a superficial character, able
to do ill with levity, the position into which desire and circumstance combined to throw him would not have upset his easy
balance. But he is a serious person, deeply self-conscious ;
witness his shocked exclamation at his father's suggestion that
he is already married and therefore cannot take Susan to wife :
" What do you take me for, an atheist ? " Frank's intro-
spectiveness must at all times have been strong enough to evoke
the beautiful lines spoken late in the play, when he has fallen a
prey to remorse and terror :

> " 'Troth, sister, thou say'st true ;
> For when a man has been an hundred years
> Hard travelling o'er the tottering bridge of age,
> He's not the thousand part upon his way :
> All life is but a wandering to find home ;
> When we're gone, we're there. Happy were man,
> Could here his voyage end ; he should not, then,
> Answer how well or ill he steered his soul
> By Heaven's or by Hell's compass ; how he put in—
> Losing blessed goodness' shore—at such a sin ;
> Nor how life's dear provision he has spent
> Nor how far he in's navigation went
> Beyond commission : this were a fine reign,
> To do ill and not hear of it again ;
> Yet then were man more wretched than a beast ;
> For, sister, our dead pay is sure the best."

*   *   *

The deep cleft in Frank's nature is symbolised, with exquisite
propriety, by the two women who allow themselves to be
drawn into the vortex of his personality—Winnifred and Susan.
Not that the first of these is evil : her obstinate, animal fidelity
is as real and generous as her instinctive movement of kindness
to her helpless rival. She has, in fact, the virtues of the gangster's
moll she is ; but her large generosity and coarse strength go
hand in hand (as we should expect) with a view of life based

on hard experience and not on dreams. In a sense, then, she is the right mate for such a man as Frank Thorney ; having lived as a serving-maid and been the mistress of her employer, Sir Arthur Clarington, she knew a thing or two before she met Frank. Thus these two meet on a level : she appeals to him because, apart from the physical attraction she exerts, she does not make him feel the duality within him. As is plain from the first scene of the play, she does not have to bear the burden of Respect.

Susan Carter is altogether another matter. Originally forced on Frank by the monetary plight of old Thorney, she is his superior both in wealth and social standing ("Marry a serving-man ? Mew ! " says Warbeck, Susan's first suitor, disgustedly), but also, unfortunately for herself, in character as well, for she is all innocence and goodness. Her meeting Frank at all was bound to be fatal to her, for his is the kind of nature her own could not even desire to resist. As the great French critic, Alain, says, speaking of Othello : " Do not find yourself on the path of an humiliated man " ; and, pointing to the inevitability of Desdemona's fate : " By the law of love the gentle Desdemona must attract the cyclone and by every movement make it turn faster. She has too much power over the meteoric whirlwind, through the disturbance which she causes in it and which the captive soul transforms into action. Just as the insomnia of a powerful man breaks the bed under him, so the tender and fragile life will be broken by that uncontrolled embrace." It is the part of unusual evil to attract unusual goodness, and vice versa. Warbeck, in spite of his bounder's manner and old Carter's suspicions, is as good as gold—and as uninteresting. Susan's pure flame would have burnt itself out uselessly, in his company ; and she knows it instinctively. He is tame and safe ; but Frank calls to something deeper in her than the need for safety—the need for self-sacrifice. From the first moment her heart is irretrievably his :

> "You, sweet, have the power
> To make me passionate as an April-day ;
> Now smile, then weep ; now pale, then crimson red :
> You are the powerful moon of my blood's sea,
> You make it ebb or flow into my face,
> As your looks change."

When he proposes to her, she says :

> "You took too sure possession
> Of an engagéd heart."

"Which now I challenge," answers Frank ; and even at this early stage it is plain that he is moved beyond all expectation by the charm of her happiness and her trust in him. But it is in the magnificently written scene of the wedding that his uneasiness, born of the immitigable conflict within him, is seen growing into a frenzy of fear. "The poor girl ! " he exclaims, involuntarily ; and his sudden determination to leave Susan, immediately after the wedding, is grounded less on the desire to see Winnifred again than on a rising suspicion that if he stays he may end by preferring Susan and thus changing the character he has wilfully embraced. Like Satan, he knows Good too well not to fear its disintegrating effect on the individuality to which he clings as to his one real possession. Having seen the highest, he must needs love it—and he dreads to do so. Hence his frienzied attempt to escape and—having failed to dislodge the vision of goodness from his soul—the hysterical rending of that vision through a totally unpremeditated murder.

Here the stage action assists the spectator's understanding of the deeper significance of this piece of the drama. For a close observation of the action reveals that the gesture with which Frank at last takes Susan into his arms, in the marriage scene, is essentially the same as that with which he later attempts to put her out of his life for ever. (In vain, of course ; for that look of pure affection, which had originally illumined the cleft in his nature, continues to regard him from the open coffin brought by old Carter to confront his tortured eyes. By which time the cleft has been widened, by the scratchings of the Dog, until it is big enough to receive not only Susan's coffin but his own.) Whether outstretched to embrace or to stab, it is the same hand, the same convulsive violence of an uncontrolled nature. But if pity, that most disruptive of all emotions, is at the bottom of his murder of Susan (and it is undoubtedly Pity, and not mere Impatience, that goes circling round him in the figure of the Dog), it is a sudden failing of respect that makes him yield even so far as to let her accompany him a little way upon his road.

A sudden movement of vanity proves Susan's undoing—the one flaw through which the Dog can creep into her soul. Not until she reveals her belief that Frank's sudden resolve to leave her is due to a desire to fight Warbeck in defence of her honour—not until she has shown him this slight glimpse of fatuity, does he steel himself to go through with the business, whatever it may be. He laughs derisively, and when she complains : " You're not so kind, indeed, as I imagined," he replies, as if released by a sudden vision : " And you are far more fond than I expected." But he adds at once : " It is a virtue that attends your kind." Had she had any skill in the politics of the heart, she would not have made this foolish blunder. Yet it is her very guilelessness that moves her husband to tenderness—a tenderness that could at any moment tip over into cruelty, for Frank is the forerunner of Byron, with Winnifred for Augusta and Susan for Annabella—a type described with excruciating precision, in our own day, in the novels of Henri de Montherlant.

After that slip on Susan's part, one trembles to think of her lot as Frank's wife, had she not compelled him to kill her. The vein of brutality in him, aggravated by his sense of her moral superiority, would have found an outlet in reminding her constantly of her folly—long after it had become only too plain to herself, what with Winnifred perpetually in the house, and one thing and another. It was by some such frantically contrived last straw that Byron achieved the final wreck of his marriage, though it is significant of his deepest feelings that, when he lay dying, it was to his wife, not to Augusta, that he turned. It is perhaps this parallel between the characters of Frank Thorney and Byron that gives to the *Witch of Edmonton* an unmistakable atmosphere of the Romantic Revival—as it were the shadow of Manfred lying back across its most poignant scenes.

★   ★   ★

And there are even remoter reverse shadows—those of the esoteric plays of Yeats and Jean Cocteau, two dramatists whose superficial dissimilarities conceal a sense of the mysterious unity

of Good and Evil which rises from the same type of imagination.
The inventive genius which created the sinister beauty of the great
scenes in the *Witch of Edmonton*—the self-wounding and binding
to the tree of Frank Thorney after the murder, the apparition
of the Dog, the knife and chicken and the sound of the lute in
the bedroom—is of the same kind as that responsible for the
beating heart of the resurrected Christ in *The Resurrection*, the
figure of Death in *Orphée*, and the sphinx scene in *La Machine
Infernale*.

In constructive ability the old dramatist is not the equal of
either of the moderns I have mentioned. While in the theatre
the interest and excitement of the play is marvellously sustained,
so that we do not care to notice the points at which the double
action fails to amalgamate, outside it we must admit that the
stories of Frank Thorney and of the Witch herself are not properly
integrated. We can, if we like, argue that the Dog acts as a
sufficient binding force ; but I do not think the argument holds,
because this figure is made to stand (since the stage is after all
a simplifying medium) for two different devils : the revenge-
lust of the witch and the self-destructiveness of Frank. As the
witch points out, at the end of the play, when she is accused of
bewitching the young man to kill his wife : " Is every devil
mine ? " For she has no quarrel with Frank—does not even
meet him till they come together on the scaffold. Her business
lies elsewhere, with the countrymen who are so wonderful an
evocation of a to us hardly conceivable age ; with the clowns
who (*pace* Miss Ellis Fermor) are of slender interest, in spite of
the grotesque, Lazarus-like figure of Cuddy Banks ; and with
Sir Arthur Clarington, who is the real villain of the piece.

Here we touch what was probably at the bottom of the
dramatists' conception : the idea that frivolity (and Sir Arthur
is entirely frivolous) is the only unforgivable sin. When all
the threads are gathered together and nothing but death remains,
the witch does her best to obtain forgiveness through public
repentance. She fails, however—at least with those she had
wronged, though perhaps not with us—for her heart is not
pure, even at the end. Life still burns within her, in spite of age
and disillusionment and grief :

> " Though 'tis true
> I would live longer if I might,"

she says wistfully (no one who heard Miss Edith Evans speak
that line is likely to forget it), thus showing that her old spirit,
which originally conjured up the Dog, is by no means dead.

Frank, on the other hand, is forgiven by all ; but he will
have none of Sir Arthur's unctuous insincerity. " Heaven send
you a new heart ! " he flares out, with some of the same vitality
that had won hearts and brought him down. He makes his
peace with Winnifred, who, ironically enough, survives to
solicit another husband, in a disingenuous epilogue. We shall
hardly blame her : the pulse of life is strong in her—stronger
really than in Frank, who burns with the hysterical violence
of an electric bulb plugged on the wrong voltage. Yet, since
Satan himself has the absolute quality essential to myths but
impossible to men, Frank Thorney is not damned for ever.
His repentance comes late, but when it comes it is sincere enough
to move even the man whose daughter he has murdered. " He
is not lost who bears his peace within him," Frank tells the
bystanders ; and there is no taint of self-pity in this his final
speech, as there is in that of the witch. The vision of reality
comes to him too late to be of use to him in this life, but Spinoza
might have approved his final frame of mind. For him, as for
the witch, the Dog has done his worst, turned from black to
white in token of indifference, and gone in search of other prey.

(1936)

9

Image and Symbol

IT is very seldom that the literature of criticism is enriched
by a contribution so succinct yet packed with thought, so
clear, well expressed and unequivocal, yet written 'from
the inside', as Mr. Cecil Day Lewis's Clark Lectures[1]; very
seldom indeed that any book so gives one the sense of being
completely filled out by its subject. That subject comprehends
the whole stuff of what we call Poetry, with the exception of
metrical technique; and the power of imagery has in itself no
necessary connection with *verse*. So that Mr. Day Lewis's book
resolves itself, as we think back over it, into an examination of
the nature of poetry.

In the most general terms poetry may be described as a
sudden moment of illumination—like the flash of light which,
when you shut your eyes, remains for a short time imprinted
on your eyeball. In one sense it is associated with the intense
conviction of sudden discovery. It is entire, involving all the
faculties in a uniform activity which is both sensuous and
intellectual. Unlike a flower, or some other natural object,
which may be beautiful in a pure sense, uncomplicated by
mental association, the poetic moment need not be beautiful:
it may be lovely or baleful; in either case its nature is super-
rational, because the elements evoking it compose a symbol the
precise significance of which eludes us. It is probable that, if
we could fix the exact provenance of the symbol evoked by the
poetic moment, the poetry itself would evaporate. The activity
of the symbol is organic.

According to this theory the material of a poem consists of
an intuition, or system of intuitions (the 'moment': Mr. Day
Lewis calls it a "state of grace"), displaying some aspect of
essential reality, in the same way that a rose may be said to

---
[1] *The Poetic Image*, by Cecil Day Lewis. (Jonathan Cape, 1947.)

reveal the intrinsic nature of the tree which gives birth to it. The vehicle of this important communication is the poetic image, and in his first chapter Mr. Day Lewis affirms the monist principle which is for poets an inescapable expression of philosophic truth :

> I should not myself go so far as Hulme and declare that, according to the Romantics, "in the least element of beauty we have a total intuition of the whole world". Even Blake would hardly have claimed that the doors of mortal perception ever could be cleansed to this extent. But Hulme's words would be a fair summing-up of the Romantic view if we changed them to "in the least element of beauty we have a *partial* intuition of the whole world". It is essential that we should make up our minds whether we believe this holds true for the images in every kind of poetry, or believe on the other hand that there is more than one basic activity of metaphor. In my opinion, it holds good for all images to the extent that every image recreates not merely an object but an object in the context of an experience, and thus an object as part of a relationship. Relationship being in the very nature of metaphor if we believe that the universe is a body wherein all men and all things are "members one of another", we must allow metaphor to give a "partial intuition of the whole world". Every poetic image, I would affirm, by clearly revealing a tiny portion of this body, suggests its infinite extension.

Proceeding on this assumption, Mr. Day Lewis tentatively supports the important theory, elaborated from Jung by Miss Maud Bodkin, of "archetypal images"—a theory which, by pre-supposing the existence of a "collective sub-conscious", provides an explanation of the power of particular images to communicate poetic experience. If this theory has any truth in it, the grounds upon which science has hitherto resisted the poetic form of perception may gradually be removed. Dr. Johnson kicking a stone in order to demonstrate the reality of matter, was adopting the poet's standpoint—which is also, in this case, the standpoint of common sense. A refusal to countenance any attitude to *sensibilia* other than the analytic, must result in a mental improverishment which would end by abolishing the analyst along with the artist.

★   ★   ★

Mr. Day Lewis is careful to stress the *precision* achieved by the image-making faculty. Since all images are rearrangements of units (often exceedingly small ones) drawn from the memory, it is natural that we should find a certain ambiguity inseparable from words used in this way : an ambiguity which does not detract from the precision of the image (as one might expect it to do) but increases the scope of its meaning and intensifies its emotional power. When Tennyson thinks of the old yew planted over a grave and proceeds :

> Thy fibres net the dreamless head,
> Thy roots are wrapt about the bones—

the beautiful ambiguity of the word *net* (among the many pictures it calls up, that of fishing occurs to us perhaps second, because we are thinking of Hallam's body being brought back across the sea to England) connects the whole of our sensibility with Tennyson's in a repetition of the poetic moment. The subconscious store, which we hold in common with the poet, has been successfully tapped, and the 'state of grace' is established.

The question of the ambiguity of an image is bound up with precision of another sort. Mr. Empson, whose work in this field has (it seems to me) been underestimated, deals chiefly with grammatical or syntactical ambiguity, and that which arises from the double meanings of nouns. An image that is ambiguous gives the same kind of pleasure as those objects in a modern picture which have been pushed so far towards abstraction that they suggest resemblances not readily discernible except to the poetic eye. The result, in both cases, is an extension of sensibility and a demonstration of the oneness of the perceptible world. To the commonsensical person who asks what is the point of painting a tree-stump in such a fashion that to one it will seem a crouching dog, to another a wig on a stand, while a third can perhaps see at once that it is 'primarily' a tree-stump, the only reply is that such ambiguities add depth to experience, enrich our imagination, and increase the stock of available images—available, that is to say, at the receiving end.

In poetry, as in painting, ambiguous images are occasions for experiencing the pleasures of *multiple connection*. Why is

such a conjugation pleasant ? Presumably because the more of
our minds we can employ at once, the greater the satisfaction—
just as a physical activity which demands exercise of all the
muscles is more satisfying than one which requires only a
limited number.

The ambiguous image, when successfully managed, is precise,
not necessarily because its outlines are sharp, but because it is
exhaustive. It fills out our interior vision, to the exclusion of
private (and therefore discrepant) images. The scope of the
poetic in differently constituted minds is a question which has
to be reviewed in every age, and much failure of communication must be put down to the time-lag which causes certain
objects—and images containing them—to resist assumption into
the vocabulary of art. In one of his most important chapters,
Mr. Day Lewis deals with the ' living ' image, and reaches
conclusion about bathos which I feel to be questionable. " The
image is a drawing-back from the actual, the better to come to
grips with it : so every successful image is the sign of a successful
encounter with the real." Agreed ; but surely it is important
that whatever represents ' the real ' should not be encumbered
with too much utilitarian association, otherwise the poem (or
line, or stanza) will refuse to rise from the ground. Mr. Day
Lewis cites the telegraph pole and thinks that the Greeks " would
have seen [it] both from a utilitarian and a poetic point of
view ". But would they ? Literary criticism in the ancient
world, from Aristophanes to Ovid and Longinus, is full of
acrimonious discussion about the vocabularies proper to certain
styles, and there is plenty of evidence that some poets (e.g.
Euripides) were felt to be insufficiently sensitive to this particular
borderland. It is all very well for Mr. Day Lewis to bid us
" experience telegraph poles poetically ". This may be done to
the extent of introducing such objects acceptably into a passage
of poetic *prose* ; but in verse I seem to feel that the attempt
could not at present meet with success. Rossetti's Woodspurge
may have coincided by chance with his hour of agony ; that
does not mean that a more utilitarian object would have done
just as well. It is conceivable that a telegraph pole might have
crystallised that poetic moment ; but neither Rossetti nor any
other poet could make us accept the phrase in a sonnet, though
it might take an equivalent place in a novel. The railway engine

in Zola's *La Bête Humaine* is indeed a poetic image ; but a hundred years have not been able to reconcile us to the locomotive which crashes into the middle of Vigny's *La Maison du Berger*. Even Cowper's sofa, his " cups that cheer but not inebriate ", are palatable only because their primness amuses and charms us ; in a modern epic by Patmore or Elizabeth Barrett Browning they would make us frown and fidget uneasily in our chairs. Nor can I agree with Mr. Day Lewis that Hardy ever wholly succeeds in infusing the necessary poetic ambiguity into the glum domestic paraphernalia with which many of his lyrics are innocently furnished.

It can be assumed, I think, that no object resists the poetic faculty for ever. As long as something remains new enough for its associations to be purely practical ; before it has had time to extend the sphere of its reference—to become ' ambiguous ' : so long as this condition persists, the object will retain the wrong kind of vitality—arouse the unsuitable smile, jump out of the page into the reader's face. Objects thus imperfectly assimilated prompt to action (however dimly and indirectly) ; art and life, instead of reflecting one another, become opposed.

Ultimately it is a question of *congruity*, which I agree with Mr. Day Lewis in thinking a more important element than either novelty or intensity. Congruity as between the various images in a single poem, but congruity also with the state of mind in which alone it is possible profitably to read a poem. Both kinds are more often achieved by the classical type of poet, such as George Herbert or Matthew Arnold, for whom a poem was before all things a construction, and imagery never an end in itself.

> With the Romantic poet, the image-seeking faculty is unleashed and wanders at large, whereas with the Classical it is tethered to a thought, a meaning, a poetic purpose already clarified, and its radius of action is thus far limited.

The time factor is important here, for—the remarks of poets notwithstanding—it is fairly clear that with the classical type of poet the idea (' thought ', ' meaning ') is to some degree detachable from the music of the poem, and therefore both precedes it and dictates what Mr. Day Lewis calls the ' pattern ' of the imagery. Not all poets whose work shows the emotional urbanity and care for form which we associate with the reaction from romanticism, can be called classical in the above sense. For all its grace and symmetry, Valéry's *Le Cimetière Marin* (it has been translated, with exquisite propriety, by Mr. Day Lewis himself) is essentially a romantic poem because its meaning is created gradually by the imagery, as this evolves its pattern from the germinating poetic moment: Valéry's "encounter with the real"—the sea, the sails, the gravestones and his own mood.

Valéry himself once said, in his snubbing way, that "it is not the poet's function to experience the poetic state of mind: that is a private affair. His business is to create that state in other minds" (i.e. his reader's). Like so many of the writer's *obiter dicta* this one is probably a good deal less detached than it looks. One side of Valéry's mind was too deeply analytical to allow the other—the poetic—side to function freely. Perhaps this is why he wrote so little poetry. A similar reflection suggests itself of Mr. T. S. Eliot. The critical writings of both poets could be charged with special pleading. In neither case can we say positively that the poetry itself has been harmed by the prevalent state of the poet's mind; but we may, I think, feel that too acute an awareness of the critic's position has precluded all abandonment to the lyrical impulse. To this extent a hostile critic of Valéry (as of Mr. Eliot) might accuse him of writing 'critic's poetry'—very much as he might condemn Coleridge or W. B. Yeats or Jean Cocteau for writing 'poet's criticism'. To which the valid reply is that there is room in plenty for both these aberrations—if aberrations they be—since neither is a mere substitute: both create effects that are new and peculiar to themselves. But the fact that Valéry's aphorism receives full confirmation from his own poetry should not blind us to what it ignores—namely, that the poet cannot set about producing the 'moment' in others unless he has previously experienced it himself. Of course the poetic state need not issue in a poem: it may be too vague and evanescent, or too trivial, or flawed by some excessive emotion. But if it does so issue, the poem will complete the thought-feeling nexus which evoked it. If there has been no 'moment', then there will be no poem—or at best a fabricated one, unlit by vision. Doubtless there is a

world of difference between the two states—that of receiving
the poetic moment and that of turning it into a poem ; but
the process must have an element of continuity, and the first
part of it is the only possible guarantor of the second.

Nevertheless, Valéry's somewhat conceited remark has a
core of truth. With the second part of it nobody would
quarrel ; the first part seems to have been provoked by a type
of wool-gathering very common to-day and stigmatised, as far
back as the 1840's, by Matthew Arnold when he spoke of " the
modern English habit (too much encouraged by William
Wordsworth) of using poetry as a channel for thinking aloud,
instead of making anything ". And we may add that although
this dart was aimed at the wrong kind of poet, it applies with
equal force to the wrong kind of reader.

★   ★   ★

Poets to whom the poetic state means sudden, implacable
investment by a symbol, run a serious risk at the moment when
the poem itself begins to take shape. Modern romantic poetry
—and there is very little of the other kind—is essentially a
poetry of images, and therefore of symbols. The risk lies in
the elliptical, as it were musical, language encouraged by a
chain of images the logic of which seems—but in fact is not—
self-evident. The dangers implicit in the romantic abandonment to the assault of images are incongruity, needless obscurity,
and the characteristic modern vice of tesselating ' broken images '
and calling the result a poem. Although one of his lectures is
devoted to the subject of ' broken ' images, Mr. Day Lewis
does not define the term. It is clear, however, that what he is
referring to is the pall mall of heterogeneous images, many of
them private or impervious to logical explanation, of which
much contemporary verse consists. The practice appears, on the
face of it, indefensible—until we remember that not all poetry
is intended to be *parsed*, and that failure to resolve a poem into
its component parts does not necessarily mean that it is worthless.
The Impressionist method in poetry is not quite as old as the
same method in music and painting, but it can be quite as
respectable, if used with restraint and above all when the aim
is unified and clear in the poet's mind. Coleridge's remark

that poetry gives most pleasure when it is only *generally* understood, may ignore some of the kinds of pleasure which poetry
can give, but of certain kinds it is undubitably true. The poetic
surd is a necessity of art. At the same time, one must admit
that modern poets have tended to abuse the privilege accorded
them by a great critic.

If the classical poet pursues his images, the romantic is
pursued by them ; and frequently overtaken. A common
disaster unites Valéry's *La Jeune Parque* and the early work of
Mr. Dylan Thomas—two poets whose minds and methods
suggest entirely dissimilar fates. To anyone who is sensitive
to the evocative power of language, a certain quality of beauty
arises from reading these extraordinary products of the æsthetic
faculty. Only the most austere minds are proof against the
charm of the rhapsodic, the fantastical, and the ingenious ; and
such minds are seldom attuned to any except epic, moralistic or
occasional poetry (the only kinds, be it noticed, which can
dispense with imagery). Nevertheless, the double risk, of
wool-gathering and of disintegration, has been thoroughly run
by modern poets. Chief among the causes of so extreme a
privacy is doubtless the fact that the nature of twentieth-
century life gives less and less scope for thinking in terms
of images.

> There is this resistance to the poetic image (and I do not pretend
> to have done much more than embroider upon the plain fact that
> most people to-day have no use for poetry)—a resistance due to
> a poverty of the general imagination. If people no longer feel the
> poetic image as a pleasurable method of exploring reality, or even
> as a pleasure in itself, or if they do not believe or take interest in
> that kind of truth which can only be revealed through the image,
> then the poet has no check on the value of his images other than
> a private and technical one. So, at the present time, we get the
> poets using a very great profusion of imagery, but with a minimum
> of support from the general imagination. That is perhaps the chief
> cause of the obscurity, the erratic touch, and the centrifugal strain
> we find in so much modern verse.

Mr. Day Lewis is, I believe, describing a malady of which the
first symptoms can be observed in poetry composed as far back
as the 1870's and the 1880's—the period which saw the birth,

in France, of the Symbolist movement. Take, for instance, the
opening lines of Meredith's *The South-Wester* :

> Day of cloud in fleets !   O day
> Of wedded white and blue, that sail
> Immingled, with a footing ray
> In shadow-sandals down our vale !—
> And swift to ravish golden meads,
> Swift up the run of turf it speeds,
> Thy bright of head and dark of heel,
> To where the hilltop flings on sky,
> As hawk from wrist or dust from wheel,
> The tiptoe scalers tossed to fly . . .

There is no ' drawing-back ' here, nor has the poet sought his
chaotic (but oddly successful) imagery in order to express an
idea : he has simply turned himself into a node of sensation,
as Swinburne was even more inclined to do. The ultimate aim
of this kind of poetry is the ' simultaneity ' for which Mallarmé
strove, and which he achieved in some of his later sonnets, where
the idea and its images do not reach us gradually, in a temporal
sequence, but are set in a timeless pattern up and down the lines,
like a constellation in the sky or a jewelled arabesque on the top
of a snuff-box. Many contemporary poems are easier to grasp
once we assume the influence (often at several removes) of
Mallarmé, and still more that of Rimbaud, who suppressed
metaphor in favour of an image, or chain of images, comporting
both the idea and its evocations. This procedure has not yet
been fully worked out ; it involves enormous risks to communication ; but it is probably the greatest invention of poetic
technique which the past hundred years have to show.

★   ★   ★

Poetry—wrote Novalis—dissolves in its own being or
essence (*Dasein*) that which is foreign to it. This is equivalent
to saying that everything in the universe is susceptible of
statement in poetic terms. No doubt it is ; but what is
' foreign ' (*fremd*) to poetry, in the sense of ' strange ' or
' opposed ' to it ? No object or aspect of Nature, surely :
nothing which precedes human perception. This limits the

scope of the unpoetic to certain states of mind—namely those
in which, for reasons of immediate practicality, the moment of
illumination—the poetic ' state of grace '—cannot arise.   Of
such states of mind that required for logical or scientific analysis
is the most striking example.   No one, it is safe to say, is
incapable of achieving, however briefly, the poetic state ; but
many people resist it because they fear it may blunt their purpose.
They have not learnt to use poetry in the shaping of means to
ends.

Ultimately, no doubt, the essence of poetry is indefinable,
though its formulations can be discussed in terms of psychology
and of religious enigma.   The specifically poetic imagination is
hardly less elusive.   Like one of those shy animals which haunt
the jungles of the Douanier Rousseau, it is not meant to be
caught and caged.   In tracking its mysterious movements and
in drawing carefully aside, from time to time, the fronds which
conceal it, we may keep track of a being we can never see in its
entirety—any more than we can see our own faces, except as
reflected in mirrors which vary from quicksilver, glass, and water,
to the accusing eyes of other people.

(1947)

10

The Innocent Heart

THERE are some writers (they are usually poets) whose views seem more fully justified by what happened after—sometimes long after—their death than by the state of affairs against which they actually inveighed. Of these Shelley is an obvious example. Europe, during and after the Napoleonic wars, was ethically a more tolerable place than it is now. Then, men did evil in plenty, bringing injustice and cruelty out of the usual weakness ; but they at least knew that these things were vile. Now millions of human beings sacrifice themselves—and, wherever possible, others—to Moloch. We have reached that nadir which Shelley imagined but never witnessed :

> Alas ! this is not what I thought life was.
> I knew that there were crimes and evil men,
> Misery and hate ; nor did I hope to pass
> Untouched by suffering, through the rugged glen.
> In mine own heart I saw as in a glass
> The hearts of others. . . .

His own experience of life revealed to him that the heart *can* die ; such a vision, whether then or now, makes the seer or poet ashamed of his human heritage, and leads inevitably, if insensibly, to the death of the body, so that the spirit may live on, undefiled by compromise. This is the triumph of life that Shelley celebrates in the poem which he left unfinished when he was drowned in the bay of Spezzia, that July day in 1822. The opening of the poem, after the introductory stanzas, draws a picture—visually distinct as an image by Dante, though a great deal more elaborate—of those who are content to live on in the body after their hearts have died :

Methought I sate beside a public way
Thick strewn with summer dust, and a great stream
Of people there was hurrying to and fro,
Numerous as gnats upon the evening gleam,
All hastening onward, yet none seemed to know
Whither he went, or whence he came, or why
He made one of the multitude, and so
Was borne amid the crowd, as through the sky
One of the million leaves of summer's bier ;
Old age and youth, manhood and infancy,
Mixed in one mighty torrent did appear,
Some flying from the thing they feared, and some
Seeking the object of another's fear ;
And others, as with steps towards the tomb,
Pored on the trodden worms that crawled beneath,
And others mournfully within the gloom
Of their own shadow walked, and called it death,
And some fled from it as it were a ghost,
Half fainting in the affliction of vain breath :
But more, with motions which each other crossed,
Pursued or shunned the shadows the clouds threw,
Or birds within the noonday aether lost,
Upon that path where flowers never grew—
And, weary with vain toil and faint for thirst,
Heard not the fountains, whose melodious dew
Out of their mossy cells forever burst ;
Nor felt the breeze which from the forest told
Of grassy paths and wood-lawns interspersed
With overarching elms and caverns cold,
And violet banks where sweet dreams brood, but they
Pursued their serious folly as of old.

Such realisations imply a fearful travail of spirit ; and
circumstances tend to govern the outcome. Shelley, in that
summer of 1822, had come to an end, and he knew it. He was
unwilling to pursue his serious folly as of old, and it may well
have been the knowledge that he was entering a new phase of
his life—a realisation accompanied by a horrifying sense of
spiritual isolation—that made him say to Marianne Hunt, just
before he ran to meet death : " If I die to-morrow, I have lived
to be older than my father ; I am ninety years of age." There
is more here than the luxurious affectation of youth ; but the
only other persons, I believe, who realised the true state of
affairs were Mary Shelley and Trelawny, to both of whom love

and hatred lent perspicacity. Yet they were powerless to avert the disaster, for when the soul is bent upon oblivion, there is no way of preventing it.

> *Ach, wer heilet die Schmerzen*
> *Des, dem Balsam zu Gift ward?*
> *Der sich Menschenhass*
> *Aus der Fülle der Liebe trank!*
> *Erst verachtet, nun ein Verächter,*
> *Zehrt er heimlich auf*
> *Seinen eignen Wert*
> *In ungnügender Selbstsucht.*[1]

Shelley's death was to all intents and purposes a suicide. He chose death rather than to become involved in the thickets of despair. The manner of his death was tragically symbolic : on the whole, it is reserved for adults to die alone, and to be killed within sight and earshot of friends is essentially a child's death.

A child. . . . The term is perhaps misleading, for it implies an absolute irresponsibility, and Shelley was irresponsible only where he and his were concerned. In this sphere his sense of reality was certainly at fault ; but when his imagination was aroused on behalf of someone with whom he had no direct connection—Byron's daughter, Allegra, or Leigh Hunt—he showed himself capable of acting with spirit and thoroughness. His generosity was far from an unacted principle ; and if it be urged that it was founded on a solid basis of money, one can only reply that open-handedness is not usually a virtue of the rich.

There is a marked difference here between Shelley, who (for all his immaturity) had character, and Byron, who had only personality and was far too indolent and misanthropic to take the line not of least resistance.

This difference between the two men showed strikingly in their attitudes to conversation. Mr. Newman Ivey White, whose judgment is seldom at fault, states that Shelley was " baffled and somewhat annoyed by Byron's constant flitting from subject to subject, his unwillingness to stick to the point

---

[1] " Ah ! who shall heal the sores of the man in whom food has turned to poison ? Who imbibes hatred of mankind from the plentiful horn of love ! First a despiser, then despised, with needy egotism he consumes in secret his own substance."—GOETHE : *Harzreise im Winter.*

and argue ".[1] The testimony is only Medwin's, but it would be gratuitous to disbelieve him on a point of this kind. Nor should his assertion cause surprise, for the discord he noticed was the natural result of two fundamentally dissimilar attitudes to life. Shelley's philosophy was in some respects vague, and its expression in poetry consequently nebulous ; but never at any time did he doubt that some things in life matter more than others, and that certain things—personal liberty, love, scientific truth, democracy—matter supremely. It is clear, on the other hand, that Byron held no such beliefs—at any rate until a year or two before he died. A strong apprehension of guilt, the features of which he took care not to inspect too closely ; a superficial generosity to anybody who did not attempt to interfere with him ; an empirical method of dealing with life, based on indolence and hedonism : a personality so constructed can hardly avoid the scepticism that is born of self-contempt. Byron's scepticism, even, was incomplete, as his emotional shilly-shally makes abundantly clear. He disliked argument, I suggest, because he had never been able to make up his mind on the essential premisses, and did not want to have to do so. He preferred the society of his intellectual inferiors—' boon companions ' like Douglas Kinnaird and Tom Moore, with whom it was possible never to be serious about anything, and women who accepted everything he said without question.

Shelley would not fit into these categories. Intellectually inferior to none, he desiderated seriousness on matters which he considered serious. He accepted nothing without examination. Where principles—rather than facts—were concerned, he was adamant. He detested cynicism. If someone—and often it was Byron—said something he thought foolish or wicked, he could not be deflected by airiness or charm ; he stood there, round-eyed, blocking the way, until he was given satisfaction.

It is evident, I think, that Byron was more than a little in awe of Shelley. No wonder, then, that he " flitted from subject to subject ", refusing to be pinned down. For to allow himself to be drawn into argument might have exposed his pretensions—the void which ached within him—the inability to choose a path and follow it—the refusal to face any conclusion.

---

[1] N. I. White, *Shelley*, vol. ii, p. 336. (Secker & Warburg, 1947.)

Yet it would be wrong to accuse Byron of self-deception. If, as I believe, he was slightly afraid of Shelley, this was because he was too intelligent not to take the measure of the moral difference between them. Since he went in chronic fear of his own feelings, he would reserve the verbal expression of them until some event or other had given their occasion an aspect of finality. Thus he waited until he himself was dying before attempting again to cummunicate with Lady Byron. That message which Fletcher failed to catch would (we may be tolerably certain) have assured her of his love and of his remorse for the cruelty he had inflicted upon her, against his better nature. And it was not until Shelley was dead that Byron could bring himself to reveal what he really thought of him : " Without exception the *best* and least selfish man I ever knew." That unequivocal tribute was Shelley's ultimate reward for scolding Byron about his selfish and irresponsible treatment of Allegra and the Leigh Hunts.

If my analysis of the relations between these two men is correct, I think we may tentatively deduce a further conclusion. Is it not conceivable that Byron's journey to Greece—the one definite plan of action to which he ever committed himself—was directly inspired by the character of Shelley, as revealed to Byron during their almost daily converse at the Casa Lanfranchi ? A strongly emotional nature, Byron had always been swayed by personal feeling, rather than by intellectual reasoning. A vague love of Liberty—even when underpinned by resentful hatred of England and English Tories—would hardly in itself have sufficed to prompt that last decision. Nor yet would the enthusiasm of Trelawny, whom Byron had never really liked (they shared too many of the same faults—always a potent cause of antipathy). But at some time after Shelley's tragic death, Byron, I believe—perhaps as he sprang into the sea and swam away from the funeral pyre—resolved to consecrate his affectionate admiration for the dead man by an act of unequivocal selflessness. He would show that he had not really been as deaf as he seemed, to Shelley's impassioned arguments. And the occasion was to hand. . . .

★   ★   ★

It is remarkable that Shelley's friends and contemporaries showed no resentment at the way he pushed them around. To posterity, no longer blinded by the dazzle of his presence, the most irritating of the many discords that sunder Shelley's character is that combination of wisdom and fecklessness which enabled him to have everything his own way. Seen from a distance, the un-unified character is bound to seem insincere. This is the price youth pays for its continuous ecstasy, never questioning the value of the sacrifice. To resolve internal contradictions seems to youth a betrayal : an elixir apparently inexhaustible is not worth husbanding. This makes young people—especially young men—dangerous ; makes them ruthless as well as tender. So that poor Harriet Westbrook, shivering on the edge of the Serpentine in which she immediately afterwards drowned her griefs, doubtless saw the worst of her bad bargain. Shelley's treatment of this well-meaning girl, whose misfortune it was to be thoroughly commonplace, began in a thoughtless impulse and ended on a note of deplorable smugness. No doubt it was very annoying to be told, as Southey told Shelley at this time, that " a man ought to be able to live with any woman " ; nor can the effect of this priggish remark have been mitigated by what followed : " You see that I can, and so ought you." It is not recorded that Shelley made the obvious retort. In any case he was scarcely in a position to take a high line with anyone just then, for his behaviour to Harriet had shocked even his staunchest friends. It was, indeed, a very bad break. But nearly everyone ' behaves badly ' to *somebody* in the course of his life. We are all due for at least one bisque, and in Shelley's case the evil arose, as usual, from a generous impulse ; which perhaps made it worse for Harriet, but better for Shelley's ultimate reputation.

At the same time, it must be admitted that in certain moods Shelley exhibited a very crude taste. What, for instance, are we to think of his jocular attitude to the affair of the anonymous letter accusing his mother of adultery with Edward Graham ? [1] Or of the ribald poem he sent to Graham on the subject ? The probability is that Shelley himself was quick to forget such incidents and so imagined that others would take them as lightly

[1] See N. I. White, *op. cit.*, vol. i, p. 139.

as he did. His changes of mood involved—it is obvious—a
faulty sense of proportion, but not a diminution of sincerity.

Sincerity is no substitute for talent or ability, but it is an
admirable fuel to either. Innocence of heart, which is related
to it, is almost equally inconvenient, and much more irresistible.
Everyone envies it, wants it for his own, in proportion as he
feels that he has eaten of the apple of knowledge. That is why,
at the moment when Shelley's breast, lying amid the flames of
the funeral pyre, burst asunder, Trelawny sprang forward to
snatch the heart from burning,[1] his own having died while
he was still a boy. Some of the symbols of genius are difficult
to recognise, but not, surely, this one. So near and yet so
far. . . .

Whether or no Trelawny succeeded in saving the poet's
heart from the fire, he singed his own hand in the attempt, an
experience shared by others who had come too close to Shelley
in his life. " I always go on until I am stopped," the poet said
once, adding : " And I am never stopped." There is bravado
here, and a kind of frivolity—the slyness of a clever child who
perceives the nature, if not the extent, of his own power. For
Shelley knew, in some obscure way, that as long as he held up
his sorcerer's wand, the world would go as he wished. If this
failed, he reacted with rage—for instance, on the infrequent
occasions when his plans were unexpectedly checked. As is the
way of genius, he affected everyone like music—put them into

---

[1] This incident is regarded, in some responsible quarters, as an absurd
invention, typical of Trelawny's inability to stick to the truth. Viewing the
story in the light of Trelawny's character, I have never seen any good reason
to doubt it ; and it was pleasant to have this conviction strengthened by so
thorough a Shelley scholar as Mr. White. The latter gives circumstantial
evidence for the preservation of the poet's heart which (it now appears) was
handed over to Leigh Hunt, who in turn—after some hesitation, occasioned
by dislike—ended by confiding it to Mary Shelley. (N. I. White, *op. cit.*,
vol. ii. p. 385.)

In spite of recent attempts to see Trelawny in a fairer light than has
hitherto been customary, the *Recollections* remains a suspect book—largely,
I think, because the author of *The Adventures of a Younger Son* forfeited thereby
any claim to general credence. Yet it seems to me difficult to read the former
book without being impressed by the air of sincerity and truth which it
disengages. His admiring love for Shelley was probably the most unalloyed
emotion Trelawny ever experienced : it made him especially perceptive ; so
did his real antipathy to Byron, though that was a less simple feeling.

what is called a 'state'. This is sufficiently obvious in the records of those who met him : men as well as women succumbed to the spell with surprising abandonment ; hard-boiled persons like Byron, Hogg and Trelawny, genial idiots like Medwin, honest yet not quite ordinary men like Edward Williams, being more especially susceptible (then as now) to the spell of this particular music—the oboe melody of cardinal innocence, of transparent liberality. When the music ceased for a moment they were irked, but while it played its phrases gave an iridescent glow to the outlines of the world, transforming them according to the principles of white magic.

★　　★　　★

Here some consideration of Shelley's relations with Hogg may throw light on his perplexing character. This is tricky ground, for the feelings of these two men towards one another were complicated and ambivalent. In cases like this it is impossible to ascertain the moment where liking ends and love begins ; or to define with exactitude the nature of that love ; or to measure the grains of contempt and hatred which adulterate yet (paradoxically) strengthen it. All we can say with certainty is that the presence and personality of Hogg—the very idea of him—threw Shelley into a state of violent and conflicting emotion. It is significant that the conflict did not arise before the Harriet affair : until then, all was harmony between the friends—a harmony intensified by their parents' attempts to separate them. It was the introduction of the sexual overtone which complicated the Hogg-Shelley relationship, and in a very special manner. Consider the following, written after Hogg's attempt to seduce Harriet :

For a month after their flight from York the mails were laden with agonised, partly incoherent letters between the two young men, whose ruptured friendship was the greatest agony that either of them had ever been called upon to endure. In his first letter Shelley wrote with reasonable control of his own feelings. He assured Hogg that he deceived himself either by false reasoning or by real passions which obscured true reasoning—and in either event he pronounced the result " disgusting and horrid ". Still eager to be a friend to Hogg, he could not help expressing a fear that his professed conversion was not genuine. Except for a promise to write again next day, it would almost appear that this letter was intended to be final. Hogg's reply was evidently an impassioned one. He was in exquisite and undeserved misery ; he protested how much he had " loved " and " adored "—apparently both Shelley and Harriet. Calmly at first Shelley answered that in the late crisis Hogg's love had really been only for himself, that this was the cause of all their present misery, and that he was as wretched as Hogg, and undeservedly so. Growing suddenly impassioned, he argued earnestly with Hogg to desert his weakness, master himself, and become again the " superior being ", the " best, the noblest of men ", whom he had formerly known and loved. Acknowledging that he was " half-mad " and was writing wildly, he declined in one breath to see Hogg again until further convinced of his recovery ; then encouraged him to hope for an eventual reunion ; then invited him to " come . . . dearest, best-beloved of friends . . . share my fortunes, enter into my schemes " ; then seemed to hint that their reunion might come only after death. " Is all past, like a dream of the sick man which leaves but bitterness. . . . Oh how I have loved you. I was even ashamed to tell you how ! and now to leave you *for ever* . . . no not for ever. Night comes . . . Death comes . . . cold calm death almost I would it were to-morrow then is another life . . . are you not to be first there. . . . Assuredly dearest dearest friend reason with me. . . . I am a child in weakness."

Hogg's letters were no less emotional. Having failed to convince Shelley that he had mastered his passion, he seems to have thought he could persuade him by a philosophic ' investigation ' that it was not evil. He urged that he could live with the Shelleys and keep his love for Harriet within bounds, and at the same time he protested that his love was undying and wrote Harriet letters filled with such fervid compliments that she was indignant and Shelley was more than ever persuaded that it would never do to rejoin Hogg at York or permit him to come to Keswick. . . . How Harriet had withstood him in the first place was frankly a marvel to Shelley. He was partly convinced now of Hogg's sincerity, but he was equally convinced of his self-deception. Hogg's vague hint of a duel was passed by Shelley almost without comment, except to Elizabeth Hitchener. More than once Hogg threatened suicide if he could not regain his friend's confidence. In one of his own moments of greatest distress Shelley spoke of dashing himself from the cliffs, but he now met Hogg's threat with the assurance that he would certainly *say* he was convinced, but that the actual state of his beliefs could be altered only by a change in Hogg himself.[1]

---

[1] N. I. White, *op. cit.*, vol. i, pp. 172–3.

When the facts are disposed in this light—when we recall, moreover, Shelley's suggestion that Hogg should become Harriet's lover—it is unwise to deduce, as many have done hitherto, that Hogg was a careless cynic with a half-protective, half-contemptuous affection for the friend whose confidence he was continually betraying.   Clearly there was more in the situation than just that—something that had its roots in the Oxford days, with their discovery of intimate companionship and the passion of shared ideas and interests.   As well as Montaigne, Shelley and Hogg might have given the same short but sufficient explanation of their long friendship : " Parce que c'était lui, parce que c'était moi."   We may discount, if we will, the high-flown, hysterical language of the Shelley-Hogg correspondence as merely the style in which people at that time naturally expressed themselves, under stress of powerful feeling ; just as we should no doubt refrain from deducing too much from the style of Chopin's letters to Titus Woiciechowski. But when this has been done it is still impossible, I think, to avoid the suspicion that there was something in Hogg's and Shelley's affection for one another which remained unsatisfied by their status as friends.   In other words, they wished for union, and tried to achieve it by the vicarious method of sharing—or attempting to share—or dreaming of sharing—a series of women.   The experiment failed, because it was extravagantly indulged, and often without reference to the inclinations of the women concerned.

It is perhaps this extravagance—the wildness of the fantasy involved—which leads Mr. White, when summing up this long process, to despair of an adequate explanation.

It was obviously Shelley's pleasure in beholding her union with Hogg that in Mary's eyes constituted the chief attraction, for both herself and Hogg, in their anticipated union !   One thinks of Shelley's desire for Hogg's union with his sister Elizabeth, of the Hogg-Harriet affair, of Shelley's later affection for Jane Williams followed by her union with Hogg.   One thinks also of Shelley's free-love theories and of the tendency to fixed ideas that he sometimes showed and wonders if this is an extraordinary coincidence, or a fixed idea with both Shelley and Hogg, or if it is not in fact slightly insane.

If, after this, Hogg is to be regarded as attempting a seduction, he must surely be conceded to be an original genius in his method. Shelley's last poem to Harriet had stated his grief that her love was for him alone.[1]

To call the embroglio "slightly insane", avoids the issue. Mr. White, whose exegesis is otherwise far more penetrating than other criticisms of Shelley, here fails to recognise the features of a quite common situation. It has been noticed that men often marry the sisters of their greatest friends : we know that Shelley wished Hogg to do this. For the same obscure reason, in the husband-wife-lover triangle, where the relationship does not result in an explosion but is regarded by all three parties as a convenience, it is apt to lead to a bond of peculiar tenderness and affection between the husband and the lover. This curious phenomenon is particularly frequent in the history of eighteenth- and nineteenth-century French society, with its tradition of the *ami de la maison*. Lord and Lady Blessington and Count d'Orsay are an example which springs to mind ; and most of us can recall cases within our own experience. Until Dostoievsky exposed it, with the tragic humour and perception of genius, in *The Eternal Husband*, no attempt had been made to analyse this situation—perhaps because it was in itself embarrassingly delicate, as well as somewhat unflattering to women.

There is no question here of sexuality, in the crude sense of the word. It ought not to be necessary to say this ; but—despite the increase in an unemotional attitude to the hidden sources of human behaviour, which we owe to the real advances in psychological knowledge made in the past thirty years—it has still to be generally recognised how wide a variety of behaviour is covered by the notion of sex, understood in its largest acceptation. By dint of close scrutiny the *tone*, as it were, of sex—however faint, still unmistakable—will be found operating in many a human relationship which by its nature might seem to preclude any such factor.

In this sense we cannot, I believe, avoid concluding that the facts of the Shelley-Hogg relationship admit of only one interpretation : the attraction which drew them together, and kept them together, was—obscurely and diffusedly—a sexual

---

[1] N. I. White, *op. cit.*, vol. i, p. 392.

one. It may be objected that sexual feeling which remains unconscious and issues in no overtly sexual act, hardly deserves the name ; to which I should reply that there is no more definite name which describes at all adequately the peculiar, compulsive and repetitious behaviour of these two friends.

★　　★　　★

The dichotomies in Shelley's character are staggering, and would account, really, for more than is required to explain his failures and successes both as man and poet. Reckless and irresponsible in his own life, but helpful and above all *sensible* on behalf of others ; vague and woolly in emotion, but hard and virile in mind ; shrill and effeminate in appearance and manner, but physically very tough, in spite of " never feeling well " [1] ; shy and shrinking in company, but quite fearless when his notions of right and wrong were called in question : these are the discords Shelley never even attempted to resolve. In several of them one notices a startling resemblance to another poet of aristocratic birth who flourished (if that is the word) at the other end of the century—Swinburne. Further comparison leads only to reflections on the decay of the Liberal tradition— reflections which bear on Shelley's case only in so far as they reveal the extent of his failure to reconcile the Paganism which he professed with the Christian ethics which he practised—to

---

[1] Of all the extant portraits of Shelley, the water-colour by Edward Williams, published for the first time in Mr. White's biography of the poet, seems to me by far the most convincing. This miniature was until lately thought to have been lost, and even now its authenticity remains incompletely established. But a single glance at it should be enough to make any doubt seem academic. The eyes, which are those of the goddess Athene, are no more striking than we should expect. Much more surprising are the short neck, the heavy, humped shoulders, the big arms, and the almost lowering attitude—attributable in part to the fact that Shelley has turned round in his chair and is leaning with both hands on the back, but instinct at the same time with vigilance, like an animal waiting to pounce. The total impression conveyed by this remarkable drawing is far indeed from the wilting flower made familiar to us by the Curran and Clint portraits, and by Alfred Sourd's sentimental attempt to assimilate the poet's head to that of Leonardo's Christ. After a thorough perusal of this drawing we need no longer feel surprised by the physical toughness Shelley seems to have enjoyed, or by the pugnacity he sometimes displayed on others' behalf.

the scandal of worldly persons. This discrepancy is more important than the others I have mentioned, because it directly affected the poetry Shelley wrote.

Here a comparison with Hölderlin becomes inevitable. The latter's *Hyperion* is a great deal more sentimental and (in spite of great incidental beauties) less firmly grounded in historical truth than Shelley's *Hellas* ; on the other hand, *Brot und Wein* is one of the most astonishing *tours de force* since *Lycidas*, while *Prometheus Unbound* cannot be considered more than a partial success. The Christian-Greek synthesis is one which has never been even approximately realised ; its realisation would mean the millennium, and there is a dismal irony in the thought that it has been the great German poets—Schiller, Goethe, Hölderlin, George, Rilke—who have tried hardest to frame this ideal.

★   ★   ★

Shelley seems to have been, on the whole, unaware of the true nature of his dilemma, though *The Triumph of Time* is some indication that he was at last moving out of youth. Where he would have arrived, had he lived, and what direction his poetry would have taken, it is useless to ask ; but at any rate we need not doubt that some genuine development would have taken place. For Shelley (I repeat) had a hard, virile mind, and no fear of what it might discover. Even outside *The Triumph of Time* there is evidence that " the gentle seriousness, the delicate sensibility ", which, in a letter to the Gisbornes of July 1808, he laid down as the first two desiderata of true greatness, and which he himself had always possessed, were beginning at long last to be supported by the third requirement : " calm and sustained energy ".

That apparently faithless friend, Jefferson Hogg, who despised all poetry (including Shakespeare), described Shelley as the acutest intellect he had ever met. And who that has read the *Defence of Poetry* will dismiss this claim as fantastic ? That essay, it seems to me, has never been surpassed, although Sidney's is hardly inferior to it. It vindicates Shelley's claim to be a thinker as well as a visionary—a claim not substantiated by much, if any, of his poetry. A true romantic, he trusted that poor lunatic shut up in the garret of the imaginative faculty :

Inspiration. No more fatal allurement ever lay in wait for any artist—though Goethe comes at once to mind as a signal exception to the rule. To succumb to the slovenly regime of inspiration means a lifetime devoted to improvisation—the art of hit or miss ; and the eight hundred and seventy-two pages of Shelley's Collected Verse contain a great many more misses than hits. As a monument it is lamentable ; but to consider it in this light is unfair. Like all improvisors (Beddoes is another example), Shelley, when not at his best, is simply negligible. Even at his best he is uneven, perverse. Very occasionally—in *The Cenci*, in parts of *Epipsychidion* and *Adonais*, in *Prometheus Unbound* and *The Triumph of Time*—his eloquence achieves a gusty splendour that is unique in his age. More often—in his shorter poems, in single lines and impassioned fragments—his poetry has the pure, astonishing beauty of natural objects—leaves, stones, flowers and skeltering water.

(1944)

11

The Legacy of Germany in
Music and Literature

How indicate such riches in so small a space, otherwise
than by a string of names ? Should I sacrifice Mozart
to Bach and Haydn, because of the Italian nature of
Mozart's music ; Schumann and Weber to Beethoven and
Schubert ; rush past Liszt to dwell on Mendelssohn and Brahms ;
find no space for Wolf because Wagner takes up too much ; and
glancing at Mahler, Strauss and Schönberg, end the list with
Hindemith ? Should I, turning to literature, ignore Winckelmann and Herder in favour of Lessing ; confound Schiller and
Goethe in a single pert phrase ; dwell on Hölderlin and pass
over Novalis, Jean-Paul, Hoffmann, Lenau, in silence ; allow
the bitterness of Heine to etch away the tenderer qualities of
Chamisso, von Arnim, Brentano ; consider the dramas of
Kleist, but not those of Grillparzer and Hebbel ; ignore the
Tennysonian beauties of Mörike, Eichendorff and Stifter ; and
wind up again with Thomas Mann, because I lack space for
Rilke, George, Kafka ? Better, perhaps, to attempt the largest
possible view and try to discern, from above that vast
Ruysdaelian landscape, the features which unify it—here the
spire, there the spreading tree or windmill, the bird on the
wing or the peasant with the plough. It is a beautiful, diverse,
yet homely landscape ; but the sky above it is neither clear nor
unbroken : a thunderstorm approaches from the right background, sinister shafts of light pick out a group of houses ; and
the colours are those of autumn.

★   ★   ★

Like England, Germany is a land of poets ; and poetry
includes music, for there is no musical version of prose. Its
nearest equivalent would perhaps be the fugue, and it is

significant that Bach's music was the perfect expression of the
Reformation spirit, by which Luther deprived Germany of the
mythology she has ever since been striving to recapture. Here,
I think, is the crux of the matter. The history of German art,
no less in music than in literature, is that of a search for a
mythology adequate to the needs of the teutonic soul. The
tragedy of that search lies in its inevitable baulking by a soul
so much at odds with itself that no mythology could satisfy
it. Symbols must not be self-contradictory. Moreover, a
mythology remains inert unless it is believed true, and to believe
it true is to live under the spell of its mysteries—to be content
not to perceive its underpinnings ; for to understand a thing
fully is to surpass it, and a mythology completely understood
becomes a fable.

Christianity, Greece, the Nordic Sagas : from Winckelmann
to Wagner, German poets and composers have wrestled with
those incompatible gods, in the effort to achieve that final
synthesis of opposites which Hegel asserted to be the key to
human life, but which may be only the expression of a peculiarly
German dilemma.

On the coast of Columbia stands one of the strangest and
most fascinating towns in the world. Cartagena was founded
by Charles V, who left it unfinished. The Indians, instead of
undoing his work and rebuilding the town on their own lines,
contented themselves with finishing the Renaissance buildings
in a style of their own ; so that the modern visitor is astounded
by the sight of an elegant classical portal surmounted by a
crazily ornate superstructure. The effect of an entire town
built on these lines is bizarre and extravagant in the extreme,
but not more so than the spectacle afforded by the great German
romantics in an effort to fit the art and thought of the ancient
world into the procrustean bed of their own strange sensibility.
This attempt, which was initiated by Winckelmann in the
middle of the eighteenth century, reached its height in the
poetry of Hölderlin, and achieved a lurid sunset in the pseudo-
philosophy of Nietzsche and the esoteric theories of Stefan
George.

The whole movement, which produced all the best of
German literature and some of the greatest poetry in the world,
was in essence the outcome of the teutonic yearning for a

mythology that should be their very own—a search the deplorable results of which we observe in the ' new ' Germany of to-day. " He bears his own pains more easily who sees his god suffer too," remarked Heine piercingly ; and the hypostatisation of reality, whether in the interests of art or of life, is a game at which the Germans have always shown themselves proficient. To see life steadily and whole is a programme which fails to commend itself to this strange people, for, as Professor Butler observes, in her capital book,' *The Tyranny of Greece over Germany* : " Accurate knowledge has little inspirational value."

Now German knowledge of Greek art was never accurate : it had little chance to be, since it was inaugurated by a man whose neurotic, if genuine, sensibility led him to see, not what was there, but what he wanted to see. Poor Winckelmann's disabilities (the expression imposes itself) landed him in the fatal error of finding all he wanted of Greece in Rome, and of refusing to look further. It was left to Lessing, a far greater man, and to Goethe, to discover the error ; but neither was more successful in rectifying it. *Iphigenia*, though a poetic masterpiece, proved in the outcome to be quite as unsuited as the Laocoon group to exemplify the serenity and noble grandeur which Winckelmann laid down as the essential qualities of Greek art. The tragedy of Goethe's attempt to scale this Everest lay in the essential un-Greekness of his mind, though in this respect he was undoubtedly nearer to his ideal than the writers who followed in his wake.

*　　*　　*

If Goethe was in some ways able to surmount the inconsistencies and unrealities of his Hellenism, Hölderlin remained the martyr of the whole disastrous movement, for his mind was soon destroyed by the Frankenstein monsters of his own (and Goethe's and Schiller's) creation. Hölderlin's poem, *Bread and Wine*, is the bridge that, in their heart of hearts, both Goethe and Schiller longed to build—and which Goethe did, to some extent, build, in *Hermann and Dorothea*. There it stands ; but, as Miss Butler points out, no orthodox Christian would dare attempt to cross it. Only a weightless spirit could pass safely across : Hölderlin did so, and in *Der Einzige* yielded to Christ.

But the gods of his imaginary Greece—the Greece of his so often exquisite novel, *Hyperion*—had their revenge in the end.

To Heine, in some ways an even more tragic figure, the problem presented itself from a rather different angle—the sceptical, iconoclastic angle of the exile and the Jew. Apart from this fact, the parallel with Baudelaire is instructive, and one is not surprised that the lover of Crescentia Mirat, a stupid, selfish sensualist who corresponds so strikingly to Baudelaire's Jeanne Duval, should have ended, after many gyrations, in substituting Dionysus for the Apollo of Goethe and Winckelmann. Nietzsche saw the possibility of making the best of both worlds, and stated the problem with new and startling eloquence, in *The Birth of Tragedy*. But the eventual result, in *Zarathustra*, was something more wildly un-Greek than anything Nietzsche's predecessors could have dreamed of, and " the deepest book in the German language " becomes, with the years, ever less convincing. Thenceforward, the battle may be considered lost, in spite of the attempts of distinguished poets, such as Carl Spitteler and Stefan George, to rejoin it.

To see life steadily and whole seems all but impossible to the supercharged mind of the Teuton ; only Goethe, perhaps, achieved that wisdom, and then only at the cost of his creative power—his demon. For us English it has been otherwise : the world of Shakespeare is our world, and his philosophy—an empirical one, which Mr. T. S. Eliot has called a rag-bag philosophy—is the one we still steer by. The pathos of the German passion for Shakespeare is an effect of their inability to accept the view of life which his dramas imply. Likewise, in their pursuit of Greek beauty, they ended by embracing a shadow : Faust's Helen is really Brünnhilde in disguise, while the method of the *Ring* is finally the result of a misconception of Greek drama which, under the aegis of Lessing, arose with Goethe's *Iphigenia* and Schiller's *Bride of Messina*, and continued with Kleist's *Penthesilea* and the stiff but noble plays of Grillparzer.

To put the matter differently : the tragedy of the German creative writers of the nineteenth century was that they strove to do what their brothers, the composers, were doing better ; for it is only in music that spiritual opposites can truly be dissolved into an organic whole. It was Beethoven, not Goethe, who achieved this miracle of synthesis : the *Ninth Symphony* fuses the pagan and Christian sacraments into a whole not achieved even by that masterpiece of German poetry, Hölderlin's *Brot und Wein*. Yet this poem is one of the keystones of German literature ; it has the supercharged quality I have mentioned— the brimming, elegiac passion peculiar to the music of German hexameters—the music of Goethe's *Euphrosyne*, or Rilke's *Duineser Elegien* (another keystone)—that unique quality which, translated into another kind of harmony, fills the Clarinet Quintets of Mozart and Brahms, saturates Beethoven's *Mass in D* (the Mount Everest of music, an unscalable peak), and can still be heard in what is perhaps the greatest symphony since the classical Viennese period—Mahler's *Ninth*.

After the composition of the *Eroica*, the complexities of human emotion tended, in the teutonic mind, to resolve them- selves in the free language of music. For the metaphysical struggle which I have represented as the basis of German art finds its most natural outlet in the allegory. Now allegory is the soul of opera, but it is the enemy of the novel. In the hundred years which stretch from *Wilhelm Meister* to *Der Zauberberg*, what of real importance has the German novel to offer ? Freytag's *Soll und Haben*, no doubt, the novels and stories of Adalbert Stifter (an Austrian) and *Der Grüne Heinrich* of Gottfried Keller (a Swiss). But no *Lys dans la Vallée*, no *Madame Bovary*, no *Middlemarch*. Poetic psychology, the development of which produced a spate of masterpieces in England, France and Russia during the nineteenth century, in Germany took form in the song-cycles of Schubert and Schumann, to issue eventually in the Wagnerian leitmotiv. In place of *Anna Karenina*, *Tristan und Isolde* ; instead of *David Copperfield*, *Die Meistersinger* ; instead of the *Mayor of Casterbridge*, Wolf's *Prometheus* ; and Schumann's *Kreisleriana* have outlived the stories (admirable as these are) which inspired them.

★   ★   ★

Yet the demonic element in the teutonic soul has not always been dominant, and quite other qualities, no less strong, have produced three interrelated kinds of masterpiece : the lyric, the short story and the song. The turn of the eighteenth century

was Germany's Elizabethan age. The songs of Shakespeare and
Ford and Beaumont remained unequalled until Goethe put
words into the mouth of Mignon, and the simplicity of the
German *Lied* is the subtlest thing their art has achieved.
Schubert, Schumann and Wolf; Brentano, Heine, Mörike and
Eichendorff; Tieck, Jean-Paul, Hoffmann, Keller, Stifter : the
names evoke a long series of lyrical comments on the extraordinary things which happen to ordinary folk and what they
feel about them.   They are discreet and perfect, the single cries
of a passionate and naïve people in love with the magic and
mystery of Nature ; they ring like a tuning-fork.   It is the
world of *Hermann und Dorothea* we are in now—the landscape
of the Rhineland in September.   We are back in the country
of *Brot und Wein* ; but it is the cosy homeliness, the tow-headed
child biting into an apple, the young lovers in the sunset, that
meet our eyes now.

German art is commonly accused of excessive romanticism.
Certainly Wagner, and before him Beethoven, have much to
answer for.   The new styles they evolved gave vast scope to the
nimiety of thought and feeling, the weathercock emotionalism,
that has ever been the bane of Germany.   Luckily for her,
however, Providence has injected her with a ceaseless yearning
after the classical south ; Austria has been (and will be again)
her corrective, and behind Austria Italy.   Few events in modern
history have been so ironically symbolic as the forced marriage
which Germany's ambivalent feeling towards Italy foisted upon
her.   Goethe and Christiane Vulpius together brought forth the
Roman Elegies ; it was too much to expect that Ribbentrop and
Ciano would be able to repeat a miracle of that order.

(1938)

12

A Poet's Evasions

B y his inheritance of the *fin-de-siècle* attitude, and by the modifications of it forced upon a central European between 1914 and 1924, Rainer Maria Rilke presents an artistic case-history of considerable importance. The stages of his life touch the nodes of significant development during the period : an unhappy childhood in Prague, spent between a shy, conventional father and an ' artistic ', silly-selfish mother who exploited her son's feelings ; a still more wretched adolescence in a military academy ; a break-away, resulting in a *Sturm und Drang* period ; then an extraordinary interlude in the artist's colony at Worpswede, where the poet evolved his cult of virginity, an obscure technique of Platonic friendship, and his characteristic symbolism of the rose. This period ended in a curiously abortive marriage, a translation to Paris and the friendship of Rodin. Then come the years of uneasy wandering, punctuated by illustrious and advantageous friendships ; finally the war and Switzerland, the gradual withdrawal into invisibility at Muzot, and at last the long-wished-for death.

This absorbing legend illustrates primarily, I think, the effect which such a childhood and youth as Rilke's must have in forcing the subconscious uncomfortably near the surface. Rilke preserved both his poetic faculty and his essential sanity, but at a cost which is an object-lesson in elaborate evasion. " Rilke was phenomenally susceptible to æsthetic influences, to atmosphere, to latitude, to landscapes, to the past, to spiritual forces . . . but not to human beings as such." [1] " He had skipped the chapter of mankind ", as he himself expressed it ; for he never succeeded in reaching the final phase of responsibility for his own and others' lives. This failure implied an ultimately meaningless marriage and a long succession of equivocal friend-

---

[1] *Rainer Maria Rilke.* By E. M. Butler. (Cambridge, 1941.)

ships ; for what Rilke always needed was not a wife or a mistress, but a mother. Affection and solicitude he could and did give in return, but he was utterly incapable of the wholemeal bread of love.

Professor Butler, in her clear-sighted biography of the poet, is necessarily rather vague about the sexual element in Rilke's relations with women, and she does not deduce (as I should) obscure repressions as the cause of the melancholia from which he suffered during the critical years 1910–14—critical because from them emerged the last and greatest phase of his poetry. But of even greater interest is the complicated rondo-form into which Rilke's compulsive alarm forced all his friendships. From the mysterious Lou Andreas-Salomé, the friend of Nietzsche, through the Worpswede sisterhood and Rodin, down to Princess Marie of Thurn and Taxis and Frau Wunderly-Volkart, the tale is essentially the same, and its guiding thread is a lack of " fundamental human delicacy "—a lack made the more glaring by the extreme superficial delicacy for which Rilke was always so conspicuous.

This fault is a typically teutonic one, for, with very few exceptions, Germans tend to understand friendship as the spiritual enslavement of others. They invade people's lives, impose their own standard of feeling—giving confidences where none were asked, extorting them in return, and betraying them with levity—abuse the emotional and material resources they find, and then, if objection is at last taken to this stupefying behaviour, show themselves affronted and accuse those on whom they have battened of being false friends. Such, in outline, is the history of Rilke's relationship to Rodin, who, with Latin *savoir faire*, resisted the siege ; Germans and Austrians, who did not resist, got at once more and less out of Rilke—less ' humble ' admiration, but more of those self-revelatory outpourings which they evidently so much enjoyed. For one of the concomitants of this man's inaptitude for direct human contacts was his passion for letter-writing, which in his case was a means not so much of bridging distance as of preserving it. Like the curious, composite angels of the *Elegies*, his letters were " a strong arm, warding off " ; hence the laborious mystification in which they so frequently indulge, and their dreadful volubility, as of a monologue spoken through a mask.

Yet, if Rilke was consistently ruthless in his determination
to keep all friends at a distance where their demands were
reduced to what he felt able to supply, his resolve that they
should minister to his own peculiar needs was no less imperious.
" So few people ever wanted to get rid of Rilke ; it was so
often the other way round that his capacity for clinging too
close was rarely in evidence." [1] It is now, however, fairly
apparent. " Alas," he wailed, as early as 1904, " that I have no
family country-seat ; nowhere in the whole world a room of
my own with a few old things and a window opening on to
great trees." All very well ; but what Rilke really wanted,
and pursued with a terribly gentle obstinacy, was a large and
beautiful house, isolated by a magnificent park, perfectly run
(free of cost to himself) by a sufficiency of domestics, and
belonging to a sympathetic, intellectual woman of the highest
nobility, who would make all arrangements for Rilke's comfort
and then remove herself to a safe distance, leaving the poet in
possession for an indefinite period ; during which an unending
stream of beautiful, fascinating, but strangely irrelevant, letters
would pour across the interval. One thinks irresistibly of
Tchaikovsky and Nadejda von Meck. . . . But even this was
not all. Having acquired the castle, the servants and the com-
placent hostess, Rilke liked to sit down and write equally long
letters to other friends, complaining of loneliness and discomfort,
abusing the people, the scenery, etc., and protesting that *any*
place else in the world would, at that particular moment, have
suited him better. This was to ask of people more than can be
expected ; nevertheless, it is evidence of Rilke's amazing tenacity
that he did, in fact, succeed in living nearly half his life, if not
more, in considerable comfort, at other people's expense.

★   ★   ★

" Reality is something distant which comes infinitely slowly
to those who have the power to wait," said Rilke, during his
Russian period. Having failed to find reality through life, he
proceeded to seek it first in works of visual art—the subtle
Neue Gedichte were the result of this phase—and then, for one

---

[1] *Op. cit.*

mad moment, in the onset of the Great War. Let me not be
misunderstood : Rilke was a great poet and a man of extremely
delicate health, and it is to the honour of Austria that she kept
him out of the war. That being so, he should have had the
taste and self-knowledge not to sound a clarion call to arms ;
as it is, his windy and romantical war poems are far more
irresponsible even than d'Annunzio's heady incitements ; for
the operatic Italian did at least know what action was and was
prepared to take it, whereas Rilke's attitude and behaviour,
once the war got going, provoke the comment that in cases
like this even poets should practise what they preach. It is even
worse to underrate humanity as Rilke—inevitably—did during
the war (" The world has fallen into the hands of men," he
groaned) ; but in that very fact lies the explanation of his
behaviour, if not its excuse. Rilke's attitude to the war was
due to that lack of proportion—that defective sense of the
actual—which led Stendhal to assert that on a day-dreaming
German the fall of a leaf and the fall of an empire have the same
effect.

★   ★   ★

Finding the reality implied by war intolerable, Rilke sought
it finally in a poetry of Death—that ' personal ' death he had
imbibed as a young man from the overwrought, consumptive
beauty of Jacobsen's novels. This desire underlies all his most
important work, from the early stories to *Malte Laurids Brigge*
and the *Elegies*. Faced at every turn by the importunate material
world, he seized and stuffed it by handfuls into his poetry, so
as to be alone with its negation. But like a *Doppelgänger* it rose
again and again before him in the guise of more and more
women, and young enthusiastic poets, and lakes and towers and
trees, and in his constant symbol of the rose, whose hundred
eyelids were folded over " no-one's sleep "—that central void in
which ached and throbbed his longing for death.
  Those who do not fear death when young, love life
instinctively and unconsciously. A *conscious* love of life nearly
always goes with a loathing of many aspects of it ; but the love
remains stronger than the loathing, unless exterior pressure, in
some more or less irresistible form, comes in to tilt the balance

in favour of death. The result then will be, not heroism probably, but suicide—although that, too, requires its own courage, if only in the discounting of posthumous contempt ; for in the end it is usually contempt which prevails over pity, in the outraged hearts of those who are left behind to face the music and have never had a thought of doing otherwise.

Rilke chose the better part, but his longing for death continued unabated. It was not merely his own death which he desired, but that of the entire visible world. Unable to accept the world, he " offered . . . to spiritualise it out of existence, to make it actually what it already practically was for him, invisible and unearthly." [1] Those months spent alone in the frozen solitude of the little old castle of Duino, when the *Elegies* were at last completed in a final frenzy of intellectual passion, are of as deep a symbolic significance as any in the lives of poets, and thus, I think, of unique interest in the history of the human spirit. The magnitude of the effort involved is comparable only to some tremendous act of faith ; for when Rilke emerged from his lonely struggle with his angels, the magical work of transformation was at last accomplished : the world and its objects, the men and women who had succoured and tormented him—all had disappeared for ever, and in their stead had arisen, as from the flames of a *Götterdämmerung*, a world of essences which spun with the serene heroic grace, the liberated universality, of a new planetary system. Musical, too, the way in which the myth is not stated in its entirety until the last Elegy, like a theme that is completely revealed only in its final permutation.

The isolation and expression of essences is the problem which faces great artists in their final period of creation ; it is the inevitable successor-phase to any kind of romanticism, and can be studied, for example, in the last works of Shakespeare and Beethoven, of Debussy and Henry James. It is, in the last analysis, the effort to solve the problem of the Pathetic Fallacy— of the evident life of inanimate objects. To Rilke some thing—a jug, a pillar—could be *felt* as a joy, or a pain ; equally, that joy or pain could exist within him, hypostatised as an image—jug or pillar :

---

[1] *Op cit.*

>   Like dew from the morning grass
> exhales from us that which is ours, like heat
> from a smoking dish. O smile, whither? O upturned glance:
> new, warm, vanishing wave of the heart—alas,
> but we *are* all that. Does the cosmic space
> we dissolve into taste of us, then?[1]

For Rilke, the Angel is the symbol of a mode in which the two rhythms of life—that of the human being and that of the thing—are united in a single harmony. For a man to attempt this precarious fusion—this parthenogenesis—is no light task; to change the metaphor, it took Rilke the whole of his life to find a way across that guarded frontier, and the *Elegies* are the considered news of what he found on the other side. The last *Fragments* are the travel-diary of that journey; from both we gather that the manner required to deal with the inhabitants was chiefly a question of pressure. The light, disinterested touch on each person and thing; the hand that clasps but does not snatch or squeeze; the eyes that regard, with neither menace nor appeal: these, says Rilke, are the tools of true understanding:

> On Attic steles, did not the circumspection
> of human gesture amaze you? Were not love and farewell
> so lightly laid upon shoulders, they seemed to be made
> of other stuff than with us? Remember the hands,
> how they rest without pressure, though power there is in the torsos.
> The wisdom of those self-masters was this: we have got so far;
> ours is to touch one another like this; the gods
> may press more strongly upon us. But that is the gods' affair.[2]

And the *Ninth Elegy* resumes the whole argument.

  The most elliptical section of the *Fifth Elegy* is known to refer to Picasso's "Les Saltimbanques". In his notes on this particular *Elegy* Mr. Leishman has, I believe, missed one connection: though he nowhere mentions it explicitly, I think it is clear that the poet was here drawing on memories of the *Stemmen*, or weight-lifting, clubs which have for so long been

---

[1] From *Duino Elegies*. Trans., T. B. Leishman and Stephen Spender. (Hogarth Press, 1939.)
[2] *Ibid.*

a feature of Viennese life and of which Rilke must, in his youth, have witnessed performances. In one passage he is even using the vocabulary of the sport :

> *wo die Gewichte noch schwer sind ;*
> *wo noch von ihren vergeblich*
> *wirbelnden Stäben die Teller*
> *torkeln . . .*

though here the actual image is, of course, not pertinent to the *Stemmen.*

★   ★   ★

Rilke's angels deserve special attention. Miss Butler goes fully into the question of their heterogeneous origins. These include Nietzsche's Superman, and have but a feeble link with Christian dogma, for Rilke was, on the whole, and in spite of his endless search for God, antagonistic to the doctrines of Resurrection and Mediation, and at one moment (1922) even went so far as to advocate a phallic religion on Lawrentian lines. The reasons for this incongruous excursion are probably no further to seek than they are in the case of Lawrence, with whom Rilke had a great deal in common, both as man and poet. I wish Miss Butler had thought it worth while to pursue this comparison, for such a course would, among other things, have thrown light on the creation of Rilke's angels—those sexless beings, " protagonists in a drama which had gradually shifted from the human to the superhuman plane ". In other words, Rilke had at last succeeded in finding adequate sub-stitutes for men and women—beings in converse with whom he was relieved of the travail of mutual responsibility ; whom he could fear, respect, *love.*

The poetic language which Rilke evolved for the expression of this difficult transformation is among the most original in modern literature. With their grammatical subtleties (recalling those of Virgil) and their hushed eloquence—as of someone whispering down a speaking-tube—surprising and seductive as the serpent's voice of Eve, the hexameters of Rilke's final period assume the dancing flight of spoken improvisation. We are reminded, now of Blake's Prophetic Books, now of Coventry Patmore, and again of the sprung rhythm of Gerard Manley Hopkins. In the search for a perfect instrument of expression even Paul Valéry was not more successful ; and Stefan George —in some respects a greater poet than Rilke—seems timid, when we compare his verse forms with Rilke's far adventure into the arctic regions of language.

★   ★   ★

Astonishing as the *Elegies* are as poetry, I agree with Miss Butler that they produce " an unquiet feeling of treacherous depth ". Rilke's attempt to give his æsthetic images the universal validity of a metaphysical system, in obedience to the *Zeitgeist* and to his own spiritual needs, ended by producing poetry which can be interpreted in a variety of ways—not to mention the enormous and pretentious prose glosses with which he gladly furnished anyone who asked for an explanation of his poetry. This fault again must be attributed to the hard core of Teutonism which not even years of Paris and Rodin and Valéry were able to eradicate. " Spiritual arrogance, intellectual confusion ", says Miss Butler severely ; and I for one feel no disposition to contradict her.

So I should not be surprised if future generations, while giving the *Duineser Elegien* their high due, were to prefer the posthumous fragments, at least some of the *Neue Gedichte*, and, above all, the splendid *Sonnets to Orpheus*—perhaps the most highly sustained body of verse produced in this century. Here, indeed, the poet succeeded in " translating things he had loved and studied in the past from the world of art into the world of myths, where they lead a double life, have a dual personality and inhabit two different spheres, each of which is an aspect of the other and both of them subject to Orpheus, the poet-god". Here, too, Rilke's rose found its ultimate justification and true being—in its own beauty and the power of the spell it could weave, through form and colour and scent. Unfolded at last, releasing death, the symbol had become the thing itself.

(1941, 1949)

13

Stefan George

ONCE, when visiting the Bargello in Florence on a singeing
August day, I had the temerity to take off my coat.
Instantly the guardian came up and, touching me on the
shoulder, required me to put it on again. "But this isn't a
church !" I exclaimed irritably. "A museum is a temple, too,"
he replied solemnly. Though we were *en plein Fascisme* at the
time (1932), it struck me that this humourless observation would
have come more naturally from a German than from an Italian.

At all events, the incident comes back to me whenever I
read anything about Stefan George, but not when I read a book
of his poems—and that is often, for George is a poet who easily
becomes a habit. Why is this ? I think because so many of
his poems are short crystallisations of moods, and because
George was in no sense an 'objective' writer, so that his *œuvre*
as a whole can become a kind of breviary to those who find
poetry useful as well as decorative. The poets who belong to
this category are comparatively few, and to enumerate them
tells us something about poetry and about them. Horace,
Shakespeare (the Sonnets, which were miraculously translated
into German by George himself), Maurice Scève, Goethe,
Hölderlin, Keats, Patrice de la Tour du Pin, Rilke, Supervielle—
no doubt there are plenty of others. I myself would add certain
prose writers, such as Montaigne, Vauvenargues, Chamfort,
Senancour, Hazlitt, and "Palinurus". It is not a question of
rushing to a poet in order to plot the graph of an exaltation—
still less to cure a moment's depression. A hot bath will do that
as well, if not better. Poetry does not ease, it intensifies ; and
what one asks of the poets and moralists I have mentioned is
that they should set our moods in the context of our whole
experience.

There is nothing obnoxious about this procedure : most
poets would, I believe, acknowledge it to be a legitimate function
of poetic communication. But we cannot imagine using Dante

or Milton, or Shakespeare's tragedies, or even Browning, in this fashion. We come to them for something else—for opportunities to sink our personalities, with their intellectual crotchets, in an experience that transcends both writer and reader. The greatest artists are always less than their best works, just as we are less than our most selfless acts.

This consideration brings me back to George, who is possibly the greatest of modern German poets. Here a comparison with Rilke becomes interesting, as well as inevitable, because it raises the question of poetic greatness in general. Let us see if the story of these two poets' different developments will throw any light on the subject.

The early work of both Rilke and George is profoundly influenced by French poetry, especially that of Baudelaire and Mallarmé. In maturity, however, the deeper natures of both men asserted themselves, Rilke remaining international in taste and general outlook, George becoming more and more exclusively German. Rilke's philosophic development was towards an increasingly remote individualism—an interpretation of life on the purely personal plane. In the end his isolation seems to have been complete. Wrapped in a cocoon of hypostatised emotions, he reached out lovingly towards death. But since he considered all *percepta* as ornamental objects of an experience irremediably private, his vocabulary of images was large. He collected the sensations aroused by people and things as other men collect stamps or waistcoat buttons. Thus he remained essentially *fin-de-siècle* to the end.

Starting from a similar æsthetic and (be it said) from a personal make-up not so unlike Rilke's as the surfaces of their lives would seem to imply, George had the firmer grasp of the important difference between a poetic and an un-poetic view of life. This is a real dichotomy, but naturally it is felt as a problem more acutely by those who share the poetic view than by the large majority who do not. Belonging, of course, to the former, George became increasingly convinced that the majority must somehow or other be made to share in the poetic vision, that the nation might thereby be raised to a higher integration of thought and feeling. This was a forlorn hope. Poetry can become a dynamic force only when it does in fact underpin the whole life of a society. This was the situation up to the

nineteenth century, when Science began to oust Poetry as a
common form of perception. Doubtless there is magnificence
in the obstinacy with which certain poets have insisted on
ignoring the removal of their function, in the last hundred
years ; but a crop of dangers has arisen from it, too, as will
always happen where confusion exists about an intellectual
status. George in particular laid himself open to the gravest of
these dangers, through failure to perceive, until it was too late,
that regeneration by means of good poetry can easily be
exchanged for regression by means of bad, through the insidious
devices of what banks call " evilly disposed persons ". Faced by
the blandishments of Dr. Goebbels, George appears to have
hesitated ; but though in some ways a vain man, he had too
much wit and intellectual integrity not to end by refusing the
Nazi regime his sanction.

Silence, departure, death : it was a beautiful and sufficient
snub, but its roots extend far back into that phase of George's
development when the pure poet was still in the ascendant. It
was a phase which, given George's character, could not last.
Nearly all imaginative writers go through at least one crisis
during which they need reassurance that what they believe to
be important really is so ; in the case of George the crisis was
expressed in *Das Jahr der Seele* and resolved in the next volume,
Der Teppich des Lebens.

> Dies leid und diese last : zu bannen
> Was nah erst war und mein.
> Vergebliches die arme spannen
> Nach dem was nur mehr schein,
>
> Dies heilungslose sich betäuben
> Mit eitlem nein und kein,
> Dies unbegründete sich sträuben,
> Dies unabwendbar-sein.
>
> Beklemmendes gefühl der schwere
> Auf müd gewordner pein,
> Dann dieses dumpfe weh der leere,
> O dies : mit mir allein ! [1]

---

[1] This burden and this grief : to ban
My once so close and own,
In vain with reaching arms to span
What now—a wraith—is flown.

This and the next example—both from *Das Jahr der Seele*—show how direct is George's descent from Heine, in spite of the French and English influences which he was fain to acknowledge, at least by implication. The plangent notes of autumnal melancholy, of proud renunciation, of withdrawal into some final sadness : this surely is the music, uniquely beautiful, of the German Lied, which alone equals the Elizabethan lyric in the singleness and immediacy of its power to move us.

> Gib ein lied mir wieder
> Im klaren tone deiner freudentage—
> Du weisst es ja : mir wich der friede
> Und meine hand is zag.
>
> Wo dunkle seelen sinnen
> Erscheinen bilder seltne hohe
> Doch fehlt das leuchtende erinnern
> Die farbe hell und froh.
>
> Wo sieche seelen reden
> Da lindern schmeichelhafte töne
> Da ist die stimme tief und edel
> Doch nicht zum sang so schön.[1]

As Dr. C. M. Bowra has pointed out, in his searching essay on George,[2] the majority of the poems in this volume take the

> This dulling without cure or stay,
> With idle no and none,
> This groundless rising up at bay,
> This course that must be run.
>
> The weighing sorrows that oppress
> An anguish weary grown,
> This numbing pain of emptiness,
> This : with myself alone !
>
> (Trans., CAROL NORTH VALHOPE
> and ERNST MORWITZ, Kegan Paul, 1944.)

[1] Sing to me once again in the clear voice of your joyful days,—for you know well that peace has eluded me and my hand falters.
Where dark souls meditate, there rise images of unaccustomed grandeur ; yet memory's glow is absent, its merry colours are gone.
Where shallow souls converse, there flattering tones assuage us ; the voice is deep and noble, but not so good for singing.
[2] In *The Heritage of Symbolism*. (Macmillan, 1943.)

form of dialogues between the opposing spirits which the poet
felt within himself. I would add the gloss that this realisation—
and its dramatised form—prepared the change which took place
in George's view of poetry. By the time George met the
youth Maximin, who, after his death, became the subject of
what is generally considered the poet's finest collection of verse,
Der Siebente Ring, circumstances—and his own nature—had
forced him to turn from the purely personal to the prophetic.

> Du wirst nicht mehr die lauten fahrten preisen
> Wo falsche flut gefährlich dich umstürmt
> Und wo der abgrund schroffe felsen türmt
> Um deren spitzen himmels adler kreisen.
>
> In diesen einfachen gefilden lern
> Den hauch der den zu kühlen frühling lindert
> Und den begreifen der die schwüle mindert
> Und ihren kindesstammeln horche gern !
>
> Du findest das geheimnis ewiger runen
> In dieser halden strenger linienkunst
> Nicht nur in mauermeeres zauberdunst.
> " Schon lockt nicht mehr das Wunder der lagunen
>
> Das allumworbene trümmergrosse Rom
> Wie herber eichen duft und rebenblüten
> Wie sie die Deines volkes hort behüten—
> Die Deine Wogen—lebengrüner Strom ! " [1]

That comes from *Der Teppich des Lebens*, but I think we can
see in it the beginnings of George's Miltonic sense of a new
vocation. The ideal took form and precision during the poet's
brief but intense friendship with Maximin. Henceforward he

---

[1] The sounding journeys you shall praise no more
Where perilous and false the water leaps,
And where the chasm rears its rugged steeps
Around whose summits heaven's eagles soar.

Learn in these simple fields to apprehend
The breath that all-too frosty spring allays,
And that which renders less its sultry haze,
A willing ear their childish prattle lend !

took up the burden of justifying Youth to Age, and, in his
final volumes, of becoming the conscience of Germany.

Du nennst es viel dass du zu eigen nimmst
Mein gut wie deins . . . noch hast du nichts genannt !
Du wurdest mitbesitzer meiner stunden
Dein bitten ist bedenklich wie befehl.
Ich muss dein schirm sein wo du dich gefährdest
Den streich entgegennehmen der dir galt.

Ich bin fur jeden deiner mängel bürge
Mir fallen alle deine lasten zu
Die als zu schwer du abwarfst—alle tränen
Die du sollst weinen und die du nicht weinst.[2]

This change of approach—from the purely æsthetic to the
didactic—represents a narrowing of purpose, which accounts for
the sense of greater austerity, of bareness, of restricted imagery,
that we feel when we turn from Rilke to George. And there
are other significant differences. Since George's purpose was a
transformation of life, his poetry leans towards life, instead of
(like Rilke's) away from it. George showed indeed no interest

You find the secret of eternal runes
Within these hills austerely drawn and pure,
Not only seas of stone with magic lure,
No more the wonder beckons of lagoons,

Of great and ruined Rome, the world-wooed dream,
As vine and bitter scent of oaken grove,
As they who guard your people's treasure-trove ;
Your waters, green with life, O surging stream !
(Trans., CAROL NORTH VALHOPE
and ERNST MORWITZ.)

[2] You say that it is much you took as yours
All I possess . . . but this says nothing yet !
You came to be the sharer of my hours,
Your pleading is precarious as command.
Your shelter I must be where you are perilled,
The blow encounter that was meant for you,
For every flaw you have, I am the voucher,
The burdens you discarded as too grave,
I must sustain them all—and all the tears
You ought to weep and that you never weep.
(Ibid.)

in death, except in so far as it deprived him of those he loved,
or as it hindered his conception of the way in which human
beings ought to develop. He did not caress Death with Rilke's
lingering and sometimes repulsive affection. The Maximin
incident, and what we can gather of George's other intimacies,
seem to indicate that for him—as for few people and fewer
poets—love and admiration were identical.

Maximin was the name George gave to a boy of thirteen
whom he 'discovered' in Munich in 1901. Poetically gifted,
as well as beautiful, Maximin became the object of a cult
instituted by George—partly for personal reasons, and partly, it
would appear, because George had reached that point in his
mental development where it became imperative for him to
present the world with some living embodiment of his ideal.
Unfortunately for George's happiness, but fortunately for his
poetry, Maximin died in 1904. This curious, nebulous and very
German affair is described in some detail, but with noticeable
impatience, by Professor E. M. Butler in *The Tyranny of
Greece over Germany*.[1] It is impossible now to discover to
what extent George believed his own assertion that Maximin
was 'divine'. It seems simpler to assume that this extravagant
claim was in the nature of a poetic image ; and to leave it at
that.

★   ★   ★

However we understand it, the incident leaves no doubt
that George was a man to whom friendship was the only bond
capable of releasing the supreme values of life. He himself
seems never to have questioned the adequacy of this view, with
the result that *Der Stern des Bundes* (his penultimate volume) is
not only the Deuteronomy of an esoteric religion, but contains
much the most obscure and least acceptable verse he ever wrote.
Yet even here, and still more elsewhere in his work, we find
that sad, melodious gravity, those perfect sequences of sound,
that mystery of difficult metres, which have their only close
parallel in Tennyson—especially the Tennyson of *In Memoriam*.
Tennyson is the touchstone for these qualities, and also for the
deep and unself-conscious expression of belief in platonic love

---

[1] Cambridge Univ. Press, 1935.

which is the most genuine emotional force in George's poetry.
I am indebted to Mr. Stephen Spender for this acute comparison
and so have less scruple in pressing it. Examples abound :

> Nichts was mir je war raubt die vergänglichkeit.
> Schmachtend wie damals lief ich in schmachtender flur
> Aus mattem munde murmelt es : wie bin ich
> Der blumen müd, der schönen blumen müd ! [1]

and from a later volume :

> Du stets noch anfang uns und end und mitte
> Auf deine bahn hienieden, Herr der Wende,
> Dringt unser preis hinan zu deinem sterne.
> Damals lag weites dunkel überm land
> Der tempel wankte und des Innern flamme
> Schlug nicht mehr hoch uns noch von andrem fiebern
> Erschlafft als dem der väter : nach der Heitren
> Der Starken Leichten unerreichten thronen
> Wo bestes blut uns sog die sucht der ferne . . .
>
> Da kamst du spross aus unsrem eignen stamm
> Schön wie kein bild und greifbar wie kein traum
> Im nackten glanz des gottes uns entgegen :
> Da troff erfüllung aus geweihten händen
> Da ward es licht und alles sehnen schwieg.[2]

★   ★   ★

---

[1] " Transience robs me of nothing that ever was mine. As once long
ago, I ran tottering into the languorous meadow, murmuring : Ah ! I am
weary of the flowers, of the beautiful flowers ! "
  Here the resemblance to early Mallarmé (*Tristesse d'Eté, Renouveau, L'Azur*)
is superficial, though striking.
[2] You, always our beginning, end and middle
  Our song of praise on your terrestrial farings
  Now rises to your star, O Lord of Turning !
  We felt a darkness laid across the land,
  The temple tottered and the inner fires
  No longer leaped for us, whom other fevers
  Had wasted than our fathers' : toward the joyful,
  The strong, the poised, on thrones unreached, that squandered
  Our noblest blood in lust for far horizons . . .
  Then you, our own, from native stock appeared,
  Confronting us in naked glows of godhead :
  No statue was so fair, no dream so real !
  Then out of hallowed hands fulfilment flooded,
  Then there was light and every yearning stilled.
                    (Trans., VALHOPE and MORWITZ.)

It is difficult not to deplore the fact that George succumbed to the German passion for teaching, since poetry cannot teach in an age in which it is not accepted as a standard of anything outside itself. This was certainly less fatal to him than to some others among his countrymen ; none the less it cast a shadow of tragedy over the latter half of his life—a tragedy very different in character from Rilke's assumption into the heaven he had built for himself. There is something symbolic in the fact that, the museum having turned into a temple, George should have felt the desire to burn it down—as he did in that brutal play, *Der Brand des Tempels*, which is a remarkably unflinching prophecy of Germany's fate. Had he lived long enough to watch the neo-Nietzschean stripling—" Der Stern des Bundes " —turn into the S.S. man, *Der Brand des Tempels* might well have been even more bitter than it is. Even so, the last poems which George published bear unmistakable signs of a new direction—or rather, of a return to the material and manner of his earlier volumes—of *Das Jahr der Seele* and *Das Buch der Hängenden Gärten*. To quote Dr. Bowra once again : " His (George's) chief figures are the young soldier and the wandering minstrel. The first is what he liked, the second is himself." In *Das Neue Reich*, it is plain, he likes neither the one nor the other.

I am aware that for a foreign critic to praise George for this change of tone is necessarily rash ; so I do not wish this view to assume a categorical air. Nevertheless, speaking personally, I cannot resist the impression that many of the poems in *Das Neue Reich* are in every respect superior to the greater part—if not the whole—of *Der Siebente Ring*, with its solemnity, its sentimental affectations, and its pretentious obscurity. Even the war poems, which one might have expected to strike a false note, have a peculiar dignity. It seems that the whole George circle was horrified by the 1914–18 war and took, from the first, the same attitude of complete abstention as earned Romain Rolland a much more resounding obloquy. Whatever one may think of this attitude, there is little doubt that any creative work based upon it will at least possess the virtue of integrity. The position of the non-combatant poet who approves a war in progress, is a very ticklish one. If he takes a resolutely elegiac tone, he will seem to many a humbug ; if he waves a flag and cheers the young on into bewilderment, despair and painful death, he becomes merely disgusting. That revolting comparison of the blood of British soldiers to " Condy's fluid " which should purge the world of accumulated moral infection, remains an ineradicable blot on the character of Edmund Gosse. More horrible even than the frivolous image is the fact that a thoughtful and sensitive mind should not have hesitated to publish it, at that moment ; and if we turn to Rilke's *Fünf Gesänge*, which celebrate, in a lengthy contrapuntal tucket, the events of August 1914, we shall be obliged to recognise just such another deplorable lapse of moral taste.

No doubt it were better if only those poets who are, or have been, soldiers took it upon themselves to write about war. We have had warnings enough in the past thirty-five years ; if one cannot achieve the tone of Alfred de Vigny's *Servitude et Grandeur de la Vie Militaire*, one had best keep silence on the subject. For it is the tone, as much as the characters and events, which gives to this great masterpiece its timeless appeal ; and that tone is as inimitable as it is faultless.

Stefan George was never a soldier : had he been one he would not, I cannot help thinking, have written *Der Stern des Bundes*, or have cherished so long the heroic day-dream. Yet when the war broke out, he did not do the expected thing. No luxurious lament fell from his pen—far less a romantic call to action. *Der Stern des Bundes* is said to have had a considerable influence among the younger officers of the German army ; but when the years passed and George saw what was becoming of his day-dream, he did not conceal his horror and dismay.

> Zu jubeln ziemt sich nicht : kein triumf wird sein,
> Nur viele untergänge ohne würde . . .
> Des schöpfers hand entwischt rast eigenmächtig
> Unform von blei und blech, gestang und rohr.
> Der selbst lacht grimm wenn falsche heldenreden
> Von vormals klingen der als brei und klumpen
> Den bruder sinken sah, der in der schandbar
> Zerwühlten erde hauste wie geziefer . . .
> Der alte Gott der schlachten ist nicht mehr.
> Erkrankte welten fiebern sich zu ende
> In dem getob.[1]

[1] This is no time for rejoicing : there will be no triumph—nothing but futile destruction. The creator has lost control of his hand, which now produces monstrous rods and pipes, inhuman shapes of lead and tin. He

The poem from which those lines are taken was not published until 1917, the ode "To a Young Captain in the First World War" not until 1921. In both the emotion is one of angry sorrow, recollected in (comparative) tranquillity. Our teeth are not set on edge, as they are by Rilke in similar circumstances; and the reason, I think, is that the Maximin incident—mistaken and slightly absurd though it may have been—had opened George's eyes to what happens in modern times when a lyric poet mistakes his vocation. Rilke, on the other hand, had risked no experience such as might have prevented him from rushing in. . . .

*   *   *

It seems improbable that anyone would class George's war poems among his best work. They are sensitive and respect-worthy; otherwise their virtues are chiefly negative. It is with some of the other poems in *Das Neue Reich* that George establishes what is likely to be his permanent position in European poetry. In the four wonderful poems "To the Children of the Sea"; in the *Aphorisms*; finally—and most movingly of all—in the section entitled *Das Lied*. In these tempered verses, where not a word is out of place, George has found his way back to the pure Tennysonian fount of his essential genius. As Dr. Bowra most truly observes, George's songs—unlike those of his nineteenth-century German forebears, Müller, Chamisso, Lenau, Mörike, Eichendorff—have no need of music to complete them. In this sense he is the real heir of Heine. It is high time we *read* the *Buch der Lieder* again, instead of only listening to the settings.

Aside from the world of his best poetry, it is George's tone of voice which should recommend him to those who seek in poetry the sanction of a mood. It is a grave and level voice, which never rises into anger or shrill admonition; a sad voice, but very alert and very proud. Yes: pride is, I think, the quality we feel most continuously below the intellectual or

---

laughs a horse laugh to hear the stale and lying eloquence of war; to see our brothers burrow like insects into the earth and crouch there shamefully; to watch them fall in a welter of mangled lumps. The ancient god of war is dead. In the general madness, our sick world languishes to its fever-death.

emotional content of this poetry. Like many proud people, Stefan George was an extremely shy man ; and the voice we hear rising from his beautifully measured lines is intensely quiet and veiled as from fear of its own intensity. His temple is fraught with pillars, and we catch sight of him only as he glides from one to another, in the intervals between his poems.

(1944)

14

The Soldier

IGNORING the advice of those who, in the first weeks of war, rushed in to tell us what we had best read, I returned at once to a classic of military life—Alfred de Vigny's *Servitude et Grandeur de-la Vie Militaire*. The form of this book is arresting : it consists of three stories, laced together by the author's meditations on the soldier's life as he had lived it. The idea illustrated by the stories is that war is a machine, in essence anti-human, and that the soldier's greatness and pathos arise from the willing submission to it of his humanity and reason. The statement that war is the continuation of diplomacy by other means may be true, but it slurs over the fact that war is as different from any other kind of violent action—a revolution, for instance—as absolute monarchy is from the constitutional kind.

Vigny was the first poet clearly to state this distinction, which his mind was peculiarly adapted to perceive ; for his naturally strong romantic feelings were held in iron control by a brilliant, jewel-hard intelligence and an exact sense of responsibility. Hence his cold hatred for all forms of vulgarity, self-deception and mendacity ; for all theatrical posturing. Almost alone of his generation he saw straight through the Byron legend and disposed of it in a single, contemptuous sentence : " La vie est trop courte pour que nous en perdions une part précieuse à nous contrefaire." He had seen too much of both sides of the medal ever to lapse into self-dramatisation —the last refuge of those who cannot face the truth about themselves. Whether he is recounting the grief of the naval captain whose duty it was to shoot the young man in whom he had become affectionately interested ; or the hideous fate of the adjutant who was guarding the powder-magazine of Vincennes on the night of the great explosion ; or the grandeur of " Canne de Jonc " who gave his life to a child in return for the life of one he had killed : in all it is the tragedy of the Unjust Necessity he is celebrating. This is the clue to the essential military character. The inexorable sadness of any great soldier's face proceeds from the knowledge that, in war, fraternity, good will and justice do not suffice. When the sticking-point comes, the military machine must surpass the human will, if the day is to be won. The untenable position must somehow be held, the limbs move when no more strength is left in them, the gun be fired when the ammunition is exhausted. "Il faut toujours exiger des hommes plus qu'ils ne peuvent faire, afin d'en avoir tout ce qu'ils peuvent faire", noted Vigny in his Journal. So the rule must be supreme and justice fly out at the shell-shattered window. So the sentry who gives way to sleep after four days and nights of vigil must be shot. This is monstrous and everyone knows it : hence that sad, inexorable face and the mild, taciturn cynicism of old soldiers.

★ ★ ★

Vigny's style is not as simple as it looks, or as cold as it has been said to be. Since it was designed to tell the truth, and does so, it is not rhetorical ; but the passionate control creates a rhythm as living as Tolstoy's, and the infrequent images, though not of the startling order, are so perfectly in harmony with the mode of thought as to provide a constant succession of just enhancements. The result is to prevent the reader from substituting his own day-dream for the author's reality.

The detail is equally precise and quite merciless :

> *Rien n'indiquait que ce pied eût jamais été chaussé. Il était comme embaumé et conservé à la manière des momies ; brisé à deux pouces au-dessus de la cheville, comme les pieds de statues en étude dans les ateliers ; poli, veiné comme du marbre noir, et n'ayant de rose que les ongles.*

Vigny's comments, too, are throughout those of a soldier. Thus, after describing the frightful scene of the explosion, when the adjutant's body appears as if engraved on the wall, he says that no one present expressed pity, and adds : " Peut-être parce que le plaindre eût été se prendre soi-même en pitié pour avoir

couru le même danger "— comment that makes rings in the
mind, like a stone dropped into water.

" Canne de Jonc " looks forward to Tolstoy's Prince Andrey,
but he has an English predecessor too—the old soldier whom
Wordsworth met that night on the mountain road, resting in
the moonlight, lonelier than the road itself.

>   Companionless,
> No dog attending, by no staff sustained,
> He stood, and in his very dress appeared
> A desolation, a simplicity
> To which the trappings of a gaudy world
> Made a strange background. From his lips, ere long,
> Issued low muttered sounds, as if in pain,
> Or some uneasy thought ; yet still his form
> Kept the same awful steadiness—at his feet
> His shadow lay, and moved not.

But the eye of genius was on him and pierced his secret.

> He all the while was in demeanour calm,
> Concise in answer ; solemn and sublime
> He might have seemed, but that in all he said
> There was a strange half-absence, as of one
> Knowing too well the importance of his theme,
> But feeling it no longer.

Such, too, are the features of the captain who furnished
Vigny with the first story in his book. These men have so long
been silent because *they know*. The young do not ; for war, in
imagination, is always conceived on chivalrous, epic lines ; its
leaden mechanism is thought of as incidental, whereas it is the
essence of the business. Thus war persists because it is a
legend—because the sense of glory and of danger—" cette
magnifique inquiétude ", as Vigny calls it—is supposed to engulf
the surrounding tedium, squalor and dread. In fact it does not
do so ; but those who return to tell the tale, find that it falls
on deaf ears. The legend cannot be exploded for more than
two generations ; after that it revives.

War cannot change a man's character ; it only modifies the
intensity of certain characteristics. The neurasthenic acquires
shell-shock, the feather-head becomes irredeemably frivolous,

he in whom the sense of responsibility has lain dormant turns
out a leader of men. Only in this sense can war be said
occasionally to benefit the individual : it may produce the best,
but it may harden the worst, in a man ; in no case will it create
anything new. Thus it is that life is hard on the hero, for
99 per cent. of it gives him no opportunity for the display of
his gift. Indeed, if he is not lucky, he may die without revealing
that he had it in him at all. And the rest of the time his other
traits—those which usually go with a capacity for heroic
action—may not be so very endearing. For strength is only
sometimes of service, and silence—if you have to live with
it—becomes an exasperating bore, as many a romantic woman
has lived to discover.

> Il n'y a que les malheureux qui se battent bien, ceux à qui la
> misère de la guerre est plus douce que la misère de la paix.

That is a hard saying and true only if the word ' unhappy ' be
understood in its profounder sense. At more superficial levels
it can certainly be affirmed that those whose lives in peacetime
are not unpleasant fight just as well as those to whom war means
only the exchange of one kind of hardship for another. But
the ultimate recklessness—the ultimate selflessness—of extreme
heroism is probably found only in those whose soul is a house
divided against itself. The integrated personality is satisfied
with less spectacular vindications and has too much to lose to
fling all away without that second's hesitation during which the
occasion passes. To act with the whole of oneself is doubtless
always the desideratum, but I doubt if it is often possible to
achieve in war : the general confusion of thought and feeling
is too great. In times of stress people resort to Public Opinion
—instead of to themselves or each other—for answers to the
questions they are asking. " What does the country feel ? "
they ask, forgetting that *they* are the country. And the questions
get answered, all too readily, by tricky persons behind desks.
But to succumb to the spell of the Press is a civilian vice :
soldiers know better than to read about what they themselves
are doing.

★   ★   ★

At least one of Vigny's points in *Servitude et Grandeur* is implicit : that what is done under pressure of the Unjust Necessity need not impair the soul. This requires to be repeated at every crisis of history. Nobility of character, generosity, forgiveness, love : these things do not depend on the State—on political systems—on war. They are unconquerably private— anti-Totalitarian. If they were not, misanthropy would not be the poor subterfuge it is and we should all be at the dictator's mercy. It is not the possession of those qualities which makes Vigny's soldiers so pathetic and so grand : it is their ability to lay them aside at the call of the monster. That is their laurel crown—the sad knowledge of a necessity peculiar to their estate and one which isolates them ; for even in these days of citizen armies, the true soldier is as rare as he was one hundred and twenty years ago. It is Vigny's distinction to have perceived the nature of his tragedy—his solitude, his horror, his silent face guarding the intolerable necessity. It is a tragedy in which the plaited skein of thought and act has been unravelled, and the threads lie side by side. For the thoughtful, sensitive man who puts his private life away to take up arms, soon abandons elaborate systems of philosophy and learns that wisdom is, after all, an affair of cracker mottoes and nurse's proverbs. Wilfred Owen knew this, and so did the anonymous French soldier who contributed to the *Spectator* on October 27th, 1939 :

> Je me suis reveillé un matin, à l'aube, dans la paille d'une grange lorraine, soldat de la République Française, l'esprit clair et dégagé de préoccupations désormais inutiles, avec le sentiment réconfortant d'une stabilité retrouvée. L'incertitude de la vie militaire a quelque chose de permanent dans quoi on s'installe avec une insouciance bénie, qui forme petit à petit, mais très rapidement, le fond du caractère du soldat et lui permet de ne jamais envisager que le meilleur des sorts et de garder intacte, en toute circonstance, une aveugle confiance en ses chefs et en son étoile personelle.

That is the voice of Alfred de Vigny, coming to us across a century of peace and war ; for, as George Santayana has said : " The truly classical is not foreign to anybody. It is precisely that part of tradition and art which does not alienate us from our own life or from nature, but reveals them in all their depth and nakedness, freed from the fashions and hypocrisies of time and place."

Servitude et Grandeur de la Vie Militaire is a classical book, for the terrible griefs and exaltations of its characters are seen as though from a great way off, from the marmoreal repose of an achieved perspective. No writer's tone—not Emerson's, not Matthew Arnold's—was ever higher than Vigny's, in this unique and beautiful book. Here speaks the voice of a completely distinguished nature, of a man who had learnt that few things are really worth saying, but that what must be said had better be said like this.

(Dec. 25th, 1939)

15

An Elegiac Novel

THE English have no time to think of happiness just now. How best to attain it, and having attained, to keep it : these are themes which war automatically obliterates, along with ' unnecessary ' luxuries and as if they were among them. In holes and corners—behind the bars of canteens, in unusual recesses of underground shelters, in messrooms and sleeping quarters, on solitary watches, and in the plagal cadence of physical love or of receding pain—individual men and women no doubt still spin for themselves brief cocoons of solitude in which happiness flowers out of memory, like a perfect concord sweetly struck and held. And for most there is the simpler ecstasy of togetherness in the present ; but this, like a drug, suffers from the law of diminishing returns. So that while endurance and suffering and anxieties continue to be the norm of existence, happiness must be content to lie in state in all our hearts. But directly the war is over it will return to life and again force itself on our attention.

Happiness has never, so far as I know, been taken as the overt theme of a novel by any except that exquisite writer, Jacques Chardonne, who, by placing a seismograph in the inmost chamber of married life, has plotted most subtly and poignantly the domestic graph. But if this writer admits that *le bonheur* constitutes his fundamental theme, *Romanesques* is nevertheless only the most recent of a long series of novels more implicitly devoted to the subject. *La Nouvelle Héloise, Werther, Adolphe, Obermann, A Hero of Our Time, Eugene Onyegin, Le Lys dans la Vallée, Dominique, Der Nachsommer, Niels Lyhne, Le Grand Meaulnes, The Waves* : the list is not exhaustive, but, I hope, contains the chief titles—enough at any rate to indicate a common quality, which I believe to be necessary to the theme I have mentioned : the quality of elegiac poetry. It is a quality supremely illustrated in the history of English verse ; but our great novelists have for the most part preferred an oblique approach, by way of relations that are generally considered less dispensable ; so that my list contains only one English novel, and that—significantly—by a woman of genius by whose death we have recently become the poorer. *The Waves* is one of the most astonishing feats of sustained imaginative writing in the language, and also perhaps the most purely beautiful of English novels ; but, my subject being Happiness, I find this more clearly and dramatically treated in another novel on my list : Eugène Fromentin's *Dominique*.

This civilised masterpiece, which appeared in the 1860's, tells the story (in the first person, except in the important prelude and epilogue) of a vine-grower of south-western France, Dominique de Bray. There are only five other characters of any importance : Olivier d'Orsel, the neighbour and friend of Dominique's youth ; Augustin, Dominique's tutor ; Olivier's two young cousins, Madeleine and Julie ; and M. de Nièvres, whom Madeleine marries. The plot is superficially simple and concerns Dominique's unhappy passion for Madeleine, her endeavour to " be a sister to him ", her failure and lapse into emotion stronger even than that which she has aroused, the preservation of her moral integrity, her separation—at last absolute—from Dominique, and the latter's marriage to another woman, with whom he finds the happiness that comes to those who have the strength to persist in the path of reality.

A dull, conventional, outmoded story ? To Fromentin, who was a painter of some distinction and knew the precise importance to be accorded to the actual subject of a picture, what mattered was, not his plot, but his theme and the application to it of his general design ; and in his choice of characters appears his consummate artistry. To be happy requires intelligence—of the heart, if not of the head—and all Fromentin's people except one are represented as accepting the major premise of living : to embrace the implications of a rather bad job. The author makes no exorbitant claims for his characters' keeping this hard truth always in sight ; yet consistency is part of his ordered, nineteenth-century point of view, and this makes it necessary for him to include at least one prize botcher—one whose extravagant demands on life continue long after the obvious answer has been made to his pretensions. The essential difference between an intelligent man and a merely clever one is that the latter nearly always lacks a sense of proportion. Dominique's sense of romance is a strong and beautiful emotion, but it yields at length before the dilemma of life or death ; whereas in Olivier d'Orsel we are shown the bitter fate of those who let the daffodils of youth wither and stink in the vase. For Olivier is the nineteenth-century Byronic man, who at once attracts and repels Dominique.

> There he was, always calm and uninhibited, ready for anything, with hints of coldness in his pleasant face, with his impudent looks for people he didn't like, and the sudden and most seductive smile which he knew so well when to use as a caress and when as a weapon.[1]

This is the kind of man who would rather offend than make no impression at all ; who plumps for facility in human relationships (" I like decisions which can be quickly made and quickly reversed ") ; and whose final words to his friend—" Try to be happy "—reveal the measure of his own failure in that respect. This self-centred, violent character is a stranger to the nobility that is willing to sacrifice itself for something unworthy‘ of it ; his opposite number in the scheme of the novel is, not Dominique himself, but Augustin. This poor, dour, painfully priggish tutor matches the unattractiveness of poverty with a strength and beauty of soul which render that disadvantage unimportant. " There were things that he didn't feel, but none that he didn't understand." It is notoriously difficult to make goodness appear interesting, as Edmund Spenser and other great writers have found to their cost ; but Augustin is a triumph for his creator. He is a Jansenist character, whose poignant interest lies in his profound resemblance to Madeleine. By the very disparity of their lives and the different conflict each is called upon to resolve, these two complete one another, as a pedestal completes and sets off a bust. Together they form a portrait of what is most truly distinguished in human beings, and the clue to their association in the author's mind lies, I think, in a passage half-way through the book, where Augustin

---

[1] The quotations in this essay are from the translation by Sir Edward Marsh. (The Cresset Press, 1948.)

says : " The question isn't whether one is happy or not, but whether one has taken all possible steps to become so." A little later on Madeleine passes this on to Dominique in a form characteristic of her own more diffident nature : " Who knows that happiness itself doesn't largely depend on the will to be happy ? "

*   *   *

Considered together, Madeleine and Augustin rise superior to Dominique, who is *l'homme moyen sensuel* of this extremely sensible book. Like many such, he is mildly romantic in youth, makes imaginary journeys on a map and writes poems of which he is somewhat ashamed (Fromentin is careful to let us know how bad they were). He, too, is conscious of " the need of being happy " ; but, being an average man, he has the average man's destiny, and that includes at least one struggle in which the life of the heart is in peril. He wins and so does Madeleine ; but because her nature is of finer grain than his, the scar on it is more cruel. And since tragedy must have its part in this most heartening book, the author gives it us first in the full orchestra of Dominique's despair. The feeling of being unhappily in love has never, I think, been better or more fully communicated ; the exact statements of Fromentin's classical prose make Proust's redundant interpretations seem horribly specialised and ornate. But (to pursue my simile) a more piercing theme is buried in the depths of the polyphony. One of the worst features of male romanticism is its inability to leave matters in a delicate balance ; the youthful Dominique, though paying lip-service to reason, belongs to the all-or-nothing school. Madeleine's effort to keep the scales evenly balanced over four heads (her sister Julie is involved, through her unheeded love for Olivier) ends by upsetting her own ; thus the tragedy lies less in Dominique's loss than in the crucial breakdown of Madeleine's character under the self-imposed strain. The lily begins to fester, and perceiving it, she gives vent to her bitterest thought in describing Olivier, of whose temperament she is perfectly aware, as " the happiest of all ". Here we reach the lowest point of fortune which Fromentin's scheme allows us to touch—the point at which Dominique understands at last that "toute petitesse est le fait d'un défaut de bonheur". The French phrase, *un défaut de bonheur*, is untranslatably exact, for the word *bonheur* contains by derivation the combined notions of luck and of the temperament which creates happiness by being on good terms with itself.

To a greater extent than Dominique, Madeleine is the victim of circumstances which required of women a stronger rectitude and a more rigid sense of self-respect than men were expected to display. Her success, therefore, is equal to those of Isabel Osmond and a kindred but even more famous heroine : Balzac's Mme de Mortsauf, who nevertheless died in achieving her aim. And Madeleine, in her last words to her lover before they separate for ever, shows her perfect realisation of the issues. "Later on, you must marry," she says, "whenever you wish. Don't imagine that your wife could be jealous of me, for when that time comes I shall be dead—or happy . . ." It is to be presumed that she had no need to die, for her husband was no M. de Mortsauf ; indeed the Compte de Nièvres is the perfect French husband—dignified, reasonable, kind. To have given Madeleine cause of complaint in this sphere would have been to ruin the story as it stands, and Fromentin has again drawn an admirably distinct portrait of the kind of man—a little stiff, a little cold—whose character commands the highest respect in his wife but leaves a dangerous amount of room in her heart.

Such is the human structure of an astoundingly faultless novel. The setting, style and tempo decorate and exhibit that structure with admirable propriety. I have suggested that Fromentin's knowledge and practice of painting influenced his narrative style. The habit of looking intently at objects and the wholes they compose, gives to his prose the unified fluency of a successful painting, in which line and colour and texture all contribute to an effect of delightful vividness and easy mastery of the exactly right touch. And in many small, discreet visions the painter's eye is obvious :

> . . . in the open spaces where the wind had room to blow, troops of children were flying kites with long fluttering tails and gazing at them as they mounted up and up, or stood still against the clear blue sky like white escutcheons picked out in bright colours.

But it is in the large Boudinesque landscapes of the opening chapters ; in the wonderfully beautiful intermezzo, which cuts the central, Paris section into two halves, and which describes late summer days in the vineyards and on a boat at sea—a passage that fills the mind with tranquillity and a sense of absolute, static happiness : it is in these extended impressions that Fromentin combines the eye of the painter with the ear of the poet, is at once Turgenev's equal and the forerunner of Virginia Woolf in *To the Lighthouse* and *The Waves*.

★　　★　　★

But the elegiac novel, of which this is a supreme example, must have another most important quality, without which it lapses into sickly dullness : the quality of movement. Tempo in large-scale fiction seems to have become almost a lost art, and here the analogy from music is more obviously useful. Professor Tovey has pointed out that stationary vibration is not movement, and that, e.g. the overture to Rossini's *Il Barbiere* simply buzzes for eight minutes, at the end of which the listener finds himself exactly where he was at the beginning. The great master of large-scale movement in music is Wagner, and his literary equivalent, for this particular feature, is clearly Tolstoy. The movement of *War and Peace*, like that of *The Ring*, is too highly organised to be grasped at any one point ; yet it is ceaseless and so wonderfully varied in rhythm that it conveys by purely technical means a sense of the time and space involved. Now Mr. Ernest Hemingway has recently published a long and portentous novel [1] which critics have invited us to regard in the *War and Peace* class. There seems no reason why criticism should lower its standards, simply because daily life has had to do so, and it should not be necessary to point out that one well-realised character (Pilar) and a dozen arresting pages in 462 do not make a great novel. But I am here concerned not so much with the exasperating falsity of what I can only describe as the sex interest (one eye firmly fixed on Hollywood), but with the appalling tediousness that results from wading through an immensely long novel of action which does not move along

---

[1] *For Whom the Bell Tolls.*

at all. For the rhythm of Hemingway's lugubrious scherzo never varies for an instant : after vibrating feverishly for 400 pages it gives a single lurch and then remains hanging pathetically over the void, like the upper floor of a bombed house. Future generations, to whom the Spanish War will no longer be a sacred subject, will surely have no difficulty in seeing that Hemingway is a meretricious writer, and no qualms about saying so. They may also, perhaps, have rediscovered the secret of tempo in fiction—a secret of which Fromentin, who neither attempts cosmic movement nor seeks to be effective through solemnity, pretentious pathos and other literary tricks, was in possession. The tempo of *Dominique* is in general a slow one, but so cunningly varied that the book never sags for a moment. The main movement is enclosed by a prelude and a final coda, and it contains a central interlude which reverts to the rhythm of the prelude—for a reminder, as it were, that the prevailing mood of the book is a Pastorale and that the author's underlying theme is the hard-won contentment of a life devoted to a small vine-growing community in one of those solitary landscapes which merge imperceptibly with the sea.

The novel might be subtitled " The Portrait of a Gentleman ", and now that gentlemen are rapidly being stifled, put down and otherwise discredited, *Dominque* may shortly acquire the ancillary importance of a *pièce justificative*. However that may be, its lesson—an eternal one—is that romanticism, of whatever kind, leads either to suicide or to misanthropy—is in fact a dead end. And it is no small part of Fromentin's achievement to have surrounded a story of uncompromising realism with an iridescent shimmer of that very romance the hopelessness of which he is pointing ; whereby the ambiguous quality which lends to life its beauty informs the style itself, as it were a piece of music tonally centred in two keys, a major and a minor. This is the peculiar music of elegiac emotion—of that paradoxical sense of happiness which comes from the courage to bid a perpetual farewell and which renews itself, phœnix-like, from the ashes of the youthful heart.

(1941)

16

Stendhal and Beyle

REFLECTION upon adolescence is, with most kinds of writer, the signal for an uprush of self-deception : from Rousseau to Flaubert the truth becomes transformed by visions which gain beauty at the expense of the real situation. All of us are apt to forget what our youth was really like—the bewilderment, the rudeness and inattentiveness, the inappropriate response to people and events, the condign losses, the advancing and withdrawing, the appalling wastage of small opportunities —because, for a number of reasons, we cannot bear to think of it as other than rapturous.

Only those to whom middle age brings an appreciable increase of happiness can look back with undeluded eyes. Among these Stendhal is conspicuous. What he did not know about being young is scarcely worth knowing. If it is true (and in the deepest sense I believe it is) that no novelist really has more than one theme, then Youth is Stendhal's. This man's career was a series of abortive attempts to relive his youth without its mistakes—and not only to relive it but to rewrite it, again and again. It is largely for this reason that the story of his life is so irritating to contemplate : if only, we feel, he would either let go and escape into one of the many ' unreal ' existences possible in nineteenth-century Europe—existences at least potentially dramatic—or else put youth resolutely behind him and embrace the dullness inseparable from real contentment. When we read about them it is difficult not to feel that men like Baudelaire, Rimbaud, even Verlaine, seized more of what was offered. Poets, they lived poetically, even when—as in Rimbaud's case—they turned their backs on literature. There is nothing poetical, or even dimly picturesque, about Beyle's life ; his writings apart, he might just as well have made a good job of his consulship, instead of a hopeless one. Dogged by ennui, he never knew what he really wanted, and if the object

of his designs for once did not elude him, he immediately
wanted something else. A maddening fellow, as women,
especially, seem to have found. "I'm afraid it's very late—
already midnight," said Beyle miserably, to one of the ladies
with whom he imagined himself in love. Whereupon, bored
to extinction by his faintness of heart, she exclaimed tartly :
" *Tant mieux ! Tant mieux qu'il soit minuit !* " And Beyle crept
away with his tail between his legs.

One must have a great deal of sympathy to spare if one is
to waste any on people who do not know what they want.
Perhaps the best way of being fair to them is to bear in mind
that their discontent implies a high standard of happiness. Thus,
in dealing with Beyle's character, we should emphasise the point
that here we have a disillusioned romantic who insisted on
clinging to a preconceived notion of what life and people ought
to be, but whose genial aptitude for intellectual analysis enabled
him to realise in literature a profoundly correct view of human
relationships. Sainte-Beuve's remark, that " the bitterness one
feels and expresses is always commensurate with the subtlety
and sensitiveness one possesses ", exactly fits Beyle's case. His
undeniable integrity made him socially all the more awkward
and agressive, so that for every friend he made he lost three
in posse. To say boh ! at once to everyone you meet, on the
assumption that he or she may be a goose, is as bad a plan as
never to say it to anyone at all. To be sure, Beyle accorded
some degree of respect and even of affection to those who took
his brusqueness calmly ; but those who resented it he wrote off
instantly as grossly insensitive to his real value. Only in rare
flashes does it seem to have occurred to him that this attitude
was pretentious and stupid.

His vanity, perpetually wounded, sometimes led him into
depths of fatuity that are astounding in so intelligent a man.
" I can't understand why she doesn't see how she is compromising
herself," he observed of his cousin-by-marriage, Countess Daru,
when she had been ordinarily polite to him at a party. The
reverse of this medal was a tendency to care deeply for those
who consistently despised and rejected him. In this connection
Mr. F. C. Green, whose critical biography of Stendhal is on
the whole the best of the many books on the subject, is no
doubt right in thinking that Métilde Dembowska was the

most important of the many women who aroused Beyle's passions.

So ambiguous an attitude could not fail to make of *De l'Amour* the ABC of philandering. It is the book of one who was in love with the spectacle of himself loving and (especially) evoking love. In spite of its brilliant analysis of certain psychological states, it no more penetrates to the heart of the matter than does Proust's more elaborate exegesis, which was admittedly influenced by Stendhal's book. Neither writer convinces us that he could ever distinguish finally between love and passion. Men who so fail may inspire affection, but seldom attach to themselves a deep, enduring love. Whence bitterness, cynicism, the " intermittences of the heart ", and other attempts to atomise the personality. It is noteworthy that these tendencies, in whatever form (and we find traces of them as far back as Montaigne and La Rochefoucauld), seem distinctively Latin. Possibly, by exercising a little ingenuity, one could establish the incidence of similar beliefs in the Italianate psychology of the Elizabethan theatre—in Webster and Chapman, more especially, in *The Witch of Edmonton*, and also perhaps in *Hamlet*, *Troilus and Cressida*, and the sonnets of Shakespeare. But in Anglo-Saxon literature between the Civil War and the end of the nineteenth century such theories are to seek, save in one bright, peculiar instance—the *Liber Amoris* of Hazlitt, a confession which, by its violence, its flouting of conventional standards, and the petulant eloquence of its tone, might easily have been written by Stendhal himself, in certain moods.

*   *   *

The famous *beylisme*, then, represents Beyle's compromise with life in early middle age—a compromise effected, not always very successfully, between the ideal of conduct *à-la*-Corneille inherited from his adored great-aunt Elizabeth Gagnon, and an æsthetic attitude to experience which was for ever at variance, not only with life as it is, but with Beyle's own preconceptions :

Je sens que je suis honnête homme et qu'il me serait impossible de ne pas l'être, non pour plaire à un *Etre Suprême*, qui n'existe pas, mais pour me plaire à moi-même. . . .
On a des devoirs suivant la portée de son esprit.

Such quotations, which could be multiplied, show the **real** strength and nobility of Beyle's intellect ; but, lest the fundamentally false basis of his theory fail to pierce, I shall quote Mr. Green's downright gloss :

> His *beylisme* was a philosophy of escape from the revolting ordinariness of existence to a vivid awareness only of life's rare and essential beauties. Its hollowness lay in the simple fact that when a man knows as much as Stendhal did about humanity it is because, whilst despising men as individuals, he has already acquired, unconsciously, a habit that nothing can destroy. Some call it the love of humanity. . . .

Beylisme has its respect-worthy side : it gave free play to the honesty which made its inventor (like Byron and Oscar Wilde) invariably nice to simple, unpretentious people. Fanatics of all kinds would be the better for a dose of it—and would forthwith cease to be fanatics. And its Epicureanism does provide a useful formula for those who, while obliged to submit to the pressure of mere business, value the life of the soul. But one doubts whether the ' happy few ' to whom Stendhal made his appeal would be, if strict adherents of *beylisme*, in fact happy. For the theory ignores far too much and, by atomising life into a series of Exquisite Moments, must lead to the discontent of the amateur, and to the hostile indifference of the rest of the world. I think it significant that only three people attended Beyle's funeral. Mr. Green feels that Beyle would have been pleased by this. I doubt it : I think he would have considered it the final proof of man's ingratitude—a quotation he would doubtless have remembered for the occasion. After all, chronic discontent such as Beyle's is not necessarily noble. " It is sad to have nothing to love ", said he, towards the end of his life, fondling his dog as he did so. To come down to makeshifts was, for Beyle, quite as much the penalty of obstinacy as it was the result of belonging to the human race, which, however, usually takes those makeshifts in its stride. And that is exactly what Beyle could never do.

His egotism was extraordinarily complete. Compare Beyle's friends—and his mistresses—with those of another vigorous egotist whom he affected to despise—Chateaubriand—and the former's appear a shabby lot. Furthermore, Beyle never succeeded in acquiring the female drudge with which men of his type insure themselves against the remorseful solitude of old age ; so that the themes of fidelity and tenderness, without which any life must be accounted a waste, are all but lacking in Beyle's story.

*   *   *

It is, then, because he carried the whole burden of his youth always with him, that Stendhal treats it in his novels with such complete realism. The groundbass of *Le Rouge et le Noir* is the obdurate fact that the blunders of youth continue to matter because they poison the ground and spoil the triumphs which succeed them. Stendhal brings the Present to the bar of the Past, thus reversing the more usual process by which human beings abuse self-consciousness in the effort to evade their destiny. The result is that observed dryness of style and comment which appeals so greatly to the twentieth century—as, in a famous phrase, Stendhal predicted it would ; the dryness of a mind in which perpetual disillusionment has sharpened the vision of reality instead of resolving it into a nostalgic dream. On the other hand, no purpose is served by ignoring the fact that to be insensible, as Stendhal was, to the qualities of fine or ' impressionistic ' writing is a definite limitation. If everyone wrote, as he did, in a style modelled on the *Code Napoléon*, imaginative prose would shrivel. Indiscreet admirers of Stendhal, reacting from the Gothic excesses of Carlyle, Ruskin and Meredith, have shown themselves unwilling to recognise this.

The tone of voice in which Stendhal speaks is not comforting, but it brings Beyle himself nearer to the reader in what seems a common conspiracy. His novels are purely astringent, and their beauty—when they have any—is simply that of truth. In his two great finished books, the otherwise shadowless surface is broken up by romantical flourishes—passionate absurdities which owe something to the melodramatic vein in his own character, and perhaps as much to the exigencies of contemporary taste. The death of Mme de Rênal, the execution of Julien Sorel, and the end of the *Chartreuse*, belong to the paradoxes of great fiction. That they are blemishes few would deny ; but the tone of feeling which dictated them is among the things which

help to endear Stendhal to us as a person. To see life too
steadily—as Laclos, Gibbon and La Rochefoucauld, for instance,
saw it—alienates sympathy, which was something Stendhal
could not do without. Indeed, it is doubtful whether a novelist
(as distinct from other kinds of writer) can ever afford to indulge
fully *le plaisir aristocratique de déplaire*.

In that sense Stendhal's instinct was sound ; but he did not
always follow it, and in his large, but unfinished, novel, *Lucien
Leuwen*, the glare is merciless, like the flat luridity dispensed by
those green or orange street lamps which make hideous the
night towns of to-day. *Lucien Leuwen*, in the state in which
its author left it, is one of the sourest books ever written, but as
a piece of unblinking observation it often reaches Tolstoyan
levels. Beneath the brilliant surface of the narrative—a surface
as ' amusing ' as anything Henry James could have desired—
burns the conviction that it is possible really to know people
as they are : this is a fundamental assumption of Stendhal's
psychological method, and it is startlingly at variance with that
of all novelists of the romantic school, from Balzac to D. H.
Lawrence. For Stendhal there were no Dark Gods except man's
self-imposed obstacles to happiness, and these did not seem to
him in the least obscure. The further he explores the depths
of tragic experience, the brighter grows the light surrounding
his characters and their doings.

Meanwhile, the plot of *Lucien Leuwen* would not seem to
promise a great deal. The twenty-three-year-old son of a rich
Paris banker, Lucien is sent as a sub-lieutenant to the garrison
at Nancy, where he incurs the hostility of his fellow-officers by
a mixture of clumsiness and ostentation. He frequents the small,
stuffily provincial salons of the town and falls in love with a
widow who is strongly attracted to him but takes pains to
conceal the fact for fear of annoying her tyrannical old father,
who disapproves of Lucien's Liberal views. What with Mme
de Chasteller's transports of nervous conventionality and
Lucien's lack of *savoir faire*, the two muff their affair (for the
time being) and Lucien returns to Paris, where his cynical
father obtains him a sinecure and proceeds, with indolent
amusement, to initiate him into the ways of the world. The
genuine affection which exists between Lucien and his mother
is the only chink in the armour of this merciless book ; but

Mme Leuwen is too busy keeping her own end up, *vis-à-vis*
her terrifying husband, to notice that she is losing the son she
loves. By the time she realises what has been happening, it is
too late : the World, the Flesh and the Devil have done their
work and the iron has entered into Lucien's soul. After taking
part in a municipal election, in circumstances which demonstrate to him once and for all the ineluctable evasions of public
life, Lucien leaves Paris for a diplomatic post in Italy, and the
novel comes to an abrupt end.

Why did Stendhal abandon a book so nearly completed ?
The ostensible reason is that he was dissatisfied with the social
scenes, especially those in the latter half of the book, and wished
to complete and rewrite those passages after having them
' vetted ' by Mme de Castellane in Paris. This is no doubt true
as far as it goes, but it does not explain why Stendhal never
returned to the book. From the marginal notes which are
printed in at least one of the most recent editions, it is clear
that the affair with Mme de Chasteller did not come to an end
with Lucien's first departure from Nancy : twice in the course
of the Paris chapters he is described as returning to Nancy,
with the express object of seeing the lady again ; but these
episodes remained unwritten, as likewise the conclusion, which
was, apparently, to have united the lovers in marriage.

It is at least possible that Stendhal simply tired of the
book—that it 'died' on him, as books sometimes do on
writers more self-confident than Stendhal ever was. After all,
the completion of a long novel involves an act of faith which
will not be forthcoming unless the original vision has struck
deep roots in the writer's mind ; and whether it has done so
or not can sometimes be discovered only when a good deal of
the book has been written. It is evident that Stendhal never
sat down to compose in a state of assurance, and the haphazard
construction of the novels he did manage to finish suggest that
he held no preconceived notion of the novel as a form of art.

In default of a clear explanation, I think we are justified in
concluding that Stendhal's visit to Paris gave him cold feet
about the political, as well as the social, aspects of *Lucien Leuwen*.
Politically, Stendhal found himself in the dilemma which faces
all writers of strong Liberal opinions in a country ruled by an
authoritarian government. Protest though he might that the

views expressed by his hero were not to be attributed to him
(" C'est un républicain qui parle ", we find, again and again, in
a footnote), Stendhal may well have been afraid lest publication
of such a book might endanger his position or even land him in
prison.

The social aspect of the novel must have caused him anxiety
of a different kind. He was the type of writer who becomes
more and more self-critical with age. Very robust men of
genius usually care little about matters of taste and even of
fact : their imagination and gusto carry them through. It is
probable that Balzac was unaware of the vulgarity of his
pictures of aristocratic life, and that even had he realised it he
would not have cared. This was not Stendhal's way, as it was
not Proust's. Paris society had, to be sure, been opened to.
Stendhal long before this, through his cousin, Count Daru ; but
there is plenty of evidence that he was never quite at ease in
le monde, and on this occasion the consciousness of his failure to
get the social atmosphere of his novel exactly ' right ' may well
have added to the awkwardness which made him rather less
than welcome in these circles. Prim persons like Mme Sophie
Gay had animadverted tartly on his ' sergeant's mess ' language
and manners. Ladies to whom he made advances tittered
behind their fans. For these and kindred reasons Stendhal never
managed to get right through aristocratic society and out on
the other side, as Proust did—Proust, who loved and hated such
people every bit as much, but saw them still more clearly. So
that the parties in Proust's novel may be felt to be more ' real '
than those in *Lucien Leuwen*, because the characters are less
inexorably witty. The terror of boredom, which seems to be
an endemic disease of the French nation, gives to Stendhal's
drawing-rooms a surface as ornamental as that of a Wilde
comedy, but at the same time lowers (at any rate for the English
reader) the sense of utter truth disengaged by the rest of the
book, since it is difficult to believe wholly in people who dare
not make a simple observation in company for fear of being
thought stupid or dull.

*   *   *

Lucien Leuwen is a wasp's nest of epigrams which recall
La Bruyère and Chamfort because they are less generalised than

those of La Rochefoucauld, and we can visualise the occasions which produced them.

> "Your skin is too thin to be proof against public contempt. Yet one can get used to it, if only by turning one's vanity in another direction. Look at M. de N——. One might say of that famous man that, when contempt becomes general, only fools continue to express it."

That last sentence strikes a shrewd blow for characters more estimable than Talleyrand, whom Stendhal had in mind. For this high-spirited and humorous man was by nature too romantic to compound for long with the drawbacks of any one state of life. In his intermittent heart a love of civilised society clashed with a vivid perception of the callousness of many civilised people. He wanted the best of all worlds—the easy-going warmth of the poor, the shrewdness of the bourgeoisie, and the graces of the rich :

> Ils me parleraient de·leurs dix vaches, qui doivent leur donner au printemps prochain dix veaux, et moi j'aime à parler de l'éloquence de M. de Lamennais, ou du talent de Madame Malibran comparé à celui de Madame Pasta ; je ne puis vivre avec des hommes incapables d'idées fines, si vertueux qu'ils soient ; je préférerais cent fois les mœurs élégantes d'une cour corrompue. Washington m'eut ennuyé à la mort, et j'aime mieux me trouver dans le même salon que M. de Talleyrand. Donc, la sensation de l'estime n'est pas tout pour moi ; j'ai besoin des plaisirs donnés par une ancienne civilisation. . . .

This passage is more important for an understanding of Henri Beyle than his many attempts at overt autobiography, fascinating as these are. A cry from the heart, it explains the inconsolable restlessness of his life. "By the time Men are fit for Company, they see the objections to it," as the first Lord Halifax put it. We need not wonder, then, at the sneer which lurks behind Stendhal's competent but hard-featured prose—the sneer which Thackeray (with whom Stendhal had so much in common) managed on the whole to suppress, because his belief in himself was stronger. For I believe we must face the paradox that, in spite of the two impressive novels which he succeeded in bringing off, Stendhal belongs essentially to the ranks of the great failures ; because the bulk of his enormous output consists of fragments, scissors-and-paste books, false starts, brilliant sketches, rough notes for novels that failed to materialise—all the Byronic paraphernalia of the over-gifted man who cannot face the fact that art involves renunciation, and who fritters away the precious months in pursuit of his own shadow.

We ought not to neglect the possibility that, armed with a little more self-confidence, Stendhal might have got the better of the lassitude which allowed him to abandon so much, and to die so largely unfulfilled. The fragmentary *Lamiel*, for instance, is big with suggestions of a whole world which Stendhal lacked the time or the inclination to explore. This is too bad ; the précis which he left, indicating how the novel was to proceed, is probably misleading (think how a précis of the last third of the *Chartreuse* would read, and compare it with what we have !), but it does hint at what might have emerged from a scheme that suddenly embraces the world of *Les Illusions Perdues*.

But the occasion seems to have passed—as with Stendhal it so often did—and the book died on him. " The reader knows everything ", he exclaimed, in one of those marginal notes which give to *Lucien Leuwen* an adventitious but very special interest. Intended as a warning to himself, the phrase rings desperately in our ears. To be too constantly aware of his audience is as bad for an artist as never to think of it at all ; and no doubt it is impossible for such a man to achieve the weight and authority—the absolute indubitability—of the great professionals. As we glance along our shelves, the collected works of a Victor Hugo, a George Eliot, a Meredith, a Henry James, seem there by right, seldom though we may feel equal to breathing their air. They withdraw from contact with us, demanding submission. But Stendhal is a writer for every day : infinitely accessible ; on the level ; one of the few friends of our early youth who do not give us the shivers when we meet them again in middle age.

(1946)

17

Zola's *La Débâcle*

O NLY a great poet or novelist, a great painter or
draughtsman, can safely be entrusted with a large picture
of war, since the inherent difficulty of the epic lies in
the necessity of keeping both the wood and the trees simultaneously in focus. In other words, the eternal must continually
be discernible as a shadow behind each particular detail ; and
the unobtrusive success with which Tolstoy achieved this effect
is largely responsible for the deep satisfaction we derive from
War and Peace. It is an effect which Dumas, for all his dash
and bravura, could never attain ; which Balzac achieved, in a
smaller focus, with *Les Chouans* ; which Dickens might conceivably have brought off, if he had attempted a novel of, say,
the Crimean War ; and which contributes largely to the success
of what I take to be the three greatest pictures of the First
German War : David Jones's *In Parenthesis*, Jules Romains's
Verdun, and Henri de Montherlant's *Le Songe*. At such a
distance from the subject, symbols become a necessity, and the
writer's constant care must be to prevent the generalised types,
which impose themselves as the dramatis personæ, from lapsing
into puppets. A large brush, then, is needed, to cover the
canvas and to keep the composition homogeneous.

Another, but much less obvious, necessity is an ambivalent
attitude to human beings. If you do not love people in some
sense or other, it is useless to attempt to deal with their corporate
activities ; and if you feel no distaste for the stupidity of the
herd spirit, and for the bodily functions of human beings, your
view will be equally ill-balanced and undiscriminating.

These considerations bring us straight up against Emile Zola,
who can scarcely be accused of not sharing Tolstoy's mixture
of admiration and disgust at the spectacle of people in the mass.
Always better at depicting the crowd than the individual, for

his psychology was of the crudest and most summary, Zola launched the Rougon-Macquart séries on its sprawling journey in 1871, when he himself was just thirty ; so it was hardly to be expected that he would permanently refrain from committing a panorama of the Franco-Prussian war. Wisely, however, he waited twenty years before making the attempt : *La Débâcle* was his last important novel.

A book of this kind prompts the immediate question : Is it a great novel ? The answer, in the case of *La Débâcle*, is emphatically no. Yet because it is informed by a certain greatness of mind—the magnanimous integrity which made Zola the overt champion of Dreyfus and which irritated contemporaries like Faguet refused to recognise—the book has an impressiveness that will make it worth reading when the topical interest of its parallel with the events of 1940 has faded.

★   ★   ★

Zola always makes a success of his first and final scenes, for he had what violinists call a " magnificent attack " ; the first pages of *La Débâcle* dispel any doubts of his claim to be an artist. The camp at night, with its wavering fires and fantastic lights, its confusion of noises, now rising into the sharp definition of a bugle-call or a shout, now sinking into a smothered blur, with here and there a groan or sigh ; the single candle in the farmhouse window marking the vigil of some staff officer : such eternal features of war are woven into a symphonic prelude out of which emerge gradually the shadowy figures of individual soldiers. The big brush is at work, sweeping them all in, filling out the background with night and fatigue, hunger satisfied and comradeship roughly mended amid the exasperation of conflicting rumours, of hope and of despondency.

Up to a point the construction of the novel is cunningly managed. As if aware that a continual series of climaxes would defeat its own end and deaden the reader's sensibilities long before the end of the story, Zola keeps the whole first part of the book out of the firing-line. The result is, I should say, even more successful in conveying the atmosphere of a war area than the terror and violence of Part II, when the fighting at last begins in earnest. Fear and doubt are after all perhaps the worst features of existence, and it is these emotions for which, in his first chapters, Zola has found such striking emblems. A perpetual twilight hangs over these pages, and in this inferno the French fight a battle with ghosts and shadows—the grey Prussians whom they are for ever glimpsing but can never properly see.

Throughout this section it is the fatigue, the discomfort, the horrible inconvenience of war, which are powerfully established in the reader's imagination ; the enemy is Matter, and when Zola describes cavalry and artillery trying to cross a pontoon bridge at night, he conveys, along with the fantastic grandeur of the scene, a sense of the horrible futility of heroism unsupported by material strength and organisation. " C'était le choc de la bravoure in intelligente contre le grand nombre et la froide méthode." As in 1914, and still more in 1940, we receive the impression of a confusion of human beings attempting to defend their land against a pest of clockwork insects.

In these opening chapters, then, Zola's perceptions are extraordinarily just. But in the appalling scenes of Part II he needs all his *bravura* to prevent the book from disintegrating through sheer violence. Luckily he was not the ' realist ' he imagined himself to be, and passages like the attack on the house at Bazeilles, and the hospital scenes, are lifted out of the merely horrible by the dramatic quality of the novelist's vision. The poetic inspiration here is genuine, if not of a very high order : it showed Zola the daisies in the courtyard dyed scarlet by the blood thrown hastily out of the hospital bowls ; it dictated the death of Captain Beaudoin trying to pull an imaginary blanket up to his chin ; it showed him the sinister calm and deceptive emptiness of the besieged Sedan at night. Above all, it created the unforgettable glimpses of the sick Napoleon III, his face the colour of paper, passing across a lighted window alone, or hurried through the streets among a preposterous rabble of cooks and attendants.

Zola is famously at his best when he allows his imagination to brood over some one thing—the staircase in *Pot-Bouille*, the mineshaft in *Germinal*, the lonely house in the railway cutting in *La Bête Humaine*, the great sale of white millinery in *Au Bonheur des Dames*, the ruined garden in *La Faute de l'Abbé*

Mouret—until it assumes the monstrous proportions of a night-mare or an hallucination. In *La Débâcle* the hypnosis is induced by the obsession of food. We watch the Prussians reeling about in rivers of wine and gorging bars of soap, while, absurd and pathetic, a horse munches the floor-boards of a cart.

Enthralling as these pictures are, they never have the final grandeur of Goya's : at best, I am afraid, it is the Baron Gros's enormous machines that they evoke ; at the worst, those of Meissonier. The arts of Zola and Wagner have important features in common, and a greater artist than Zola would have refrained from prolonging Part III so as to take in the Commune. The final scenes are in every way the equal of those in Part II, but we are too much exhausted to assimilate them, as most people who have listened attentively to two and a half acts of *Die Meistersinger* are simply not in a position to respond to the beauties of the last scene.

★   ★   ★

" Je n'ai pas besoin de psychologie ", Zola is said to have retorted to a critic. In a sense he was right, and never more so than in *La Débâcle*, where the individual characters are adequate in number and variety to fulfil the transitions in what is essentially a tragic landscape. Their subsidiary role has other advantages ; in particular, the depressing and monotonous crudity of Zola's attitude to sex (" Et il la renversa, la prit brutalement, par terre ", etc., etc.) is less oppressive here, partly because, by the time he wrote this book, Zola had come to have a better opinion of mankind than is evident in *L'Assommoir* or *Nana*. This does not prevent him from noting what few writers on war ever care to mention—that disgraceful hatred of civilians for the soldiers who are protecting them. It is a phenomenon that even ' total ' war has been unable wholly to expunge, for it has a deep and double root, in the humiliating difficulty of gratitude and in those long ages when the " brutal and licentious soldiery " were mercenaries who battened ruthlessly on the civilian population. Such memories lie dormant in the blood of generations and each new crisis brings them to light. In the case of France there is, too, that hysterical defeatism which is the curse of ardent minds ; which Zola depicts in the manic-

depressive outbursts of Maurice Levasseur ; and which reached
calamitous depths in Pétain's groan : " Nous sommes foutus ! "

★   ★   ★

Uncommonly ill-read—especially for a Frenchman—in the
literature, history and philosophy of the past, Zola was no
thinker. You may search his novels in vain for a single interesting comment on life : everything is implicit. This, for a
man whose stock of ideas was not only small but often fallacious,
is unsatisfactory. Zola demands, in fact, too little of his reader.
If he had been the exquisite type of artist, this might not matter ;
but he was slovenly and tasteless, he had more than a touch of
Hall Caine (*Fécondité, La Faute de L'Abbé Mouret*), occasionally
even of Marie Corelli (*Le Rêve, Rome, L'Œuvre*). His illiterate,
slapdash methods brought their own punishment : they robbed
him of recognition by the best contemporary critics, who were
so outraged by the vulgarity of his style and of his plots that
they failed to perceive the rare epic quality of his imagination ;
and they firmly implanted in the public mind the image of a
gloomy pornographer who thought the very worst of people
in general and of his countrymen in particular.

It is easier to be fair to Zola now than it was at the end of
the nineteenth century ; to-day we can see why he was so
universally but so erroneously regarded as a black-hearted
pessimist. For if he was ignorant of any literature but that of
the Romantic Movement, he was at least steeped in that ; and
his direct masters were Chateaubriand and Flaubert. Those
two writers were of course genuine pessimists, and the characteristic cadences of Flaubert's style, which are imitated in
almost every paragraph of Zola's, are so full of the music of
sadness and resignation that they confer a specious pessimism
on material that was really not designed to that end. For it is
surely all but impossible to produce a sanguine impression in
those immense descriptive arcs, often beginning with the word
cependant, which rise and fall with the melancholy wail of a
wind at twilight. This music was more or less forced upon
Zola by the literary tone of the times ; but in himself he was
a believer in Humanity and Justice, and their ultimate triumph
through Progress ; his deepest convictions were those of 1848

and of Renan's *L'Avenir de la Science*. Had he been born a contemporary either of Stendhal or of H. G. Wells, his generosity of mind, his vigorous and confident imagination, and that genius for broad depiction which triumphs over even the most commonplace and insistent detail, might have been expressed in a style better suited to vindicate his own dictum that a novel is " life seen through a temperament ".

(1941)

18

André Malraux and the
Novel of Action

As a result, apparently, of reading the works of Edgar Allan Poe, the brothers Goncourt jotted down the following note : ". . . the literature of the twentieth century : the scientific miracle, algebraic construction (*a* plus *b*), a literature at once monomaniac and mathematical. Sudden strokes of the analytical imagination. . . . Things will play a more important part than human beings—and love, which has already been diluted, in Balzac, by money, will become a secondary source of interest. In other words, the novelist of the future will be called upon to write the history rather of what goes on in people's minds than of what passes in their hearts."

That prophecy is dated July 16, 1856. It has been more precisely fulfilled than the Goncourts probably expected ; for those two originators of the æsthetic movement were fond of throwing out startling suggestions, paradoxes, *fusées*, in their journal as in conversation—so as to keep alive, in a society of competitive intellectuals, the legend of their extreme cleverness. But since they were genuinely clever, what was meant as not much more than a flash of wit sometimes turned out to be a visitation of the *Zeitgeist*. The reference to Poe need not detain us : it is characteristic enough, but—like the incidence of less exotic fashions—the profound influence of Poe in France is easier to assess than to explain. We may say, if we will, that his work is intrinsically of slender importance ; yet to many Frenchmen, both then and since, Poe has been the tablet of Benzedrine which made their brains function even more brilliantly than usual.

Implied by the Goncourts' prophecy is the future "novel of action", as it is called, to distinguish it from the novel of psychology. It is perhaps significant that in the same year as the passage quoted (1856) appeared Flaubert's *Madame Bovary*, a book which, more than any other, carried in its bones the necessity of that distinction. For until Flaubert and Turgenev decided that plot was to be subsidiary to analysis of motive and the (outwardly static) exhibition of spiritual process, critics had not found it necessary to scrutinise fiction with any such discrimination in view. In fact they might justifiably have done so : *Werther*, *Adolphe*, the novels of Richardson and of Jane Austen, on the one hand, much of Balzac, the whole of Smollett, *Les Misérables*, *Nicholas Nickleby*, on the other, were already there to nudge the minds—so alive to subtle differences— of a Sainte-Beuve or an Arnold. And there had been several borderline cases which will not, even now, fit conveniently into either category. Stendhal resists any such definition, and examination of his very peculiar case may enlighten us a little further.

Stendhal is praised nowadays for his ' modernity ', for his anticipation of changes that were taking place in the life of the race (the phrase is Mr. Martin Turnell's). But too much has been made of Stendhal's famous prophecy that he would be read in 1935. Wise after the event, we discover in the great novels (*Lucien Leuwen* is here included) a forward-looking vision for which there is remarkably little evidence. For all their acerbity and the crackling, aphoristic style from which the smart novelists of to-day have derived so much, Stendhal's writings are those of a disillusioned idealist. And since to dislike the age one lives in implies a certain amount of imagination, haters of the Present usually live in a dream of some chosen Past. After Rousseau the disease became increasingly common ; in the nineteenth century it was endemic—and has remained so to this day. Stendhal by no means escaped the disease, and his chosen refuge was, not the desert island of Bernardin de Saint-Pierre, still less the rococo paradise constructed by latter-day æsthetes, but the Renaissance. All Stendhal's most cherished creations—Julien Sorel, Fabrice del Dongo, the Sanseverina, Lucien Leuwen and (more particularly perhaps) that young man's father—are pure types of the Italian Renaissance, as the art and history of that period had suggested them to Stendhal's disgruntled imagination. Clelia Conti is a heroine of Shake-

speare, and even Count Mosca owes more to Machiavellian
legend than to the real Metternich, who is supposed to have
been responsible for him. As comment on French society under
the Restoration, all this was quite legitimate : the parallels were
real enough ; but to call it " anticipation of changes that were
taking place in the life of the race " is to impute too much
purpose to the hazards of temperament. That by 1935 some of
the more disagreeable features of Renaissance life had crept
back into the European scene, was one of the forms in which
history is seen to repeat itself. For Stendhal it was a lucky
accident that his nature inclined his taste towards Renaissance
behaviour, its means and ends. There is no reason to assume
sociological prescience.

★   ★   ★

Within the realm of invention, however, Stendhal can now
be seen to have pursued a fictional method which, because it
issued from his preoccupation with Renaissance man, in time
gave rise to a new genre. The basis of this method is the
report, a text the value of which depends upon the degree of
its acceptability as evidence in a court of law. It is this specialised
attitude to truth, rather than the romantical elaborations of
plot, which gives to Stendhal's novels their curious air of
authority. This is the essential thread which connects Stendhal
with André Malraux. The point should emerge later : for the
moment we are concerned with the earlier history of the novel
of action, which remained ambiguous until the First German
War uncovered the paths down which European society had
for some time been unconsciously travelling.

In fiction, of any sort whatsoever, action must be a function
of character ; so much is obvious, although in the lower reaches
of the thriller or detective novel the emphasis on sheer physical
activity tends to obscure the connection, both for author and
reader. Novels of action, then, must deal primarily with men
of action—and this means men whose lives are based on the
assumption that physical violence need not be confined to
self-defence. As a definition, this has the merit of including
characters whose bent is partly, or even mainly, intellectual : it
invites us to regard, say, the works of Dostoevsky and of Joseph

Conrad as distinctly novels of action. No doubt those authors would have greeted the description with surprise and resentment ; yet it covers their most characteristic work : *The Brothers Karamazov* and *The Possessed*, *Nostromo*, *The Secret Agent*, *Victory* and *Suspense*.

Violence is of the essence of all these stories, however long it may remain beneath their surface. If civilised behaviour consists in proceeding in such a way that each step leaves the agent free to retreat from a resort to force, then both Dostoevsky and Conrad must be said to commit their ' heroes ' to a perilous borderland. The Russian in particular permits his characters emotional outbursts which are equivalent to acts, since they produce a physical effect on others not less wholly upsetting than that of a blow or a caress. That neither of these writers was of English—or even west-European—nationality seems even more capitally significant to-day than it would have seemed in 1914, before the onset of what we now see as a new and crucial phase of history. Yet it is worth noting that in the previous phase both Hardy and Zola took the ' spectacular ' view of human life which issues naturally in the novel of action, although they left it to Conrad to state this view in so many words. The later decline in Christian belief, which has been steep, has elaborated the ' spectacular ' theory without, however, adding usefully to it. As a philosophical foundation for art, Existentialism may be even more immediately intoxicating than Vitalism or the theories of Bergson ; it seems unlikely to prove more fertile.

In the meantime what Unamuño called " the tragic sense of life " is all that is left to those who cannot accept the sanctions of a metaphysical system. The phrase covers a multiplicity of possible beliefs, none of them leaving room for hope, all of them stoical in implication and having their origin in the experiences of the war of 1914–18, which were new in the sense that they revealed for the first time to Renaissance man the hollowness of his pretensions. In the general disarray which followed this revelation creative writing throughout Europe submitted to its disintegrating force. The years immediately after 1918 saw a considerable atomisation of all those forms of art which had consolidated themselves between the turn of the eighteenth century and 1914. The more conscious artists turned in upon themselves, tessellating recondite emotions as it were stones in a mosaic. There was, of course, a simultaneous movement outwards ; but in either case emphasis was upon the possibilities of the Here and Now.

In these circumstances the novel of action became a militant force, politically and socially. The problem for the writer of such books is to avoid creating an impression of adolescent romanticism. Conrad sometimes fell into this trap (e.g. in *Romance*, *Victory* and *The Arrow of Gold*), and in recent times Ernest Hemingway has wholly failed to escape it. Reasons for the inflated reputation at present enjoyed by that writer are not far to seek : no violence at all was needed to turn *For Whom the Bell Tolls* into a film possessing all the ingredients of popular success in those countries which knew nothing of the subject at first hand.

More interesting in every way are the comparatively few contemporary instances of a major writer who has chosen the novel of action as a vehicle for the communication of an adult conception. Of these André Malraux is unquestionably the first : in intellectual depth and in the scope of his imagination he must be counted among the most important creative writers of to-day. No other living novelist, it is safe to affirm, so possesses, and is possessed by, that tragic sense of life which Unamuño found in men of genius as different one from another as Marcus Aurelius, Pascal, Chateaubriand, Leopardi, Vigny, Kleist and Kierkegaard. There is hardly a corner of his published work in which it is not to be found, in more or less explicit form. When Malraux sprang to fame with his first novel, *Les Conquérants*, it was as a more or less overt supporter of Communism that he did so ; and perhaps it is the anonymous character of modern warfare that makes him the supreme poet of collective suffering. When, as so often in his novels, he describes someone in agony, with the terribly tender gravity of a surgeon or a judge, we have the impression, vivid and mysterious, that as the torment increases so the individual disappears beneath the human mask. The portrait darkens into a silhouette, like the Adjutant in Vigny's *La Veillée de Viencennes*, whose outline was " lithographed on the barrack wall by the explosion ". And Vigny's comment on that sight has many an echo in Malraux's tragic pages : ". . . nobody uttered a word of commiseration—perhaps because to have done so would have seemed like pitying ourselves for having run the same risk."

★   ★   ★

Like Vauvenargues and Alfred de Vigny, Malraux knows war too well to have any illusions about it ; and in him, as in them, the tragic sense of life is sustained by a sense of glory—the glory, not of men conquering other men, but of faith conquering doubt. His heroes never stop to ask themselves whether their frightful lives are worth living, because they would in fact have to stop in order to answer such a question. To stop is to cease, for the time being, to act ; and if these people ceased to *act* they would cease to *be*. Even when they talk about themselves and generalise about existence (as they occasionally do) we can see their thoughts crystallising into action. Glory may be tragic, but for them it is all there is. The exercise of mentality is never admitted by Malraux as an excuse for not proceeding to the acts which it may suggest. Violence may be only the ultimate expression of personality, but it always *is* ultimate—i.e. at the farthest remove from the reasoning spirit—as we see from the fact that when it is a first, rather than a last, resort the agent is deemed criminal or mad or both. Malraux knows the price of violence, is prepared to pay it, and, incidentally, to make others pay it too.

To such a writer war is the subject *par excellence* : the Sino-Japanese war (*Les Conquérants*), the Communist rising in Shanghai (*La Condition Humaine*), the Spanish civil war (*L'Espoir*). Only in two shorter novels has Malraux approached his central theme from a slightly different point. In *Le Temps du Mépris* Kassner, the Communist prisoner of the Nazi Government, is entrusted with the whole burden of the action. This is exceptional for Malraux, who is more at ease with a large canvas and a multiplicity of characters ; but it was in the circumstances a wise decision, since the book deals with frustration and hope, a condition capable of being more sharply focused by concentrating on a single character than by dispersing the interest. As an interpreter of the crisis of his time Malraux has seen to it that his novels exactly followed its course : *Le Temps du Mépris* marks an interlude in his work, between

the two big historical machines, *La Condition Humaine* and
L'Espoir. At the same time it describes the dead point between
a climax of the Chinese war and the explosion in Spain.   In
this *nouvelle* we see the workings of a police tyranny through
the narrow window of Kassner's vision, a window strong as a
porthole to resist the forces outside it. The action here is all in
the battened-down, vigilant suffering of a body and soul that
are both under lock and key—a condition which, of course,
increases, and is meant to increase, the suffering. In this contemporary version of political imprisonment Malraux is perhaps
at his nearest to Dostoevsky ; and the novelist of action does
not fail to suggest that his prisoner is more intensely alive than
those who persecute him.   " In a recoil of fear the chest is
behind the legs, not in front of them."   An observation like
that is typical of Malraux, who is seldom content to allege
spiritual processes without proving their existence from physical
behaviour.

★   ★   ★

Le Temps du Mépris, eloquent and impressive as it is, has
one flaw : the style extrudes nostalgic overtones that accord ill
with the author's attitude to his subject.   Strangely enough
this is the only novel, before *La Lutte avec l'Ange*, in which
Malraux, usually so little concerned to be ' literary ', has allowed
a literary tone to intervene between the reader and the subject.
The results are not fatal to the novel as a work of art ; but it
is fair to assume that Malraux here intended something rather
different—namely, a tract for the times.   On that score Arthur
Koestler's *Darkness at Noon*, which treats a similar theme in the
spirit of sensational journalism, must be considered a greater
success.

In the earlier of the two stories which do not deal directly
with war Malraux is once again nearer to Conrad than to
Dostoevsky. *La Voie Royale* is at once the record of a journey
into the Indo-Chinese jungle in search of lost cities and the
sculptures they contain, and a prowl round the central mystery
of a personality imprisoned, this time, by himself. It is a pity
that this fine story has been eclipsed by the more spectacular
success of *La Condition Humaine* and *L'Espoir*, for Malraux has

never invented a more effective symbol of the tragedy of human effort. As an example of furious will-power Perken is the direct heir to the sinister realm of Conrad's adventurers. The essential aim of such natures is to create—at first perhaps some particular thing, but eventually anything whatever—through destruction. Negative characters sometimes begin by destroying themselves : they always end by doing so ; and Perken is no exception. His insistence is suicidal, although he sees it as something else. " Suicide," he says, " does not interest me. . . . The man who kills himself is pursuing an idea he has formed of himself. One commits suicide only in order to feel that one is alive. I don't care to be duped by God."

Here two parallel passages suggest themselves : one from *La Condition Humaine*, where the terrorist Chen snaps out : " One doesn't go and get killed to order. Or kill other people that way. Except in the case of cowards." [1] The other, more general, comment comes from Unamuño : " The greater part of those who seek death at their own hand are moved thereto by love ; it is the supreme longing for life, for more life . . . that urges them to death, once they are persuaded of the vanity of this longing."

In forms that are more or less disguised, all Malraux's earlier heroes seek death as the supreme gesture of defiance in face of a life they have found intolerably humiliating to their pride. This is true no less of Kyo, in *La Condition Humaine*, than of Perken, who is untroubled by a social conscience ; yet we may find the latter's struggle with his demon the more terrible of the two to witness. The passage which describes the later stages of his lingering death is a peculiarly intense expression of poetic sympathy—of *Einfühlung* :

Perken plongeait dans l'hébétude. Tout près de ses oreilles, des moustiques croisaient leurs fins bourdonnements ; la douleur des piqûres, transparente, recouvrait comme un filigrane celle de la blessure. Elle montait et descendait elle aussi, envenimant la fièvre, contraignant Perken, pour qu'il parvînt à ne pas se toucher, à une lutte de cauchemar—comme si l'autre douleur eût été à l'affût de lui-même, avec celle-ci pour appeau. Un son de chair le surprit : c'était ses doigts fascinés par la brûlure des insectes qui tambourinaient

---

[1] Quotations from this novel are taken from the English translation by Alistair Macdonald. (Methuen, 1934.)

convulsivement sur la charrette, sans qu'il s'en fût aperçu.   Tout
ce qu'il avait pensé de la vie se décomposait sous la fièvre comme
un corps dans la terre ; un cahot plus brutal le ramenait à la surface
de la vie. Il y revenait en cette seconde, tiré vers la conscience
par la phrase de Claude et le mouvement en avant de la charrette,
qu'il ne pouvait séparer ; si faible qu'il ne reconnaissait pas ses
sensations, que cet intolérable réveil le rejetait à la fois dans une
vie qu'il voulait fuir et en lui-même qu'il voulait retrouver.
Appliquer sa pensée à quelque chose ! il essaya de se soulever pour
regarder le nouveau feu, mais avant qu'il n'eût bougé, une mine
sauta, loin devant lui : la terre retomba avec un grand mouvement
mou. Les cheins des Moïs commencèrent à hurler.

Here the union of the sufferer's personality with the sense of
suffering—Baudelaire's " Je suis la plaie et le couteau . . . les
membres et la rcue "—is all but complete : the individual soul
is dissolving away, because the body which is its form is fast
becoming indistinguishable from its vegetable and mineral
surroundings (and origins). The wound in Perken's knee—
guilt-ridden as the wounds of Tristan and Amfortas—throbs
with the rhythm of the jungle heat and the hum of the stinging
insects.

If the end of *La Voie Royale* goes about as far as it is possible
to go into the actual process of dying, right up to the ineffable
moment where being passes into not-being, *La Condition
Humaine* and (in a lesser degree) *L'Espoir* are concerned to trace
the frontier between the private and the public instincts within
individual minds. A frontier presumes, even where it does
not evoke, some possibility of conflict. In Malraux's novels
conflicts are always fought out to the end, which is bitter for
everyone concerned. The scene of *La Condition Humaine*
inevitably reminds us of Loti and Claude Farrère ; talent apart,
the enormous difference of tone is an expression of the increase
in ' awareness ' and responsibility created in serious writers
by the 1914–18 war. Both Loti and Farrère show a sense of
the low ebb to which their world was sinking, but, in common
with such recorders of private life as Henry James and Proust,
they did not face at all squarely the possibility of cataclysmic
change. Aware of social decadence, they wrote as if it could
persist. Many Western writers continued in this somewhat
desperate frame of mind after 1918, since in neither France nor
England had the war produced any violent social change, while

in Central Europe attempts at revolution all flashed in the pan. No writers were absolutely required to change their tone.

★   ★   ★

Temperamentally averse to that (or perhaps any) kind of safety, Malraux sought and found the intrinsic condition of humanity, not in Paris or London or New York, but in revolutionary China and the Spain of the civil war. This paradox was a *parti pris* which subsequent events have seemed to justify. To a generation imbued with theological despair, or at least with a profound disbelief in the efficacy of moderation, the tormented agents of Malraux's two largest novels must seem to assent to the logical issue of their situation. Kyo, the central figure of *La Condition Humaine*, is obsessed by the desire to transform his own emotions into their ' mass ' equivalents : to be himself is for him not enough—or too much. It is impossible not to suspect Kyo of a simple fear of solitude— that is, of the human condition as conceived by Stoics and by most Christians, but which Unanimists like Jules Romains deny and political thinkers like Malraux seem to believe can be abolished. Nevertheless, compared with the terrorist Chen, Kyo is a genuinely tragic figure. He is too intelligent not to be aware, even if his wife's defection had not made him so, of the many difficulties inherent in his assumed position. That these difficulties are insoluble is implied by Kyo's father : old Gisors is a wonderful portrait of the wise man, the perfect intellectual, lifted beyond Good and Evil by the pacifications of the opium habit. When all is over and his son has met the violent death he so plainly sought, Gisors is capable of expressing deep grief through an accession of clear-sightedness :

> You can go on tricking life for a long time, but in the end it converts you into what you were intended to be. Every old man is an admission of defeat, believe me, and if old age is often so empty, it is because so many of the elderly are themselves empty and have concealed the fact. But that in itself is unimportant. Men should be able to comprehend that there is no reality, but that worlds of contemplation exist—either with or without opium —where all is vain. . . .

What helps the old man to speak like this is no doubt the persuasion of another idea, expressed at the beginning of the book : " One possesses only that part of another person that one has been able to change." We do not doubt that so steadfast and pungent a personality as Gisors has changed at least some part of his son, so that behind Kyo and his will to action the changeless figure of his father is always felt to stand. Behind Chen, on the other hand, stands nothing—*le Néant.* The difference between the two young men is perfectly illustrated in a conversation which is central to the book : the passage is lit by those bleak metallic gleams which confer poetic beauty on Malraux's haggard prose :

Kyo felt at once both the nearness of Chen as a comrade, there beside him in the night, and a great sense of dependence ; the anguish of being only a man, of being only himself. . . . He was certain that at that moment Chen too felt drawn to him, that they were fellow-prisoners. Chen spoke :

" Can't tell. . . . If it's a question of killing Chang Kai Shek, I can see my way. And I suppose it's the same with Vologuin ; only in his case, instead of being murder, it's obedience. A life like ours must have something solid behind it. And there's no doubt executing orders does the same thing for him as killing does for me. There must be something that is definite and secure. There absolutely must."

He was silent.

" Do you dream much ? " he continued.

" No. Or if I do I don't remember much about it."

" I have dreams almost every night. Then there are day-dreams too. Sometimes when I let myself go, I see the shadow of a cat on the ground : more terrifying than anything real. But the dreams are the worst of all."

" Worse than anything real, no matter what ? . . ."

" I'm not the sort of person who gets conscience-stricken. The difficult part of murder isn't the actual killing. It's keeping a tight hold over oneself : rising above . . . what one is going through just then."

Was there bitterness behind his words ? The tone of his voice gave little indication, and Kyo couldn't see his face. In the empty streets outside, the faint hum of a distant car died away in a gust of wind which left a scent of orchards behind it, to mingle with the camphor-laden air of the night.

" . . . If that were all. . . . But that's not the worst. It's the Creatures."

Chen repeated :

" Creatures. . . . Octopuses, especially. They keep coming to my mind."

Despite the vastness of the night around them, Kyo felt as near him as if they were shut in a room together.

" How long has it been going on ? "

" A long time. As long as I can remember. It hasn't come so often just lately. And I don't remember anything else. Only . . . that. I hate remembering, as a rule. I can't cope with it : my life isn't over, it's still going on now."

Silence.

" The one thing I dread—dread—is going to sleep. And I go to sleep every day."

Two o'clock struck. Somewhere there in the night an argument was going on ; a high-pitched, staccato, Chinese argument.

" Or going mad. Those tentacles, night and day, all one's life long. . . . And lunatics never commit suicide, so they say. . . . Never."

" Does killing alter the dreams ? "

" I don't think so. I will tell you after . . . Chang."

Kyo had definitely come to realise that he was risking his own life, was living among men who knew that their lives were in danger every day : courage held no surprises for him. But it was the first time that he had seen death fascinate a man, as it fascinated this friend of his, scarcely visible in the darkness, who spoke so abstractedly ; as though his words had been inspired by the same strange nocturnal force as his own anguish of mind, by the compelling intimacy of their uneasiness, of the silence, and of fatigue. . . . But his voice had a different note in it now.

" Does the thought of that . . . worry you ? "

" No. I feel a kind of . . ."

He hesitated.

" I'm trying to find a stranger word than joy. There isn't one. Even in Chinese. A kind of utter relief. A sort of . . . what does one call it ? of . . . I don't know. There's only one thing which goes deeper still. Takes a man further from himself, nearer to. . . . Do you know what opium is like ? "

" Not really."

" Then it's difficult to explain what I mean. Nearer to . . . ecstasy. Yes. But heavier. Deep. Not light and soaring. An ecstasy which . . . plumbs the depths."

" And there's an idea which gives you that feeling ? "

" Yes : my own death."

Still that far-away voice. " He'll commit suicide," thought Kyo. He had listened often enough to his father to know that a man who seeks the absolute with such unremitting zeal will only find it in a form of sensationalism.   Thirst for the absolute, thirst after immortality, and so fear of death : by rights Chen should have been a coward ; but like all mystics, he felt that the absolute was only to be attained through the moment.   Whence, probably his disdain for everything which did not lead directly to the moment when he would enter into breathless communion with himself.   From that human frame which Kyo could not even see, emanated a blind force which held it in thrall ; the raw material of inevitability.   There was a touch of insanity in that comrade of his, silent now, brooding upon the horrors of his nightmare, but there was something divine also, something of the mysticism which is always present in the supernatural.   Perhaps he was going to kill Chang first and himself afterwards.   Trying in the dark to visualise that pointed face with the full lips, Kyo felt that he too was a prey to the same elemental distress which drove Chen on towards the writhing tentacles of his dreams and to his death.

   " My father thinks," said Kyo slowly, " that anguish of mind lies at the very root of human nature ; that man is conscious of his destiny, and that all fears arise from this, even the fear of death . . . but that opium provides a means of escape, and that that is its justification."

Malraux has here pushed a step further Dostoevsky's analysis of the nineteenth-century Nihilist, Nechayev (" Verkhovensky " in *The Possessed*).   Chen is not tragic, only pathetic ; we feel interest in his maniacal obduracy, but no sympathy.   In terms of humanity Chen is a zero.

In a very interesting letter published by *The Times Literary Supplement*, in which this essay originally appeared, Mr. G. Ionescu objected (if I understand him aright) that, in writing of Malraux's heroes—and especially of *La Condition Humaine*—I first assumed their state of mind to reflect his own, and secondly, failed to distinguish the fundamental difference between Kyo and the Nihilist, Chen.   The first charge, if true, would be extremely grave ; but I should have thought it disposed of, if not *passim*, then at least in the concluding paragraph of my essay, in which I have tried to emphasise the humanity of Malraux, a humanity rendered the more profound by a very rare ability to combine action with detachment.

M. Ionescu's second objection seems to repose on a verbal misunderstanding.   In suspecting Kyo of " a simple fear of solitude ", I had no intention of particularising the fear and so reducing it to one of many different kinds.   It is the fundamental fear inherent in the human condition—in other words, M. Ionescu's *l'angoisse*—which I impute to Kyo ; thus distinguishing him essentially from Chen, whose aim is to get rid of humanity by destroying it within himself, as a step towards the final zero of a suicide which shall involve others besides in violent death.

The extent to which Malraux himself shares Kyo's " anguish of spirit " must, I should have thought, remain open to question ; but at least it is clear that, in imagining the dialogue I have just quoted, the author is in no doubt of the important distinction between the two men. And to distinguish is, almost inevitably, to judge. In terms of Malraux's *Weltanschauung*, Chen is rejected, though with evident grief. There are many stages on the Nihilist's road which leads outward—away from the common life. The mystique of violence is not, in Malraux's scene, confined to one political side. König, Chiang Kai-shek's chief of police, is quite as terrifying in his sadistic hatred of himself and therefore of mankind. The dealer in *objets d'art*, Baron Clappique, observes him with the disobliging clarity of the self-seeker :

> He felt fascinated by this utter intoxication which only blood could satisfy ; he had seen enough of the wreckage of civil war in China and Siberia to know what a negation of the world intense humiliation produced ; only blood deliberately spilled, drugs, and neuroses, are nourishing to such loneliness ; now he understood why König had so enjoyed his company, for he knew quite well how all reality faded away in his presence.

König, we deduce, is of the same race as Perken of *La Voie Royale*, of whom it is said : " Acquiescence in the regime of a childless and godless man is the most complete of submissions to death."

Such are the types of character in whom, it is clear, Malraux is primarily interested. At the same time it must be repeated that this novelist prefers a full canvas and is never at a loss to give life to any kind of person, male or female, which his theme may require. Of course, he takes sides ; but he is seldom unfair to his characters. It is a sign of his comprehension that, when one of them is speaking from the heart, we are never quite sure whether Malraux is inside or outside him. In this sense, at least, *L'Espoir* is a profounder study of character in action even than *La Condition Humaine*, although the latter is more deliberately designed, more closely knit, and therefore, as a work of art, more satisfying.   Whereas in *La Condition Humaine* the author claims sympathy exclusively for the party of revolution and implies disapproval even of Gisors, in *L'Espoir* he does not fear to confer dignity—not indeed on the overt partisans of Franco—but on those whose distaste for extremes has landed them in absolute refusal.   Such generosity is a peculiar kind of courage, for to display too imaginative a grasp of the opposite view may be to spoil the impact of one's own purpose—and to deny that Malraux is a writer with a purpose would be idle. It is impossible not to wonder whether, ten years earlier, he would have cared to put into the mouth of a mere intellectual a statement as unambiguous as that of the art-historian Alvear, in *L'Espoir* : " Man entrusts but a fraction of himself to any act ; and the more committal the act, the smaller will be the fraction engaged."   And he adds, drily : " It is hard to be a man . . . harder than the politicians think."

Perhaps the clearest statement of method to which Malraux has committed himself is to be found in the preface to *Le Temps du Mépris* :

More than any other, the distinguished example of Flaubert confuses the issue.   For Flaubert, to whom the æsthetic was the highest value and who actually elevated the artist above the saint and the hero, created only characters who did not subscribe to his own beliefs, and went so far as to write of them : " I will roll them all together in the same mud—because I believe in justice." Such an idea would have seemed inconceivable to Aeschylus or Corneille, to Hugo or Chateaubriand—even to Dostoevsky ; yet it would have been—and is—accepted by many writers who could not be mentioned in the same breath with them.   Two radically different conceptions of art are here in question.   Nietzsche thought Wagner insincere to the extent in which that artist put his genius at the disposal of his characters.   On the other hand it is quite justifiable to use the word art in the sense of an attempt to awaken human beings to an awareness of their own potential greatness.

It is not passion which spoils a work of art, but the desire to prove something ; the value of a work is a function neither of the passion nor of the detachment which has produced it, but of the harmony that exists between what is expressed and the method of expressing it.

A loftier credo for a novelist would be scarcely possible to frame, and it realises its most perfect expression in Malraux's latest novel, *La Lutte avec l'Ange*, of which, unfortunately, only the first volume (apparently one-third of the projected whole) has as yet been published.

To possess only the first part of this most impressive novel is tantalising and awkward : tantalising because Malraux's MSS. are said to have been destroyed by the Germans during the occupation of France, so that we cannot tell when we may get the sequel to this volume ; awkward, because without the continuation it is very difficult to foresee how the trend of thought is going to be worked out. For *La Lutte avec l'Ange* is a philosophical novel, of an ambitious order, and it continues the debate on the limits and respective value of Action and of Intellect. In the first volume we are given—to borrow a simile from music—the exposition and part of the development of a sonata first movement. We await the rest of the development section, the recapitulation and (most important) the coda. Until that arrives we are reduced to a provisional judgment. This important but enigmatic work was first published in a limited edition in Switzerland, during the war, and although it has since been re-issued in Paris, the edition was again a limited one, so that it seems worth while to discuss it in some detail.

Volume one falls into five parts, in each of which an experiencing figure stands at a different remove from Action.

(1) *Immediate Action*. The hero—" I "—among other French prisoners at Chartres, during the last days of the fall of France. · As the battle recedes, the prologue ends with the significant words : " In this place writing is the only way of continuing to live."

(2) *Mediate Action*. The diplomatic intrigues, *à-la*-Papen, of " my father " in Turkey, in the years preceding the 1914–18 war. His mission ended, this rather sinister figure returns to his brother's home, a forest-bound castle called the Altenburg, in Alsace.

(3) *Inaction*. On the eve of war, a conference of European *savants* takes place at the Altenburg. Subject of discussion : Man, changing yet eternal.

(4) *Mediate Action*. On the Eastern front, in June 1915, " my father " takes a spectator's part in the first experimental gas attack by the Germans against the Russians.

(5) *Immediate Action.* " I " am in a tank which is attacking the Germans in the spring of 1940.

It will be observed that Malraux's aim, in constructing his book from these oddly disparate elements, is to focus our eye, as it were, down a funnel on to the object of his greatest disapprobation : the intellectual divorced from ' life ', who sees the world through the distorting lens of books, as a kind of chess problem. These central scenes in the great Gothic library of the castle, with the rain hissing relentlessly down outside among the immemorial walnut trees, are written with a sardonic dignity and a loftiness of tone which few, if any, other novelists of to-day can even approach. The rather grim satire of these pages makes the most destructive fun of the Kayserling type of ' thinker ', with his addiction to pretentious phraseology. " In these circles an idea never arose from a fact, but always from another idea." It is all very brilliant, and very telling, while it lasts ; but the dice are loaded : History and Science and Art are down the drain before we have time to grasp the enormity of the sacrifice we are being asked to make. The trouble is that, in order to drive home his point, Malraux is more or less obliged to blow up the subject from inside : only an intellect of the highest order could have delivered so formidable an onslaught on its own methods and conclusions, or have imagined the *mise en scène* with so Flaubertian an aptness and exactitude. That this attack comes from a noble source does not prevent it from being deplorable, since it ranges Malraux willy-nilly alongside the zanies who wave their arms and shout : " *A bas* Flaubert ! *A bas* Mallarmé ! " Malraux's own war-cry (in this book, at any rate)—" *A bas la psychologie !* "—may seem rather different ; but the result of taking it literally would land us (as Malraux sees, with apparent approval) in an oriental fatalism which could not but alter fundamentally the moral basis of our civilisation. Perhaps this might be a good thing, but it is hardly compatible with the strong neo-humanitarian bias which is Malraux's most striking quality as a thinker. " Man is what he does " is, I take it, the central idea of this book—as it is of *La Condition Humaine* and of *L'Espoir*. Its corollary : " And if he *does* nothing, he *is* nothing ", is unavoidable. We need make no bones about this ; but after reading *La Lutte avec l'Ange* and recalling its predecessors, it is impossible to avoid the suspicion that by action Malraux still means violent (i.e. warlike or revolutionary) action. This is the ancient, endemic illusion of the intellectual—the kind of view we might well expect to hear voiced by one of the *savants* at the Altenburg conference ; a view quite unworthy of a man of Malraux's experience. Try giving vent to it to anybody who served in the late war and you will get a horse laugh. Violent action, he will tell you, is " before, a joy proposed, behind, a dream ". It is like the rainbow : you cannot be inside it and intellectually aware of it at the same time ; and afterwards the memory is distasteful and nugatory. The only action which really justifies both itself and the agent is that of creation, and this is never violent, wasteful, or destructive of individual integrity. One is reminded at this point of Goethe's remark that to *do* anything one must first *be* something. Too many ' men of action ' are— in a spiritual sense—nothing to speak of. Which will not do.

It is in the third part of this volume—the narrative of the gas attack—that Malraux rises to his full stature as a master of descriptive prose. There is not a word too many, not one out of place ; the cold, precise bitterness with which the destruction wrought, in plants, animals and men, by the advancing cloud of corrosion, renders these pages as frightful, and as unrivalled in their art, as the etchings of Goya. The moral protest against man's inhumanity to man, has never been more trenchantly made. Malraux's N.C.O. sums up the horror he has witnessed in a phrase that will have other echoes for the contemporaries of Buchenwald : " No. Man is not meant to moulder away." The implications of the second half of this volume run counter to those of the first ; and we are left with the impression that, while war may destroy life, it is condemned to remain for ever outside it.

In his brilliant and profound essay on Goya's Prado drawings Malraux throws much light on his own aims, particularly in the following sentence : " He cared less for faces than for the whole scene, less for the scene even than for *a kind of complex dramatic symbol the unity of which holds the entire picture together and creates what he intends by a work of art.*" (The italics are mine.) This form of intensity places Malraux among the very few writers of our age whose claims to greatness are obvious, even to those who are politically out of sympathy with him or who are alienated by the remorseless tone of his narrative.   Where Alain Fournier could feel, and write, that "life is everywhere beautiful and serious", it seems likely that Malraux would suppress the first of those epithets.   Likely, but not certain. Even at. his grimmest—at the end of *La Voie Royale*, in the description of the gas attack in *La Lutte avec l'Ange*, amid the wounds and tortures of *L'Espoir*—Malraux, on the whole, contrives to keep before us the notion of organic splendour.   This is not simply another way of saying that he is a literary artist of a high order :   there are plenty of good writers who portray life as a sentence from which there is no appeal.   Malraux, for all his severity, leaves behind a rather different impression, which is a result of his rooted belief in strenuous action and the spectacular value that accrues from it.

Although a born writer, Malraux can hardly be considered a born novelist, as Dickens or Balzac or Mauriac may be said to be, for his technical faults are such as no born novelist would be guilty of.   The worst of these is the habit of describing in minute detail scenes of complicated physical activity.   This is a pitfall into which the novel of action most easily falls.   Conrad succeeded, on the whole, in getting round the occasions for tedious confusion offered by his plots ;   but all the lesser novelists of action, down to Harrison Ainsworth and Henty, indulge it to the full.   Malraux is here no exception ;   as if unaware that violent action in a novel must be brief in duration and relatively simple in outline, if we are to grasp all that is happening, he attempts protracted scenes of the wildest visual complexity, which batter the unfortunate reader into exhaustion and, eventually, boredom.   At moments, it is true, the minuteness of the observed detail produces an effect on the reader which is almost as painful—*physically* painful—as the event described. While reading the following paragraph from *L'Espoir* one finds oneself shrinking as from a real flame :

The jet of the flame-thrower, phosphorescent in the darkness, came out of the passage and swept the ceiling, the opposite wall and the floor of the cell as with a slow spray, as if the fascist who was holding the nozzle were lifting a long column of petrol. Bounded as it was by the doorway, the wave of liquid fire could not reach either side of the room.   Despite the energy with which the militiamen hurled bucket after bucket of water on the wall

and the crackling flame, Hernandez guessed that they were waiting
for the moment when the fascists would appear in the doorway.
From the way in which some of them were pressing back against
the wall, he judged that they were getting ready to give ground.
This struggle between man and an element had no connection
with war : the advancing wave of flaming petrol, the militiamen
staggering about among the splashing water, the hiss of steam and
the desperate coughing of men stifled by the acrid stench of oil
and the dreadful whining of the flame-thrower. As the crackling
sheaf of fire came nearer and nearer, the frantic agitation of the
militiamen was multiplied by the darting blue flames which threw
on to the walls great bunches of mopping and mowing shadows, as
it were a pack of phantoms unleashed by the frenzy of the living.
And in the asphyxiating fog which transformed every form into
a silhouette, the men themselves counted for less than their lunatic
shadows, less than the furious sizzling of the flames and the water,
less than the little barking screams of a burnt man.

    " I can't see any more ! " The cry came from the level of the
floor. " I can't see any more. Get me out of here ! "

    Hernandez and Mercery had got the man by the shoulders and
were dragging him to one side ; but still he went on shrieking :
" Get me out of here ! "

On such occasions as this there is no questioning the validity
of what Malraux himself sees and hears ; the units are severally
vivid enough, even if they do not add up to a single impression.

    But too often, both in *La Condition Humaine* and *L'Espoir*,
there is an apoplectic congestion that is most un-French, in the
sense that analogous passages in Zola are un-French. To borrow
a simile from music, the material is symphonic and the music
well composed, but the *tutti* are grossly over-scored. As we
plunge breathlessly through the breakers of *L'Espoir* we cannot
help thinking, however unwillingly, of the later tone-poems of
Richard Strauss. As in the middle sections of *Ein Heldenleben*,
we are impressed by the vitality and assurance, but confused
and distracted by the elaboration of the material : the counter-
point crowds along, pushing and shoving like people trying to
enter a tube train in the rush hour.

    It would seem as if Malraux had become aware that in
L'Espoir he had gone too far in the direction of the film scenario.
Even those who affect to despise art seldom disdain its methods ;
and Malraux, who has never despised the more serious forms of
art, in that novel finally exhausted the possibilities of the

Stendhalian report.   From a technical point of view *L'Espoir* is the dead-end of the novel of action.   Some kind of retreat was necessary.   This was made in the best order : even in its unfinished state *La Lutte avec l'Ange* is a wonderful specimen of novel writing, and a remarkable proof of the author's power of self-criticism.   Malraux has lost nothing in the process of reducing the reckless density of his earlier manner.   The conversations in the Altenburg are more impressive than similarly reflective passages in the preceding novels, because Malraux has given the tempo of his prose time to slow down and scope to expand.

The violent scenes which frame the book are much better managed than the hectic agitations of *L'Espoir* ;   and the description of the gas attack, although long and minutely observed, is perfectly clear and easy to follow, because each phase of it is carefully established in our minds before the next is introduced.

The increase in technical accomplishment to be observed in *La Lutte avec l'Ange* naturally involves formal improvement. To judge by the passage quoted from the preface to *Le Temps du Mépris*, and in spite of the diffusions of *L'Espoir*, it seems unlikely that Malraux would repudiate the importance of the formal element in a work of fiction.   It must, however, be admitted that *Les Conquérants*, *La Condition Humaine*, and *L'Espoir* are formally uninteresting.

In the matter of style Malraux has always been a highly conscious artist ;   but the exigencies of the themes he has chosen—the very nature of the novel of action—involved him from the first in the one-way traffic of a Picaresque scheme. *La Lutte avec l'Ange*, on the other hand, already possesses the circular form we are accustomed to find only in the ' purer ' works of fiction.   The result, needless to say, is a substantial increase of communicative power.   Perhaps we may attribute the development of this aspect of Malraux's genius to his preoccupation with visual art.   At all events the change is very much for the better.

In treating the relations between the sexes Malraux assumes a harsh, sardonic attitude.   He is not embarrassed by the subject, as English writers often are ;   but he seems to prefer to take it for granted.   One senses impatience, and even contempt, when

his characters compel him to attend at all closely to this aspect
of their lives.   As part of the human condition, sexual love
exposes men's weakest side, and as an analyst of human character
Malraux is as ruthless as Savonarola.   An idealist *à rebours*, he
shows an instinctive dislike of those velleities which detract (or
seem to detract) from the divinity of the human soul.   The
affair of Ferral and Valérie, in *La Condition Humaine*, is as hateful
and discordant as most of the other personal relationships in
that acrid masterpiece, and for reasons which do less credit to
the pair concerned.   In fact, Ferral's attitude to his mistress is
most trenchantly described in a passage which refers to another
woman.

> His pleasure sprang from putting himself—clearly that was it—
> in the place of another, a creature in constraint, constrained by
> himself.   In fact, he never achieved enjoyment of any one but
> himself—yet this was a joy that could only be attained in the
> presence of someone else.   He understood now what Gisors had
> only suspected : yes, that was it, his thirst for power was never
> quenched, was kept alive by being renewed ; but even if he had
> never in his life before possessed any woman, he *had* possessed, he
> would now, in this Chinese girl awaiting his embrace, possess, the
> one and only thing he hungered for : himself.

It is the skilful juxtaposition of the scenes of desolating
intimacy with those of anonymous violence which gives this novel
an extraordinary power.   Yet the final impression produced by it
it uniquely depressing in Malraux's work, because once our
sympathy has been successfully claimed for his characters the
author proceeds to involve us in moral confusion, by plunging
those same characters into a mælstrom of violence that reduces
the political issue to a struggle between Wrong and Wrong.
In so doing he illustrates, even more convincingly than in
L'Espoir, the fatality which lies in wait for the novel of action
when carried to its logical extreme.   It is significant that in a
single reference to Kipling—an author to whose ideas and
literary methods he seems to owe not a little—Malraux attributes
to one of his characters this cynical thought : " Now let's go
over to the other side and listen to some more lies."
   Like all who are obsessed with the realisation of a political
idea, Malraux suggests in everything he writes too little belief

in the value of Pleasure. The recent change in his political views may well be more apparent than real ; in any case it has not affected his status as a novelist. The admiration for Power has the same effect upon the mind which harbours it, whatever may be its ostensible aim. To the political revolutionary the exercise of power is a substitute for other (and it might be added, less harmful) forms of pleasure. It leads, by the only route available, to a puritanical disapproval of what is simply agreeable. Malraux's novels are full of *obiter dicta* indicative of this point of view, to which his recent essay on Goya gives open expression. Eloquent and penetrating as it is, this study betrays too narrow a sense of the legitimate scope of art. The practice of robbing Peter to pay Paul is of all critical methods the least convincing. Malraux's resentful scorn of any form of decoration (a Tanagra figurine, a Buhl clock, a Meissen bowl, would, one feels certain, make him frown) leads him to depreciate, not only the Baroque, but all Italian painting, in order to represent Spanish art in general—and that of Goya in particular—as more profoundly concerned with the human situation. This is true if to be obsessed by Pain and Death is the only valid sign of real contact with life. But is such an obsession, in more than a narrow sense, more *real* than that simpler acceptance which permits the delight in natural beauty, and in the caprices of human character, to come uppermost ? Largely the question must remain one of temperament, though it is easy to see why, in our day, the tragic sense of life should recommend itself to the serious artist as inherently superior. Error arises only when it is assumed that tragic art is in some absolute sense superior to any other : that the work of Zurbaran and Goya is *truer* than that of Velasquez and Murillo.

Remaining for a moment in the domain of painting, we might say that to André Malraux has fallen the task which in the last century fell to Courbet. Both practise an art of realism which extracts beauty, as well as truth, from subjects that in weaker imaginations (such as Daumier's) aroused only the rhetoric of romanticism. Courbet's " The Burial at Ornans " is a Malraux scene translated into terms of paint. The comparison need be pushed no further, and is made here only because of the misleading voice which might otherwise be heard murmuring something about Picasso's " Guernica ".

Malraux's novels give no purchase to those who seek in fiction the resolution of personal discords. Man, he seems to say, can fulfil his nature only by aspiring to a super-personal ideal—never by the exercise of private virtues alone. If man is to retain his humanity, the human situation must be surmounted.' So strict an assertion, and one so wholly lacking in humility, could be made only by a mind in which pity had been purged of self-regard by an experience of suffering on the largest and least individual scale. No doubt there is, and always must be, something shocking about the ability to experience an emotion that is both intense and impersonal. Such a feat is paradoxical, inhuman. We may expect it in men of action, and perhaps we should find it easier to forgive in Malraux if he were less fine an artist. The case of Vauvenargues shows that in similar circumstances it is possible to love humanity without bitterness or loss of detachment. Yet it may be objected that at the crises of history the relation of the individual to society is strained to breaking-point, and then the artist who would express that relation (not all will wish or need to) must be something more than a witness. Such, at former periods of crisis, were Langland, Cervantes, Mathias Grünewald. To-day André Malraux, alone among novelists, can claim to possess something of their stature. Intellects as imaginative and as logical as this do not easily abide by the concept of union. It is well that, at the present juncture, the nations of western Europe should be able to boast a mythologist whose vision is guaranteed by a passionate love for the simplest of those feelings which bind men together.

(1948)

19

The True Realism: François Mauriac

I N a short essay on "The novelist and his characters", which is distinguished no less by the modesty of its tone than by its complete insight into the subject, M. François Mauriac places himself, by implication, among those creative writers whose concern for the living soul raises them above the contingencies of journalism and political party. "The distinction", he says, "is not between bourgeois (*mondains*) and proletarian writers, but between good and bad writers." And further on he fills out this distinction by a more explicit statement of the serious novelist's aim: "I believe it is our justification . . . that we create an ideal world thanks to which living men may see more clearly into their own hearts and so may show each other more understanding and more pity."

It is refreshing to come upon a contemporary imaginative writer whose moral values do not wear a provisional air. Pity and understanding are certainly the most striking qualities of M. Mauriac's novels; but both are edged with the sternness that comes of an absolute religious conviction, bred in the bone and fostered by strong attachment to a traditional way of life in a remote and self-contained corner of France. With its tracts of sand dune and pine forest, its vines, its lost and crumbling manors, its proud peasantry, its torrid summers and dank winters, the Gironde is a gift to the novelist, for it contains those extremes of habit and circumstance which he need not describe but of which he must be constantly aware. Though on the same latitude as Liguria, this uncompromising land is turned towards the Atlantic and its mists. M. Mauriac derives the simplicity and vigour of his style from the classical south, but from the north and west his passion for the human soul. If he does not really count among the 'regional' novelists, this is because the fervently Catholic cast of his mind gives to his picture of life a universal quality which is lacking in the deliberate and emphatic provincialism of writers like Gottfried Keller or Jean Giono. Mauriac writes always of the Gironde, not in order to celebrate it, but because a lifetime's knowledge of the place and its inhabitants offers him all the material he needs for the exploitation of his theme.

★   ★   ★

Unlike most contemporary novelists, Mauriac is primarily interested in the problem of Good and Evil ; and here it must be remembered that while to the atheist or agnostic evil is simply the anti-social urge within an ill-balanced personality, to the Christian it is a hierarchy of its own, parallel to the human system. It is also essentially parasitic—a wandering force which, in order to maintain itself, fastens upon the unwary, the violent, or the desperate soul, taking possession of it so that it becomes separate, terrible. " Every time we do good, God works in us and with us ; on the other hand, our bad actions belong wholly to us. Where evil is concerned, we are in some sense gods." And in *Les Anges Noirs*, which is Mauriac's most unflinching examination of the hierarchy of evil, the action of the story is constantly being snatched away from the characters themselves, so that everything is made deceptively easy for them, as in some kinds of dream. . . .

> His experience did not deceive him : all through his life these sudden, unpremeditated journeys had always meant a putting into play, or the accomplishment, of some plan. At such times he felt himself gently rocked to and fro, like a stone held in a clenched hand. . . . Yes : inert as the pebble that a child's hand is about to throw at a harmless animal. Never, so strongly as that evening, had he had this feeling of terrible passivity.

This strong conception of the nature of evil renders it terrifying to the imagination in a manner, and with a power, which are not available to those writers (nowadays in a majority) who entertain a negative idea of this reasonless force. Mauriac—like Graham Greene and (in a different way) Kafka—is a great adept at the art of gathering two or three together so that Evil is conjured to make a fourth in the game. A suddenly intensified *usualness* in the appearance of everything—a quietness replete with signs : the fire burning just too brightly ; the pictures on the wall edged with intent ; outside the burnished window the landscape dissociating itself. There is no escape, and the scene is set for a proud exaltation of the self which organises a cold and careful demolition of the subtle structures of love. The agents of evil in these novels are superficially various : they range from weaklings like the gigolo, Bob Lagave, of *Destins*, and the furtive rake, Hervé de Blénauge, in *Ce Qui Etait Perdu*, to professional artificers of ill like Gabriel Gradère (*Les Anges Noirs*) and Hortense Voyod (*La Pharisienne*). These are extreme cases, and it is perhaps natural that Mauriac's most famous character, the murderess Thérèse Desqueyroux, should also be the one which has aroused the liveliest interest and sympathy among his readers.

*   *   *

It was some years after writing the first part of her story that he returned—like one irresistibly drawn back to the scene of his crime—to discover what had happened to Thérèse " in the end ". Yet still it was not enough, either for him or for us ; and back he went again—once, twice—to take soundings in the Sargasso Sea of her middle years. He has since hinted that something yet remains for him to tell.

The first part of the novel displays this writer's narrative power at its most compelling. From the moment when we first catch sight of Thérèse in the train, white and tense and desperate and more than ever alone, returning, after her acquittal, to the home she loathes—from this moment we retrace, through her own stumbling memory, the steps of her moral disintegration. At the end of Part I we lose sight of her, free as a bird of prey, in the crowd of a Paris street. The two episodes from *Plongées* give us glimpses of a Thérèse growing old in vicious despair. In the first of these she is shown telling a smart-alick psychologist the story of her utter betrayal by a lover ; in the second she returns the look cast at her by a young man in a hotel dining-room, only to discover that he is studying for the priesthood and that it is her soul, not her body, he is after. Finally, in " The End of the Night ", we assist at Thérèse's last struggle with her demon, and leave her, old and sick and longing for death, in the house lost in the depths of the Landes, which had witnessed her first, and perhaps most pardonable, crime.

It is an appalling story, and I am not surprised that some critics should have called Thérèse Desqueyroux a " monster " ; nevertheless, I think this judgment fails to take account of the profound humanity, and the Christian charity, of M. Mauriac's portrait. What was fundamentally the matter with this woman —so intelligent and gifted, so charming, so vital, and capable so often of good and generous actions ? For in brain Thérèse is as much superior to Emma Bovary as at heart she is better— far better—than Hedda Gabler ; and there is much in her of both those tragic creations. The impulse which prompted her to start poisoning her unattractive boor of a husband, was originally much vaguer than that which drove Madame Bovary to eat arsenic, or Hedda to press the trigger of her gun. Consciousness of ability stifled by a narrow, conventional environment ; a dynamic will turned in upon itself—then, in rage, facing round to destroy what it has failed to make its own ; realisation of a vicious circle creating an ever deeper hatred of self : such is M. Mauriac's vision of the earthly hell to which defiant self-will drives its victims. This arid fever is purely cerebral : it makes use of sex only in order to enslave and destroy. In a wonderful passage of analytical description Thérèse, a prey (of course) to insomnia, is shown as deriving solace only from reliving in fantasy one or other of the innumerable *passades* by means of which she has tried to affirm her own dwindling reality.

As a rule, though all hope was dead in her, she was too proud to have recourse to drugs. But to-night she could not resist their promise of help. In the day-time it is always easier to be brave. What, at all costs, she must avoid was waking up in the middle of the night. She dreaded sleeplessness more than anything else, that awful lying in bed in the dark, powerless against the horrors of imagination, a prey to all the temptations of the mind. In order to escape from the agony of knowing herself for what she was, to avoid becoming the victim of that crowd of silent presences, among whom she recognized the sickly, heavy-jowled face of Bernard, her husband and her victim, and Marie's too, her daughter's, tanned by the sun—all the many faces of those whom she had threatened with destruction, who had fled from her—that she might not be overwhelmed by this surge of ghosts, she had but one recourse in the long nights when sleep would not come—namely, to choose from among them, to get on terms of comradeship with, just *one*, one who did not really matter, and so relive in imagination some brief experience of happiness that would perish with the moment. Only what had counted for little in her life, what had occupied the tiniest place in her experience, held now the promise of a mite of joy—friendships which had come to nothing, love which had not had time to grow corrupt. During her periods of insomnia she would wander in thought about the battlefield of memories, turning over the corpses, seeking some face that still was recognizable. How many were there now of whom she could think without bitterness ? It had needed no long time for most of those who had once loved her to discover the power she wielded for destruction. Those only could bring her aid to whom she had vouchsafed but a glimpse of herself, who had moved only on the outer circumference of her existence. From them alone she could draw comfort—strangers met some night and never seen again. But, as a rule, even these casual acquaintances slipped from her hold as she thought of them. They melted away, and suddenly she noticed that they were no longer there, that her thoughts were wandering far from them. Even in the land of reverie they refused to be her friends, but left her alone to struggle against the surging onset of others. How she longed to escape from the presence of those others ! They woke in her a sense of shame and humiliation. Almost always there had been a moment in their wretched histories when she realized that the familiar friend was out after his own ends. . . . Always had come that moment of the insidious word and the outstretched hand, the exploitation of friendship had taken many forms, from the loan openly requested to the " promising investment " in which it was hoped to enlist her interest. All through the hours of deepest quiet, when the silence of the countryside descends on Paris, she would think, over and over again, of all the money she had lent or that had been wormed out of her by dishonest means. Now that she was herself reduced to the bare necessities of life, it annoyed and exasperated her to set the total of her losses against the figure of her debts. She had surrendered utterly to that " dread of being in want " to which the elder members of her family had always been a prey.[1]

Such a character would be nothing but an object of aversion if, like Jean-Paul Sartre, M. Mauriac thought life pointless and

---

[1] From the translation by Gerard Hopkins. (Eyre & Spottiswoode, 1947.)

absurd. It is because his religion impels him to seek a reason for evil that his full-length portraits of wicked people move us so strangely. Like Gabriel Gradère, in *Les Anges Noirs*, Thérèse is a deeper excursion into the jungle of human motives than those characters who are less completely divided against themselves. Faced by her anomalous nature, we are forced by an overwhelming sense of pity to accept the dichotomy of good and evil as a conflict of absolutes. Seen in this light, the soul of Thérèse reveals a purpose beyond itself—a purpose which the author states at the very end of the book : "It was her mission to force an entry into half-dead hearts and there turn up the soil . . . with her sharp share she cut deep into the waste stuff of men's souls, making them, at long last, fruitful."

★   ★   ★

All the persons of this memorable drama have been seen and heard and experienced by the author with such terrible acuteness that his presentation of them is entirely without the emphasis of the artificial. Like all true creations of the imaginative intellect, they persist behind scenes in which they play no part ; if they die or disappear, their spirits continue to haunt the living. When Thérèse's daughter reappears, grown up, at the beginning of the last part of the novel, we do not ask ourselves what she will be like : we know in advance. The door opens and there she is. It is her mother alone who is surprised.

This effect of inevitability is the reward of an integral vision of human life, achieved through personal suffering—for it is the paradox of great fiction that perfect objectivity is attainable only through perfect sympathy. Such an effect provides, I suggest, the only sense in which the word *realistic* can properly be applied to fiction. M. Mauriac's method of selecting detail is very different from that of a Meredith or a Henry James : he catches his people at work or at play, in dignified or undignified postures ; their natures are exhibited at every level of consciousness ; no detail of their lives is deliberately ignored. Yet, like Tolstoy and Dostoevsky, M. Mauriac never loses sight of the fact that the only thing of permanent interest about human beings is the making of their souls. The nature of the material assembled to reveal this process is in itself indifferent.

The author has stated that he may, at some future date, give us the scene in which Thérèse is finally absolved, by a priest of peculiar saintliness, from her entire burden of sin. At the risk of impertinence I must hope that he will do no such thing. All that is necessary to our comprehension of this woman's life is fully, and most movingly, implied in the masterly final pages of *The End of the Night*. *Le mieux est l'ennemi du bien.* The marriage of heaven and hell is already consummated : to insist further might easily injure our impression of a nearly faultless work of art.

★   ★   ★

Thérèse was a very special case : her intelligence alone would single her out in any milieu. M. Mauriac's most recent creation—and, I think, his finest, just because so rich in those complexities of motive which are still observable in the 'average' person—is a woman whose character suffers all but total ruin through the irreconcilable claims of the religious and the secular forces within her. In other words, Brigitte Pian— *La Pharisienne*—is devoted to the forging of an " armour of perfection " around her soul, the corruption of which is hidden from her by egotism and a self-righteous striving for power. In this superb portrait, which has the grandeur and pathos of a Rembrandt, M. Mauriac observes his subject with extreme detachment and with a dry humour which exposes Mme Pian's pretensions as essentially comic. When one of her victims becomes restive under her relentless interference, this is the author's comment :

> But Mme Brigitte would not listen. She had been wounded, but forgave the hand that held the weapon. She always behaved like this when people told her that she had been wrong or had committed some injustice. Instead of frankly admitting her fault and sitting in sackcloth and ashes, she turned the other cheek, protesting that it was well she should be thus misunderstood and vilified. In this way she added another link of mail to the armour of perfection and merit in which she went clad from head to foot. On such occasions her interlocutor was driven to speak angry

words, and this gave her a feeling of still greater excellence at the
bar of her own conscience and in the sight of God.[1]

M. Mauriac has shown us the male, and even more sinister,
equivalent of Mme Pian in the spoiled priest of his play, *The
Intruder*, and has commented upon the type in an interesting
essay on Molière's Alceste, which contains the following acute
remark : " He feels no horror for what is horrible—beginning
with himself : all his attacks are turned outwards ; he compares
himself with others only to his own advantage." In the
Christian sense, then, Brigitte Pian's self-satisfaction is comic ;
meanwhile, the harm it does to others is frightful, and nowhere
does the power of this novelist's imagination operate to such
admirable effect as in the success with which he engages our
sympathy for the miserable woman, when, at long last, the
results of her acts begin inevitably to recoil upon herself.

The subject is a large one ; it requires both time and space
for its deployment ; and the author's management of both is
that of a master of fiction. When the story opens, three of the
principal characters—Mme Pian's stepchildren, Louis and
Michèle, and Louis's school friend Jean de Mirbel—are children ;
but the narrative is so cunningly contrived that before we
realise it years have passed and the children are grown up. The
tragedy of the saintly Abbé Calou, the deterioration of Jean de
Mirbel, are contributory stages in the same sequence ; but the
factor of space is equally important, and the irregular intersection
of diverse destinies (a constant feature in all these novels) is
managed with an effortless ease and a completely firm grasp on
the realities of the situation, which make the laboured counter-
point of Aldous Huxley and others look very clumsy indeed.
For although the progress of the Pharisee is the centre of the
book, the individual histories which contribute to it are made
to seem no less interesting, because the author's grasp of his
characters is both firm and tender.

It is an absorbing spectacle, not only because we feel so
lively an interest in these people, but because—to put it very
mildly—M. Mauriac knows how to tell a story. In fact, I can
think of no other living novelist whose sheer narrative power

---

[1] From the translation by Gerard Hopkins. (Eyre & Spottiswoode,
1946.)

is at all comparable with his. Impossible to stop reading any
of his novels, especially this one. His method is traditional and
presents no difficulties or obliquities such as we find in writers
like Bernanos or Elizabeth Bowen (to take two very dissimilar
examples). Reserving all complexity for the analysis of character
and interplay of shadowy moral forces, M. Mauriac's prose has
the close, economical texture, the hard definition and the smooth
serenity of Racine's verse. And because he never flinches before
the worst, he is an entirely unsentimental writer. In the hands
of a cynic or Existentialist a novel like *Les Anges Noirs* would
become a mere piece of Grand Guignol ; Rose Révolou, the
only character to survive the general cancelling out in *Les
Chemins de la Mer*, would be a first cousin of the Constant
Nymph ; and Jean de Mirbel would be indistinguishable from
one of Mr. Koestler's emaciated heroes. M. Mauriac, on the
other hand, regards his creations, not as figures in a day-dream
nor yet as social or economic pawns, but as individual objects
of love. Since he loves them, he can afford to display their
vileness, as well as to conceal, if necessary, their nobility—for
" not all mysteries are shameful ", as he says in the second
volume of his *Journal*. In the same way, he knows that his
Pharisee will never wholly outgrow her evil propensities, even
when events have shown her to herself as she really is. So he
allows us to witness the change in her, reasonably confident
that we shall not be deceived.

This judgment is so beautifully balanced, so just and sober,
that the effect of pathos is overwhelming. When the young
lovers—so long, so ruinously, so uselessly, kept apart by Mme
Pian's abstract jealousy—are at last in a position to defy her,
they find there is nothing left to defy—only a broken old
woman holding out a tray of tea-things. For all three the
tragedy is crippling, because each has lost the basis of judgment
upon which, up to then, the tensions of life have existed.
Whether they cling to one another or fall apart, certainty has
given way to doubt. Jean and Michèle will marry and go away ;
but we know, before we are told so, that they will tear each
other to pieces ; and Brigitte Pian will die alone, in possession
of the truth at last, but too late to make use of it—too late to
rebuild the life of the guiltless priest whose career she has ruined
by her campaign of traducement—too late even to transform

the surly suspicion of her stepson into the love she has so long despised.

With the possible exception of *Les Anges Noirs*, in which, I feel, it is very difficult to accept the author's belief in Gradère's change of heart, all Mauriac's novels achieve a perfect catharsis, so that the sense of disaster, though predominant, does not leave behind it an impression of gloom or futility. This is perhaps due in the main to the charm and sincerity of his pictures of young people. Those of us who saw *The Intruder* acted in London before the war will scarcely have forgotten the beautiful simplicity with which the boy and girl were drawn ; and it is the same with the three young victims of *La Pharisienne*. Our pity for and understanding of their agonies evoke all the helplessness and ineptitude of our own youth, and leave besides a conviction of the ultimate value of their ordeal.

(1946)

20

The Personality of Eugène Delacroix

THE well integrated person rarely keeps a diary, unless it be of the strictly factual order. The commonsensical adult, calmly equipped to deal with eventualities, may, for practical reasons, find it useful to retain a list of the things he has done. In which case, if we peep into his diary at random, we shall find something of this sort :

July 16. Rainy and rather cold. Letters received : Rawlinson (4 cords of wood already despatched), Aunt Millie, John (asks for money—again ! !), General Hitchener (why ?). Elinor left for London by the 9.5. 10.15 : Milk Marketing Board. Lunched early (remember to tell Elinor *one* course enough when I am alone). Drove into Frumpton to beard Petroleum Officer. Not in (of course !). No satisfaction from idiotic assistants of nineteen, obviously snowed under with bumf. 1½ gallons of petrol wasted. Evening : Symphony concert on wireless. Eileen Joyce in the Rachmaninoff concerto. Can't help wishing they'd just play the tunes and leave out all the dull stuff in between. Bed at 10.45.

Now turn to the diaries which have been thought worth publishing : here it is not mainly the record of activity (often non-existent) which interests, but the comments on it. Intro-spection (Amiel, Barbellion, Kafka, Julien Green) ; professional utility (Mauriac, Hebbel, Grillparzer, Jules Renard, Henry James) ; vanity, secret malice (Goncourt, Benjamin Constant, Jules Renard again) ; eye on posterity (Gide, Vigny) ; *goût de l'abîme* (Marie Bashkirtseff, Montherlant, Senancour) : in each case one motive preponderates, though it is seldom the only one. Underlying all is the minor melody of loneliness—the inescapable solitude of the divided soul, whose two halves try to unite by means of a perpetual dialogue. It must have been some such inner loneliness which drove men like Evelyn, Parson Woodford and Kilvert to talk to themselves, though they were

comparatively normal personalities and did not suffer overmuch
from accedia. Writers are naturally more prone than most
people to this compulsive muttering ; but there are good
reasons why all kinds of artist should indulge it, and we may
legitimately wonder at the almost entire abstention on the part
of composers, who (with the signal exception of Tchaikovsky)
have tended, prudently, to prefer the tidier evasions of autobiography.

The Journal of Eugène Delacroix is neither tidy nor evasive,
but it shuns, with quiet and persistent dignity, the shrill tones
of self-pity, exhibitionism and neurotic emphasis. Less consistently introspective than Amiel or Kafka ; remarkably free
from vanity and the intermittent silliness which afflicts most
diarists ; obviously indifferent to what posterity might think of
him personally : the great painter of the Romantic Movement
describes his thoughts and feelings with a sobriety that is only
occasionally disturbed by irritable exaggeration. Whatever he
may have been as man and artist, as a writer Delacroix is neither
clever nor profound. He was far too sincere to write up his
diary with a view to impressing himself. His comments on his
friends, on politics, contemporary novelists, and the vicissitudes
of life, are immediately intelligent (sometimes supremely so),
but they lack those sudden gleams of intellectual brilliance
which start from the pages of Hebbel and Alfred de Vigny and
André Gide. Instead, we assist at the spectacle of a deeply
sensitive man who trusted his judgment—however much it
might alter—but not his heart. The result is an unfailing
lucidity expressed in an even, gracious prose. There was
nothing amateurish about Delacroix except his reactions to
music ; and these are always interesting.

In personal relationships his natural warmth was interfered
with by an uneasiness which he never mastered. Unlike Henry
James, who managed to turn a passion for society into a professional asset, Delacroix continued throughout life to hover
between the solitude demanded by his art and an irresistible
hankering after people who wasted his time. Upon this
insecure basis he founded his personality : it was definitely a
construction, and we can watch it going up in the pages of his
journal. As a painter, and a French one, his care for form
refused to be content with the rag-bag type of character so

dear to the English. Delacroix's earliest and most discerning
admirer, Baudelaire, noted that his life was not rich in outward
incident : his struggles were with himself, and " one of the
great preoccupations of his life was to conceal the violence of
his nature and not to appear a man of genius ". After this we
are not surprised to hear Delacroix described as having much
in common with Stendhal and Mérimée—though even more
revealing, perhaps, is the comparison with that gentle naturalist,
Victor Jacquemont, whose charm and distinction reach us even
to-day through his letters and the unanimous tributes of friends
more worldly than himself. Only the truly good compel
admiring affection in hard-boiled, ambitious people.

A constant, self-imposed control induces a certain melancholy
in emotional natures, and Delacroix's journal bears witness to
this particular form of strain. With his slight figure, large head,
prognathous visage and swarthy complexion (" son teint de
Péruvien ou de Malai "—to quote Baudelaire once more),
Delacroix charmed people as various as Dumas, Chopin, George
Sand, and Princesse Mathilde Bonaparte, by a mixture of suave
attention and sudden, unexplained abruptness. The violence of
his character had to come out somehow : it does so in the
acerbity with which he describes the tedium of social gatherings ;
in impatience with his own slowness at work ; in his capri-
cious judgments on music. Above all it shows in the scenes of
frenzy and bloodshed which he loved to paint and around
which his imagination continually played. This taste was far
from being a mere love of movement. In his many pictures
of animals fighting, the masks of tigers and horses assume
expressions of malevolence that are disconcertingly human.
" The work of Delacroix forced the doors of drama, dragging
in some of Rubens with it ", writes André Malraux, in his
vigorous, sweeping manner. We agree, but enter the caveat
that Delacroix's genius absorbed three only of Rubens's traits :
the love of diagonal composition, the huge scale of passionate
colour, and the concentration on contour as a means of
expressing the quiddity of natural forms. Otherwise, the
difference between these two great painters is profound and
rooted in opposed temperaments. Delacroix, with his ill-health
and his habit of worrying, had none of Rubens's gaiety and
high spirits. A capacity for intense enjoyment, such as the

Journal displays, does not imply a light-hearted attitude to life.
Delacroix's bravura has a sinister, unsmiling quality, just as his
imagination has always a touch of the morbid about it. Like
Titian and Tintoretto, he wields his brush as a violinist his bow ;
but whereas the great Venetians regarded the world of their
day with minds for which the Golden Legend was still true,
Delacroix lived in an age which forced him to take as the
subject-matter of his art a romanticised view of history. It was
a makeshift which sufficed men of lesser genius—the historical
painters of the Empire and the minor epic poets who swarmed
throughout the century ; but, although the Journal affords no
evidence that Delacroix was aware of the anomaly, there is in
fact an immense pathos in the persistence with which his
imagination raked over the junk-shop of history and legend, in
search of adaptable material. The results are magnificently
dramatic, but inevitably they lack the sincerity which results
from a deep conviction, whether it be that of a traditional
belief or of some new spiritual discovery.

Nevertheless, if we do not look for joy in the work of
Delacroix, we shall find the emotional violence of his nature
translated into terms of colour—colour that glows luridly among
the swirling, fuliginous shadows of a general conflagration.
Such is his vision of experience : his men and women and
animals live dangerously in a world that is always smouldering
and often bursts into flame. The superb rutilance of the colour
distracts us from what is happening to the persons depicted ; the
wonderful painting of the madmen's clothes, in the *Tasso in
Prison*, excludes the emotion which Delacroix most wants us to
feel, namely, the desolation of the poet's condition.

The tragic sense of life was with him from the start ; the
earlier journals (1822–4) are instinct with it. But for a painter—
however intentionally romantic—this is not enough. By 1831
Delacroix had reached a nadir of depression and inertia, as a
result of living continuously in his imagination alone.

" No news could have given me more pleasure ", he wrote,
in May of this year, to his old friend, Raymond Soulier, who
had announced his intention of getting married. " One of us
at any rate has found a shelter against misfortune. The very
thought makes my heart beat—I who avoid emotion and whom
it avoids. The idea of your future happiness distracts my

thoughts from the monotony of my life. You are going in the right direction—towards peace—and that is all that matters. There is no worse position to be in than never to know how you are going to eat in eight days' time—and that is how I am placed. Give me a desert to live in, rid me of my last wretched stump of self-love, and I might still have a chance of happiness in this life. But reputation, success, the fame one never achieves—is all that worth ruining one's life for ? . . . Ah ! my dear Raymond, my character is going through a nasty crisis, and one to which you too are no stranger. I haven't yet succeeded in coming to terms with the blows life deals one, nor yet in being content with the few good things it has to offer . . ."

Allowing for a certain amount of affectation and self-pity in the style of this letter, we can see that it contains the truth about Delacroix at this time. He was thirty-two years old and the faceless sphinx—*le mal du siècle*, nowadays known as *Angst*—had him in her claws. He no longer cared even to keep the diary of his unhappiness—a very bad sign, apparent since the end of 1824. But life was not as obdurate as he imagined. The means of escape from his impasse was at hand, in the shape of an invitation from the Comte de Mornay, who had been entrusted by the French Government with a mission to pacify the Sultan of Morocco. No special duties seem to have fallen to Delacroix and it is clear that Monsieur de Mornay, who was an extremely intelligent and civilised man, regarded the painter simply as an agreeable companion.

The importance of the Moroccan journey to his development is too obvious in Delacroix's work ever to have escaped the notice of critics ; but the results, in the tone and tempo of his *Journal*, are quite as startling. The adagio of the introspective paragraph gives way to the staccato bustle of direct observation. Helter-skelter come the sentences—often minus verbs.

> Mounted Cadour's horse, mine being sick. Again saw the fine olive trees on the slope of a hill. Observed the shadows formed by the stirrup and the feet. A shadow which always draws the outline of the thigh and of the leg below it. The stirrup coming out while the straps remain invisible. The stirrup and the clasp of the breastpiece very white without any gloss. Gray horse, a bridle at his head, worn, white velvet.

I must mass the human figures in dark colour, and then put light touches on to bring them into relief.[1]

The artist's eye flickers to right and left, snapshotting everything it sees. Page after MS. page is illuminated with scribbled drawings. For the first time in his life Delacroix has given up his laborious search for the picturesque detail : the whole visible world has suddenly presented itself to him as equally worthy of the painter's attentive love. From now until the end of his life he observed and compared natural objects with a minuteness that, when we meet it in his Journal, reminds us of the notes of Ruskin and Gerard Manley Hopkins.

The rapture did not last. Echoes of it grow fainter and fainter in the years that succeeded Delacroix's return from North Africa. Its influence never faded altogether, of course. The voluminous notes for a Dictionary of Painting are probably more interesting in their raw state than the finished work would have been—just as Delacroix's sketches exist in their own right, and not merely as suggestions for pictures. Morocco and Algeria conferred on him the gift of inspired improvisation, together with power to observe the contemporary scene. Yet in the main he settled back into historical painting on the grand scale, with sorties into portraiture of astonishing brilliance. The Journal is full of evidence that he projected far more pictures than he ever painted. The wonderful sense of colour never failed : it earned him the title of father of modern painting among a generation of critics who abhorred the ' literary ' aspect of his art. The melancholy and the sinister vision persisted too. Delacroix had not been dead many years when the Impressionists rediscovered joy in the ecstasies of pure sensation.

After reading his Journal we shall conclude, I think, that Delacroix was as happy as any highly conscious person ever is. Possibly, like a good many men, he was not interested in happiness for its own sake. Throughout life—it is evident—he pursued, and in the end achieved, an equilibrium in which his visual imagination was left undisturbed by extraneous desires. At the same time he remained too intelligent to fall a victim to the spurious wisdom of successful old age. " Taste is the

---

[1] From the *Journal of Eugène Delacroix*. Trans., Walter Pach. (Secker & Warburg, 1948.)

maturity of the mind ", he wrote, six years before his death. No
doubt ; but with Delacroix taste remained a most uncertain
quantity. One of the delights of his Journal is the diarist's
moody inconsequence, his readiness to admit changes of mind.
This is but one of the signs of his immense vitality. Delacroix
seems to have found it hard to decide what he really thought
about his friends—except Chopin, of course, whom he adored
to the end with a touching lack of reservation. In what we
may agree to call love he is even more elusive : the figure of
Jenny Le Guillou appears as the solution of a time-wasting
problem. Perhaps she was more : Delacroix is very good at
hinting. . . . In any case he remains enigmatic on this point.
We may, if we like, deduce something of his attitude to the sex
in general from his abiding taste for the memoirs of Casanova.

In politics he was conservative, because he hated disorder.
Yet time and again we find him girding at the dominant
bourgeoisie for their inability to provide artists with inspiration.
It was the refrain of Matthew Arnold, and indeed of every
considerable French artist of the later nineteenth century, from
Flaubert downwards.

Apart from painting, music was clearly Delacroix's chief
passion, and his comments on the music he heard are always
interesting, though they are often inconsistent and sometimes
quite beside the point, as when he condemns Schubert as a
" dreamer ", or remarks testily that the slow movement of the
Eroica has " nothing beautiful or sublime at the beginning ".
The virtue of these *obiter dicta* lies chiefly in the light they
throw on Delacroix's fundamental æsthetic leanings. Mozart,
Cimarosa, Chopin : these are seldom if ever allowed to be
wrong ; but Beethoven, Berlioz, Donizetti, Rossini, while they
earn much praise, have to run the gauntlet of the diarist's wild
irritability.

But if Delacroix blew hot and cold on most subjects, he
had no doubts on one cardinal point :

What is beautiful is beautiful : I don't care in what period it
was done or for whom : as soon as there are two of us to admire
Charlet and Géricault, you have the proof, in the first place,
that they are admirable, and in the second, that they can find
admirers. I shall admire what deserves it to the day of my death,
and if I am the last of my race, I shall tell myself that after the

night which is to follow me on the hemisphere that I inhabit there will be a daybreak again somewhere, and that man still having a heart and a mind, will get his enjoyment from those two things.

The point needs making in most periods, including the present. The night which Delacroix expected was in no hurry to descend. It may never do so, though the signs are far from propitious. But it is always there, waiting. The heirs of European civilisation, of which Delacroix was consciously one, bear the responsibility of preserving their own convictions, in the face of neglect, ridicule and malevolence. The belief in an absolute standard of beauty is ultimately as insusceptible of proof as the kindred belief in the divinity of Christ. Both conceptions are rooted in a moral attitude from which we secede at peril of our humanity. To believe in them to-day is not a source of immediate comfort, for they still have some authority to lose—and are losing it. It is more than possible that we stand on the threshold of a night deeper and more extensive than any known to history. If so, that is matter for sadness, but not for despair. The cycles of history may be very, very long ; but they are cycles : what has been won is never lost for good and all. Thus we have good reason to believe that, if the barbaric night should indeed descend, and however long it may last, there will at length come an age which will rediscover Baudelaire, Debussy, Valéry, Renoir, Matisse, and all the other great artists of the individualist tradition ; just as the Renaissance rediscovered (since it had never been entirely lost) the art and thought of the ancient world. Like the monks of the Dark and Middle Ages, those of us to-day who cleave to the heritage of Western Europe must contrive to keep that heritage alive, for the nourishment and delectation of a far distant future.

(1948)

DATE

Randall Library – UNCW
PN511 .S15, 1967   NXWW
Sackville–We / Inclinations.

304900141850Z